COOPERATIVE LEARNING ACTIVITIES
IN THE LIBRARY MEDIA CENTER

Cooperative Learning Activities in the Library Media Center

SECOND EDITION

Lesley S. J. Farmer

1999
LIBRARIES UNLIMITED, INC.
and Its Division
TEACHER IDEAS PRESS

Copyright © 1999 Lesley S. J. Farmer
All Rights Reserved
Printed in the United States of America

No part of this publication may be reproduced, stored in a retrieval system, or transmitted, in any form or by any means, electronic, mechanical, photocopying, recording, or otherwise, without the prior written permission of the publisher. An exception is made for individual librarians and educators, who may make copies of activity sheets for classroom use in a single school or library. Standard citation information should appear on each page.

LIBRARIES UNLIMITED
and Its Division
TEACHER IDEAS PRESS
88 Post Road West
Westport, Ct 06881
800-237-6124
www.lu.com

Library of Congress Cataloging-in-Publication Data

Farmer, Lesley S. J.
    Cooperative learning activities in the library media center / Lesley S.J. Farmer. -- 2nd ed.
    x, 166 p. 22 × 28 cm.
    Rev. ed of: Cooperative learning activities in the library media center. 1991.
    Includes bibliographical references (p. 153) and index.
    ISBN 1-56308-542-9 (softbound)
    1. School libraries--Activity programs--United States. 2. Media programs (Education)--United States. 3. Education, Secondary--Activity programs--United States. I. Farmer, Lesley S. J. Cooperative learning activities in the library media center.
II. Title.
Z675.S3F234   1999
027.8'223--dc21   98-53623
                                                        CIP

P

> In order to keep this title in print and available to the academic community, this edition was produced using digital reprint technology in a relatively short print run. This would not have been attainable using traditional methods. Although the cover has been changed from its original appearance, the text remains the same and all materials and methods used still conform to the highest book-making standards.

Contents

Introduction ix

1 The Nature of Cooperative Learning 1
   What Is Cooperative Learning? 1
   Key Elements of Cooperative Learning 2
   What Teaching Factors Make It Work? 4
   Variations of Cooperative Learning 9
   Tips 12

2 Inclusive Ways of Learning 17
   Learning from the Inside Out 17
   Learning 17
   Processing 19
   Variables Influencing Learning 21
   How Can Educators Maximize Learning? 23
   Tips 24

3 Outcomes-Based Education 27
   What Is Outcomes-Based Education? 27
   Standards 28
   Authentic Assessment 29
   Rubrics 30
   Aligning Instruction 31
   Implications for Cooperative Learning Activities 32
   Tips 32

4 Information Literacy ... 35
- Models of Information Literacy ... 35
- Instructional Strategies and Information Literacy ... 37
- Current Trends in Information Literacy ... 38
- The Impact of Information Literacy on Cooperative Learning ... 39
- Tips ... 40

5 Building a Learning Community ... 43
- The Cooperative School ... 43
- Resource-Based Learning ... 43
- Fostering Cooperative Learning in the Library ... 44
- Cooperative Planning ... 44
- Structuring the Learning Environment ... 45
- Facilitating Learning ... 46
- Tracking and Assessing Learning ... 47
- Using Benchmark Projects ... 48
- Expanding Cooperative Learning ... 50
- Tips ... 50

6 Activity Plans: An Explanatory Key ... 53
- Basic Activity Plan Format ... 54

7 Activity Plans for Art ... 55
- Virtual Art Museum Tour ... 55
- Persuasive Art ... 57
- Artistic Brochure ... 58
- Masking Art ... 61
- More Idea Starters ... 62

8 Activity Plans for Domestic Sciences ... 63
- Housing A.D. 2020 ... 63
- Raising Kids, Raising Money ... 65
- A Clothes Horse of a Different Color ... 66
- Dr. Fix-It ... 68
- More Idea Starters ... 69

9 Activity Plans for English ... 71
- Literary Walkabout ... 71
- Guest Author ... 72
- Word Family Trees and Journeys ... 75
- I Say… ... 76
- More Idea Starters ... 78

10 Activity Plans for Foreign Languages 79
Slice of Life 79
Food on the Internet 82
Visual Dictionary 83
Cartoons and Photo Novellas 84
More Idea Starters 85

11 Activity Plans for Health and Physical Education 87
Emergency Preparedness 87
Nutrition Survey 88
Exercises by Body Parts 89
HIV/AIDS: Fact or Fiction? 91
More Idea Starters 92

12 Activity Plans for Mathematics 95
How Do You Measure Up? 95
Earth to Mars 96
Mathematical Crossword Puzzle 97
Numbers Through Literature 99
More Idea Starters 101

13 Activity Plans for Music 103
G(ender) Notes 103
Composing a Database 104
Playing Musical Instruments 109
Music Media 110
More Idea Starters 111

14 Activity Plans for Psychology and Sociology 113
I've Got a Problem 113
Multimedia Dating Game 115
Age Is in the Eye of the Beholder 116
From Barbie to Barbarella 117
More Idea Starters 118

15 Activity Plans for Science 121
Travel Agent 121
Dinosaur Field Guide 124
Environmental Summit 125
Machinations 126
More Idea Starters 127

CONTENTS

16 Activity Plans for Social Studies 129
    Time Capsule 129
    Immigrants All 132
    1776 News Break 133
    Mapping the Economics Picture 134
    More Idea Starters 136

17 Activity Plans for Technology 137
    Read My Chips 137
    WebQuests 139
    Mirror, Mirror on the Wall 141
    Computer Ethics 142
    More Idea Starters 143

18 Activity Plans for Vocational Education 145
    Minding Your Own Business 145
    Behind the Job Scene 146
    Trendy Careers 147
    Biography Resumes 149
    More Idea Starters 150

Glossary 151

Bibliography 153

Index 161

Introduction

1991. My first book is published: *Cooperative Learning Activities in the Library Media Center*. Since then I've talked with librarians from California to Canada about the benefits and processes of cooperative learning. I've written articles and books about working cooperatively with teachers. I've moved to a new school where, as librarian, I continue to encourage cooperative learning. Fast forward to 1997. My first book is almost out of printed copies; it's time to either reprint it or revise it. The time is ripe for revision. I reread my book and realize all of the changes that have occurred in a short six years: the SCANS report, the rise of outcomes-based assessment, the push for national standards, the ubiquity of rubrics, work on new national guidelines for library media programs, school-to-work issues, and the continued rise in information. When I started to revise the book, I looked for my original disks and realized that they were 5¼-inch floppies, and I didn't even have that kind of disk drive anymore! So, yes, the time has certainly come for a new take on this important topic.

The first chapter is probably most like the first book. Cooperative learning hasn't changed much. However, the term collaborative learning has taken on new meaning to press the fact that students needn't have a deep-seated relationship with their peers in order to work with them. In that respect, the current work on small group tasks has become more realistic, reflecting the short-term relationships that occur in the real world.

The second chapter is a spin on the original chapter on critical thinking, then a hot concept. This time I wanted to emphasize diversity: different kinds of learners, different ways to learn. I believe in deep learning on a conscious level, which encompasses far more than analytical metacognition.

The third chapter could well have been placed first. That's because the concept of outcomes-based education forms the basis for my discussion on benchmark projects and processes leading up to them. What should students know and do? What will it look like? How can it be measured? How should instruction be aligned to meet those outcomes? What prior skills do students need? These are issues raised.

The fourth chapter speaks to the importance of information literacy. Particularly with the wide integration of the Internet, the ability to critically analyze information is vital. The projects and activities in the book reinforce the need for students to shape information according to their own needs and abilities and to share that synthesis.

The fifth chapter broadens the concept of team planning to involve the student early on in the process and to provide a community context for learning. Just as each learning activity gains significance if conceived or created to further the purpose of a course, so all courses become more meaningful and interdependent if aligned with the school community's mission.

As before, the second part of the book provides a variety of lessons that culminate in benchmark projects. Some of the original lessons have been kept, but most have been modified to incorporate educational technology, and many new lessons have been introduced. The other change in this part is the introduction of a multifaceted project for each subject. This feature highlights the possibility of in-depth student work over time.

As always, the main message is "Many minds can be better than one—and more fun!"

CHAPTER I

The Nature of Cooperative Learning

Have you ever tried to accomplish an overwhelming task, only to find that it could be achieved beyond expectations and even fun when other people worked with you? That's the spirit of *cooperative learning*. Particularly as education seeks to provide in-depth learning and realistic experiences, cooperative learning offers a way for students to master complex concepts in a meaningful way. How does cooperative learning work, and how can it improve student learning? This chapter explains the theory and practice of cooperative learning.

WHAT IS COOPERATIVE LEARNING?

Basically, cooperative learning involves a structured group of people who have a specific learning task to accomplish together. Every group member contributes. Both group results and individual accountability are necessary components of effective cooperative learning. In addition to the academic task, a social task is involved in cooperative learning, for a significant part of the cooperation includes social interaction. Interaction, usually face-to-face, and positive interdependence mark successful social characteristics of cooperative learning. (An easy way to demonstrate to students the need for interaction is to have them assemble a puzzle or build a model without talking or writing to each other.)

What Are Its Benefits?

Over the years, cooperative learning has been found to be an effective teaching strategy for a variety of students in a variety of situations. As early as in the 1920s, studies examined the impact of this approach to learning. Students of all grade levels and of all achievement levels can learn to the same degree. Students are placed in an all-win atmosphere where prior knowledge and experience can be pooled. With cooperative learning, students have been shown to improve their self-esteem, their attitude toward school, and their ability to work with others.

With the influence of their peers, students are more motivated to work; they know that others depend on their efforts. Additionally, because these cooperative-based projects often approximate real-life situations or have concrete applications to daily life, students see the reason for the work and so are more apt to put forth honest effort. Their problem-solving methods improve too because group members can test ideas on each other. Having a range of judgments makes each person revise and improve group opinions, and students see the need for gathering data to justify their stands. This interchange also helps students transfer learning, applying concepts or skills from one experience to help in another; this practice also reinforces retention of ideas. Partly because of the nature of many cooperative activities, students learn how to manage resources and time for complex tasks. Indeed, the interdependent nature of cooperative learning results in improved information literacy skills by students.

The social benefits of cooperative learning are equally significant. At its most basic, students engaged in cooperative activities learn to like their peers. They exhibit increased prosocial and altruistic behavior. This impact is particularly meaningful for cross-cultural relationships and for acceptance of students with special needs.

Some other positive outcomes from participating in cooperative learning activities include increased sense of control in the learning process, increased time on task, and better attendance. Quite frankly, we all live most of our lives in groups, and learning group skills is vitally important.

KEY ELEMENTS OF COOPERATIVE LEARNING

Cooperative learning consists of specific structures and practices. In combination, they maximize the benefits of students working together.

Heterogeneous Groups

Students' backgrounds, experiences, and skills can be recognized and used to best advantage when groups are arranged to maximize diversity. At its most basic level, group membership can be comprised of varying ethnicities, genders, and learning styles. Depending on the task at hand, the teacher can divide the class to create the maximum differences within small groups so as to encourage more dialogue and opinions; for instance, a project dealing with affirmative action would mix gender and socioeconomic background. For complex projects, students can share their individual expertise: researching, organizing, writing, drawing. Ideally, group members discover each other's gifts on their own; particularly when group membership remains constant for a long-term project or several smaller tasks, students can develop sophisticated strategies of dividing the work.

Academic Objectives

Obviously, a main focus of cooperative work is academic progress; it is not an encounter group or group therapy session. The group can be successful only if the teacher provides adequate instruction and orientation. The directions should also be accompanied by the eventual assessment so students can measure their progress against some objective criteria. Thus, they know ahead of time what they need to know and do—and what that looks like. Particularly when the teacher and librarian plan cooperative activities, both content and information literacy concepts should be determined.

As students work together to accomplish their project, several group tasks need to be carried out to fulfill those academic demands:

- Sharing information
- Checking for information
- Keeping track of time
- Following directions
- Keeping the group on task
- Paraphrasing, elaborating, summarizing, testing, and other ways of clarifying information

Social Objectives

Students also need to learn how to be effective group members. In fact, the 1991 Secretary's Commission on Achieving Necessary Skills (SCANS) report (U.S. Department of Labor 1991) considered interpersonal skills—working on teams, teaching, negotiating, and serving customers—as one of the five essential competencies needed for high-performance work. Teachers and students need to unbundle these complex and interdependent skills so they can focus on specific aspects. (This approach resembles the practice of grading student-written products. In some cases, if the teacher marks every grammatical, spelling, organizational, analytical, and conceptual error or misunderstanding, the paper will be covered in red ink and the student will be demoralized. And the teacher will be able to mark only a handful of papers. Instead, a teacher will focus on one technical aspect of writing and one analytical task when grading a set of papers.) Important group maintenance tasks include:

- Checking for agreement
- Encouraging group members
- Addressing group members by name
- Sharing feelings
- Responding to ideas
- Maintaining eye contact
- Listening
- Gatekeeping
- Mediating
- Setting standards
- Easing tension
- Showing appreciation (Dishon and O'Leary 1994, 57; Jaques 1984, 29)

Distributed Leadership

Another important characteristic of cooperative learning is its democratic structure of authority and responsibility. Every student has a voice in decision-making and implementation. No one student is supposed to command the others. For that reason, cooperative learning usually involves structured leadership roles. For working groups, several such roles are useful:

- Materials handler, who gets any materials needed and keeps track of them
- Data gatherer or reader, who reads the task and clarifies group opinions
- Assessor or observer, who makes sure that cooperative skills are used
- Recorder or secretary, who documents the group's answers
- Checker, who makes sure that all members get the right answers
- Coordinator or facilitator, who makes sure that everyone participates
- Timekeeper, who makes sure the group stays on task
- Reporter or representative, who shares the group's work with the rest of the class

In a smaller group, one person may assume two roles. Alternatively, the teacher may assign specific roles, depending on the task involved.

Each role needs to be explained to and practiced by the students. Every student should experience every role at some point. Usually at the beginning of the year, group and role assignments change frequently so students can get to know a variety of peers and remain flexible in terms of group roles. Additionally, the teacher/librarian can observe how students work together and modify practice. At this point, the cooperative activities are also smaller in scope and less complex. After a month, group membership can stabilize and students can self-select their group role. Still, it's a good idea to change groups somewhat for each major learning activity because each project, ideally, takes advantage of different skills and learning styles.

Group Autonomy

A basic tenet of cooperative learning is that students have significant control over learning through autonomy and key decision-making. They are responsible for their own learning both in terms of the outcome as well as the process. The teacher and students are "on the same side" of learning; a strict hierarchical system is replaced by equitable transaction. The sage on the stage must become the guide on the side. For some teachers, cooperative learning can be threatening: How can students do as well without the teacher's immediate presence and direction? A great deal of trust and mutual respect must be established before an atmosphere conducive to cooperative learning can exist.

As with other cooperative skills, the ability to work autonomously doesn't come automatically. Teachers/librarians have to instruct students in self-governing techniques. At the start, the adult usually provides a structure in which the groups work, defining short-term time frames and dividing the activity into small, manageable steps. Monitoring is close and extensive, and the class spends considerable time discussing group dynamics and brainstorming ways to improve group management. As groups become more functional, they can assume more autonomy. But, whatever the degree of self-management, groups as a whole and individuals within each group are always accountable for their work.

Group Accountability

If everyone does his or her own thing, independently, then it's not cooperative learning, even if the students are sitting at the same table. Ideally, the outcome should be substantial enough that one student alone would have difficulty doing it and complex enough that teamwork makes it happen. Getting a ship across the ocean is one apt analogy. So is winning a baseball game—an activity that is easily understood by students. Each student might have a specific task, but all need to depend on each other. The group should be responsible for every member's learning. It is important to note the difference between coming up with the right answer and learning. In the first case, students who know the answer typically give it to the others; math homework assignments get copied in this scenario. But did the copiers really learn anything? Only if the answer-giver *explains* the answer and how it was derived will others have the opportunity to learn. Otherwise, studies indicate that *less* learning will actually occur. If the focus, instead, is on *learning*, then all students need to know how to do the math skill. They have to ask clarifying questions and practice on different problems together in order to ensure that everyone in the group can solve the problem the next day in class.

Individual Accountability

Just as a chain is only as strong as its weakest link, so is cooperative learning dependent on the best efforts of every single person. The laggard can demoralize the group, the undependability of one person can throw off the group's schedule. Some practices can ensure individual accountability: assigning specific roles and tasks to each person, having students each bring in individual work before collaborating, monitoring student participation in group discussion (through teacher or student observations and checklists), giving extra points to groups where every person does well on a follow-up exam.

Some high achievers may fear cooperative activities because they worry that they may find themselves doing the lion's share of the work or the tutoring. They have two consolations: The person who teaches actually learns the material best, and each activity should include assessment of each individual. Again, the simplest assessment is a formal written test. But groups can also assess their members, noting the contribution that each person made to the final project. It should be noted that accountability should be seen from a very broad perspective. Contributions such as organizational ability, patience, neatness, ability to keep the group on task, negotiation skills, and dependability should all factor into the assessment. Sometimes the brightest person isn't the most productive or helpful.

WHAT TEACHING FACTORS MAKE IT WORK?

Just as a good lesson may be poorly taught, so cooperative learning activities can fail to impact students meaningfully. Even though students are largely responsible for their work, the teacher/librarian needs to structure the learning environment to facilitate cooperation.

Quite frankly, some activities lend themselves better to cooperative work than others. Take reading: Silent reading and journaling are obviously independent tasks. Writing a five-page report on an author is probably best done on an individual basis. Essay critiques and coaching are typically done in dyads. However, a hypermedia stack on Steinbeck and his works is a natural for cooperative effort. A cooperative activity should be multidimensional and complex, and it usually results in a product.

Likewise, teaching attitudes and strategies may advance—or detract from—cooperative learning. If a teacher tends to lecture or present information to the whole class, such as with a video, the tone for small group work will not be established easily. A problem-solving approach to classroom activity, on the other hand, lends itself to cooperative learning. With this strategy, emphasis is placed on data gathering and analysis. Divergent thinking and group brainstorming are encouraged. Particularly in cooperative learning, a balance must be struck between content and process, presentation and interaction. Additionally, the community within the classroom and library needs to value relationships and the skills of helping others.

For cooperative learning to be implemented effectively, the teacher/librarian must put several factors into place:

- Classroom management
- Clear definition of the specific tasks
- Group assignment
- Instruction on group processing
- Monitoring and assessment

In defining the task for students, the teacher/librarian should begin by giving very specific directions so that the groups can concentrate on the tasks. Written instructions, worksheets, or checklists to guide group discussion should be provided, and each group must understand the task goal and directions before beginning the process. Because cooperative learning activities involve social interaction, a group maintenance goal or social skill task should also be stated. Again, as you begin to use this group structure, you will want to give a very specific social skill task assignment, such as making sure that everyone verbally participates or that every idea is understood by all the members before another idea is put forth.

The time frame also should be stated at the start—and adhered to. One student in each group can act as the timekeeper. Time should be allocated not only for group work but also for whole-class processing. The time factor should be considered not only within the class period but also for the entire project. Particularly for middle schoolers, there should be immediate goals set for each class period. As students gain more experience in accomplishing complex projects, they can be given more autonomy in time management.

Dividing students into groups is the next step. Groups should be small enough to ensure participation by everyone but large enough to accomplish the assigned task. For buzz sessions, in which a specific concept is discussed and responded to by clusters, groups of three are very workable. When a range of ideas and approaches is needed, group size should probably consist of five or six members. As stated earlier, groups should be heterogeneous, bringing together students of different abilities and learning styles. Interestingly, when students self-select group members, they tend to choose those students most like themselves. When teachers make the decision about group membership, students do not act as cooperatively as when they self-select, so it is useful for students to create their own groups occasionally.

Seating should also be arranged. The most effective arrangement is a close circle, which requires portable desks. The second best arrangement is one group per round table. The surface is great for working, but the space adds a barrier to communication.

Group Processing

Telling students to work cooperatively isn't enough; they must be taught *how* to work together effectively. All of us coexist—as a class, as a family, as a neighborhood. Yet relationships can be dysfunctional; some students experience few positive models of group behavior. Generally, each group session should include these points:

- Introduction of clarification of member roles
- Restatement of the assigned tasks
- Open-ended discussion about the activity, possible problems, and related issues

- Decision about strategies to use to achieve goals
- Work toward goals
- Assessment, including check for clarity and quality of work
- Summation and thanks

The group should focus on solving the problem or completing the task at hand, while ensuring participation and understanding by all group members.

Group roles should be explained and practiced before being used to achieve a significant task. Students need to see the need for group skills and know how they will be assessed accordingly. They must understand the skills and know when to use them; this requires demonstrating and modeling the behaviors. The teacher needs to set up practice situations, including process time to assess the results. And students need to persevere in practicing the group skills until those concepts become well-honed and internalized. Some signs of positive group interdependence include:

- Drawing together physically (e.g., heads close together)
- Talking about the task
- Sharing materials and answers
- Only one person writing (Dishon and O'Leary 1984, 80)

At first, students may be awkward in their roles and wish to resort to other learning modes. However, as they continue they will improve quickly until they plateau for a while.

The teacher may share with students the usual stages of cooperative group skills: from self-consciousness and phoniness, to skilled (but mechanical) functioning, to routine ease. Groups may start tentatively, consciously looking for participation by all members and using names to elicit responses. As groups move to the functional level, they become more supportive of each other and help clarify problems through paraphrasing and other descriptions. At the formulating state, groups vocalize more—summarizing, correcting, elaborating, and inventing. They may swing from an overeagerness to placate everybody to a critical stance about the group's progress. When groups mature, they work more in-depth: integrating findings, critiquing ideas but not people, generating new directions, and making reality checks (Johnson and Johnson 1987).

Usually the classroom teacher handles this group development. Each class has its own dynamic, which the teacher works with daily. The teacher may assign different social tasks for each project, concurrently with the academic task, depending on the class's needs. As the teacher teams with the librarian, such social tasks should be communicated so that the librarian can assess group processing during the activity.

Though each class has its own characteristics, the general nature of cooperative learning should look similar. A good activity to reinforce cooperative process norms is class development of a cooperative learning rubric. Each aspect of cooperative learning, group accountability, and so forth, should be discussed and described so students can identify good practice. For each feature students can then differentiate among levels of cooperation. For instance, within the social task process, one of the behaviors is participation. Using a four-point rubric, the descriptors might be as follows:

4: Every group member participates equitably and positively, and offers unique and valuable suggestions.

3: Most group members participate, usually in a positive manner; some members talk more than others. Most members offer good suggestions.

2: Some group members participate, offering suggestions. Some behaviors may be neutral or somewhat negative.

1: Few group members participate. Group members disrupt participation or block useful discussion.

The resultant rubrics can be posted and used to monitor group behavior. Classes can compare the rubrics and come to consensus about the descriptors.

Monitoring and Assessing

For a learning activity to be beneficial, assessment must be an integral part of the process. What is happening? Why is it happening? What is positive about the process and the result? What change would improve what happens? What difference does it make? While these same questions could be posed for any school work, the discussion in a cooperative learning situation makes the ensuing decisions and modifications more powerful.

To know what is happening, all persons associated with learning need to modify behavior. Teachers and librarians need to modify students and themselves, and student groups need to self-modify their progress. Monitoring, a form of feedback, reinforces positive behavior and signals dysfunctioning behavior. As students self-monitor they attain self-control; they determine their own success.

During group work the teacher/librarian monitors behavior mainly by observing student behavior. Are social skills being practiced? Are academic goals being pursued? In general, students should work independently from the teacher, even when group conflict occurs. If students ask for help, the teacher/librarian should ask questions of clarification:

- What are you trying to accomplish?
- What is happening?
- What is working well?
- What obstacles exist?
- What needs to be done to overcome the problem?

The situation should be resolved by the group, unless concerns about safety arise.

Additionally, teachers/librarians should monitor their own behaviors during group work:

- Do you set an open atmosphere?
- Do you move around the classroom?
- Do you encourage students to seek alternative answers?
- Do you help students become self-directed?
- Do you point out negative or nonsupportive behavior as well as cooperative behavior? (Note that the most effective reinforcements are specific and based on observed behavior.)

During group work, one student may act as assessor or observer, noting the social and academic behaviors demonstrated by individuals. If specific social tasks are given, the observer may list the individuals' names on a piece of paper and make a check mark each time someone performs the social task.

Assessing Group Behavior. Teachers and librarians may use one of the observer forms included in books about cooperative learning such as titles by Costa, Johnson, Sharan, and Slavin. Such forms provide models and standards for measuring group behavior. They organize the tasks for easier group management and accountability. They also allow groups to be responsible for their own success.

Class-produced rubrics or questionnaires encourage student ownership in the group process. Especially when long-term groups are used, students can begin to determine which social skills need attention. They can then concentrate on these areas of concern.

When the class regathers at the end of the activity, further assessment occurs. Essentially, such assessment provides the opportunity for synthesizing learning and giving a sense of closure. In all cases, the assessment process should be prepared and be timely, brief, and specific.

First, each group reports out, sharing its project and findings. The class as a whole discusses the activity and underlying concepts. Feedback is all-important: within groups, between groups, and between teacher/librarian and students. Feedback provides a reality check to assess how groups are working. If one group experiences a difficulty, other groups may offer suggestions for improvement. Perhaps one group found resources that would help another group.

Both negative and positive experiences of both academic and social tasks should be considered grist for the assessment mill. This synthesizing process also sets the stage for determining what skills need to be practiced in the future. For example, if all groups have a hard time locating current information in newspapers, then a brief lecture on analyzing news format might be in order.

For feedback to be productive, it should satisfy the following criteria:

- Be descriptive rather than judgmental.
- Be specific rather than general.
- Focus on the receiver rather than on oneself.
- Be accurate.
- Be clear.
- Request or suggest rather than impose.
- Focus on the achievable.

Groups may use a variety of assessment tools in critiquing their efforts. The following are some useful methods:

- Groups may analyze observer sheet results or rubrics.
- Groups may be videotaped for detailed analysis (with or without assessment forms when viewing).
- Groups may use thumbs up for good work, thumbs down for negative reactions, thumbs sideways for neutral situations.
- Students may draw faces—or make faces. Faces range from positive smiles to downcast frowns.
- Students may react to group work by forced quick decisions. If an open space for movement is available, the teacher/librarian can line students along the middle of the room. The teacher/librarian calls out statements, such as "My group talked like giraffes—or like monkeys." Students who think the giraffe metaphor better describes their group go to one side of the room, and those who think the monkey metaphor is more fitting go to the opposite side of the room. The teacher/librarian reassembles the class, then makes other evaluative statements. This approach, which eases the tension associated with assessment, is best used with younger students. Alternately, students may stand up or sit down as a particular behavior applies to their group.
- Students may use a number range from 1 to 10 to indicate relative success. To signal their response, students or groups may raise placards, as athletic competition judges do.
- Students may rank order social skills according to their group's performance. That is, which skill was best accomplished? What one was done second best, and so on.
- Students may complete open statements such as, "I wish my group…" or "My group helped me…."
- Students may circle adjectives that best describe their group, or they may write their own adjectives.
- Students may describe their group work using analogies or metaphors, such as an animal, a song, or a season: "Our group is like a pine tree: prickly at the end, straight and narrow at the heart."
- Students may rank skills in response to specific statements about the group work (see fig. 1.1). Other scales that students may use to measure their relative response include:

positive _____ negative
always _____ never
rigid _____ chaotic

Assessing the Activity. The activity is also assessed. Both group results and individual effort should be measured. The group grade or reward should align with the specified goals or projects assigned. Because group success demands individual effort, separate scores for each member should be included. This approach emphasizes individual accountability and encourages peer tutoring. Group and individual progress should

THE NATURE OF COOPERATIVE LEARNING

sedentary _____ active
immediate results _____ long-term goals
object-oriented _____ people-oriented
concrete thinker _____ abstract thinker
having variety/unpredictable _____ routine
needing close supervision _____ autonomous
small-motor coordination _____ no fine coordination
high communication _____ low communication
little organizing _____ much organizing

Figure 1.1 Skill line spectrum.

also be taken into consideration. This factor helps equalize the opportunity for success; even the slowest learner can improve over time.

Each student and each group may begin with a base score, determined by the first activity. The teacher/librarian may assign the group score for each project, based on predetermined grading criteria (e.g., appropriateness, accuracy, thoroughness, creativity, neatness). Each criterion, by the way, may be weighted; for example, accuracy may be considered more important than neatness. The group sum is then divided by the number of group members. Test scores may be calculated for each person to demonstrate what students have learned individually. Improvement scores may also be included in the final grade calculation. As with individual criteria, scores for team results and individual achievement may be weighted differently. Although some high achievers may initially question the validity of team scores, teachers/librarians may point out that the best way to attain both goals is to learn the material. It should be noted that both academic and social progress are assessed.

Although grading is a traditional measurement and reward system, other reward systems may be incorporated. Ideally, the internalized enjoyment of learning is a powerful reward. Teacher-initiated rewards may come in the form of recognition: a smile or gentle word, announced or displayed achievement. However, some cooperative learning activities include concrete rewards for working together, such as certificates, food, or special privileges. Outer rewards provide incentive, but in some cases, such rewards can actually *lower* performance. For example, if a student who likes to do bulletin boards receives extra credit for doing them, he or she may lose interest in doing bulletin boards when the credit is no longer offered. Part of the problem is that the evaluative piece or reward distracts the learner from the work; part of the problem is that the learner may feel controlled by the reward. The reward replaces learning as the motivational factor. Outer rewards usually need to reinforce inner satisfaction. Of course, the greatest reward may be the ability to work cooperatively with others, a lifelong skill and often a source of pleasure.

VARIATIONS OF COOPERATIVE LEARNING

Though cooperative learning maintains some consistent features, such as a balance of academic and social tasks and a balance of group and individual accountability, the structure can vary in its implementation. Some practices are commonplace in classrooms: brainstorming to elicit a wide range of new ideas, and using case studies to identify ways to deal with situations. A few other models follow.

Buzz Session

Buzz groups pool ideas in response to presented concepts. Typically, the teacher summarizes or outlines the ideas, defines tasks and roles for the groups, sets the time limit, and floats from group to group. Students usually report out the main points derived. This process is effective when a controversial topic is introduced and the teacher wants students to discuss implications and options.

Snowballing

This process develops class consensus—and also recognizes divergent thinking. A quick activity, snowballing provides a nonthreatening way for students to interact. Questions posed might be "What are the key qualities of a democracy?" "What is the most important scientific discovery of the twentieth century?" or "What constitutes a masterpiece?" The process is simple: The class is divided into pairs to discuss the topic. The pair reaches consensus, and then joins another pair. The two pairs reach consensus, then join another quartet. Eventually, the entire class becomes one group, with one consensus response.

Numbered Heads Together

As a simple way to familiarize students with cooperative learning, this structure works well. It also counteracts the competitive and exclusive nature of whole-class questioning, where only one student gets a chance to answer the question. Basically, the teacher/librarian divides the class into groups of fours; within each group, students number off 1 to 4. When the teacher/librarian asks a question, the student groups put their heads together to come up with an answer. The teacher calls a number (1 to 4), and students with that number may raise their hands to answer. Group members who know the correct response share the information because they realize that anyone in the team could be called upon, and the group wants to do well. The other group members listen carefully so they will get the right answer as well.

Student Team Learning

Student Team Learning (STL) is based on the idea that students work together to *learn* something, which may seem reminiscent of college study groups. There are important differences, however: In STL, teams are likely to be heterogeneous. Teams are consciously assessed on their ability to make sure that everyone is prepared to do the work if asked to perform individually. Teams are rewarded if everyone meets a certain predetermined goal; they are not measured against any other team's performance. In addition, STL offers equal opportunities for individual success; that is, each student is assessed according to his or her progress over past performance. Each student's prior knowledge is valued, whether that student is a traditional low, middle, or high achiever. In this model, a traditional high achiever is challenged and does not lose status by sharing knowledge to help others learn. On the other end, the traditional low achiever need not despair but actually has the opportunity to gain knowledge from several "experts."

Jigsaw

The Jigsaw model breaks down content matter into manageable pieces and encourages cross-fertilization of ideas by mixing groups (see fig. 1.2).

The basic Jigsaw process works as follows: Suppose students are studying the American colonies. Four groups are formed, each one taking a colony. Each student in the group studies one aspect of the colony: politics, daily life, resources, demographics. These aspect experts meet together (cross-fertilizing in a different group configuration) to compare and contrast their findings. Afterward, the aspect experts return to their original groups. Within the original groups, teammates teach each other about the colony *and* about cross-colony aspects. Culminating individual assessments measure how well students learned from each other.

A variation of the model begins with every team examining a single source, but assigning each team member a different aspect of the source to focus on. For example, all students

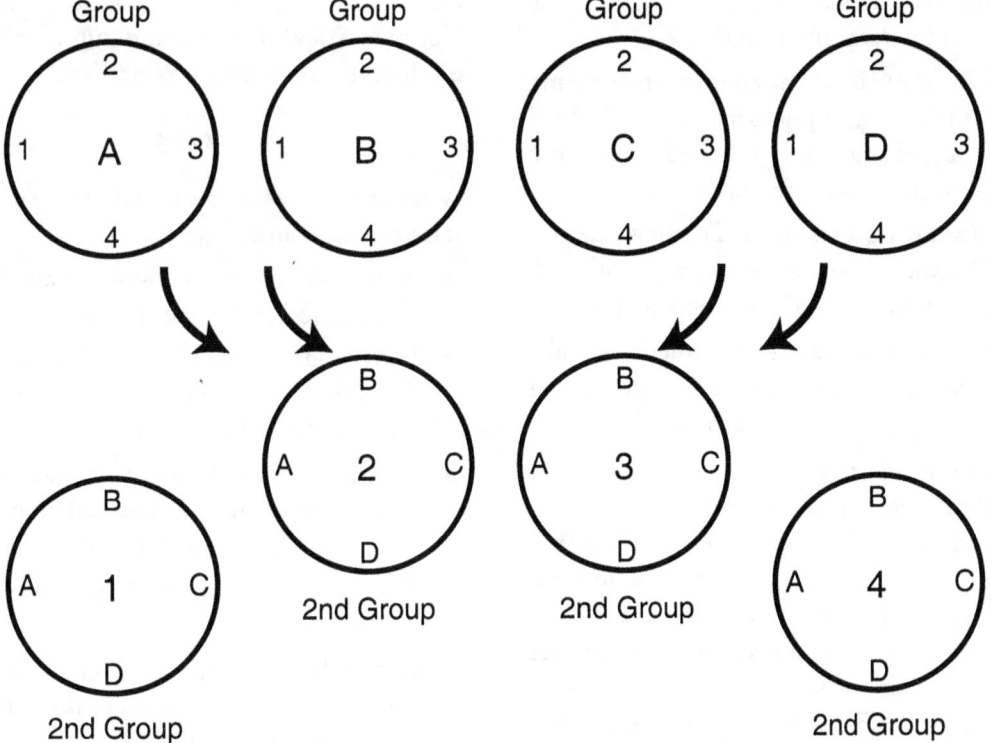

Figure 1.2 Grouping: cross-fertilization.

watch a play by Shakespeare on video. Each student within each team is assigned a number; all "ones" focus on the setting, "twos" focus on character development, and so on. After watching the video, the aspect experts meet to discuss their focus. Then they return to their original groups and teach each other about the play.

Group Investigation

This format supports problem-solving situations where a truly puzzling scenario or issue is presented to the class. It could be an economic crisis or seemingly impossible physical phenomenon, for instance. The groups discuss their reactions to the problem, then strategize how to study it and what resources they need to solve it. The teacher/librarian acts as the content or information literacy advisor. The groups can compare notes along the way or work independently until either the problem is solved or the time limit is reached.

Role–Play

When exploring human interactions, students experience powerful learning when acting out social problems. Situations that lend themselves to role–plays include political issues, such as immigration or affirmative action, and psychological traumas. Simulations, say of life in the Middle Ages or of a political hostage crisis, constitute one type of role–play activity. The problem presented should be open-ended with several possible resolutions. The teacher/librarian usually structures this activity carefully, from defining the problem to identifying the way groups should observe the role–play. Student responsibility lies in the research and presentation. Role–play involves several steps:

- Introducing the problem: Groups may go into a buzz session to explore immediate implications.
- Setting the stage: Establishing the parameters and intended goal.

- Group work: Researching the issue, defining roles, and determining action.
- Enacting the play: Usually one group performs while the other groups observe; alternatively, groups could act/observe in paired groups and then report out to the rest of the class.
- Discussion and assessment: The class examines the role–play in terms of group work and of the consequences of the proposed action.

For extensive role–plays, the enactment can take place over several sessions, with group processing and reflection at the close of each day.

Technology-Based Collaborative Learning Services

Increased use of cooperative learning has teamed up with technological advances to raise collaboration to new levels of interactivity. More and more, teachers are posing cooperative ventures on the Internet, asking for remote classroom partners. Global Schoolhouse lists ongoing cooperative projects, from simple foreign language key pals to international weather watches. Video conferencing between schools enables students to work together while apart, sharing their findings and synthesizing them to create Internet products.

Even commercial ventures have entered this field. CNN offers Internet field trips. The Jason Project, supplemented with curriculum material from Mind Extension University, provides an interactive field trip program with project scientists. AT&T Learning Network matches classes from around the world in "learning circles." The businesses facilitate classroom networking so students can work together on a specific task—for a subscription fee.

Sometimes these distance cooperative activities are more like field trips than true collaborations. The key is in teacher planning, project structure and student autonomy. One successful innovation in Net-based collaboration is ThinkQuest, an annual contest to design educational Web pages. A basic Web structure and process is presented, and students create their own collaborative teams with representation from at least two schools. They contract their plan with an adult advisor, work together via the Net over a few months, and submit their final product to a nationwide exhibition.

TIPS

What are some ways I can help students get started with cooperative learning?

- Help students get to know one another through icebreaker games.
- Have students quickly interview the students sitting beside them and introduce them to the rest of the class.
- Pair students for drill-and-practice sessions in which students quiz each other, providing the correct answers for the partner.
- Pair students for writing. Each one edits the other's work.
- Pair students for reading. One student reads a paragraph, which the other then summarizes. The two switch roles.
- Create focus trios, in which students find out how much their teammates know about a subject. They may also decide that they collectively want to learn about that subject.
- Have group members round robin a topic; students sit in a circle and take turns sharing their thoughts.
- Provide just one sheet of paper, one book, and one pencil per group.

How can I help students build a sense of team cohesiveness?

- Have each group design a personal coat of arms, collage, or mural.
- Have the group put a puzzle together, preferably without speaking.
- Have each group choose a slogan, flag, group colors.
- Have each group present a skit about themselves.
- Have each group create and maintain a group scrapbook or video.

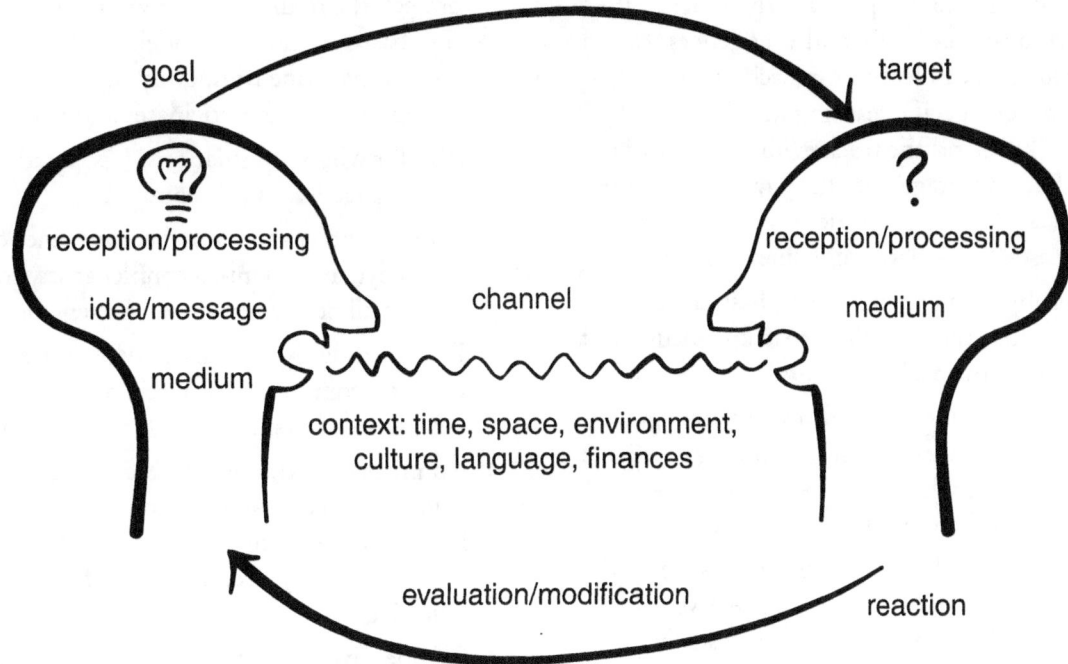

Figure 1.3 Communications model.

How can I help students learn to communicate more effectively?

As the illustrated communications model (fig. 1.3) shows, a good deal happens between the time of the original idea and the time of the audience's reaction. The idea is formulated relative to the sender's personal internal system, an idiosyncratic system of inputting and processing information. The idea is translated into an expressed medium, with the goal of reaching some target audience. The channel of communication between sender and receiver is hazardous, affected by a context of time, space, environment, culture, situation, and so forth. As the audience receives the message, the information is translated into another personal internal system. Only then can a reaction occur. And only then can the original idea be evaluated or modified. Sometimes it may seem miraculous that ideas are communicated accurately at all.

Keeping this model in perspective, some practical techniques can help the communication process.

- Demonstrate how to communicate effectively—and ineffectively.
- Have students perform skits that demonstrate effective and ineffective communication.
- Point out times when students communicate effectively.
- Observe if the verbal and nonverbal messages are consistent.
- Observe if statements are complete and specific.
- Ask students to paraphrase another student's statement before giving their own statement.
- Have students draw a picture based on a verbal description given by their partner.
- Have listeners describe the communicator's feelings.
- Limit the amount of time each person may speak.

How do I maximize diversity within each group?

Because each group develops its own dynamic relationship, allow groups to exist for at least a month. Ideally, the same groups should work on two or three different projects so they can experience significant social growth. In general, strive for group memberships that represent a variety of learning styles, skills, and experiences. In that way, students can learn from each other.

However, specific learning activities highlight special skills, and the teacher/librarian may want to take advantage of the available student resources to present a variety of viewpoints. For those cases, some basic guidelines follow:

- If subject knowledge is emphasized, group together students with broad knowledge and those with specific insights.
- If information skills are accentuated, group together students with such prior knowledge with those who are more expert in the subject area than in information skills.
- If a variety of information sources are used, group together students who receive information in different ways (e.g., visually, aurally, kinesthetically).
- If information processing is the main task, group together students who analyze information sequentially with those who process it creatively or globally.
- If the presentation format is the main interest, group together students who approach that particular media in different ways (e.g., group detail-oriented learners with holistic learners, and technically competent students with those who have good ideas but are less competent in using technology).
- If social tasks are important, group together students with different social skills.

How do I help students resolve conflicts?

Preventative group groundwork lowers the probability of group conflict. Building an accepting, trusting atmosphere in which students can take risks safely short-circuits conflict. Maintaining a calm, respectful attitude in the middle of conflict provides a healthy model of behavior for students. Other suggestions follow.

- Develop class rules about individual and group responsibility. This may be a class project, the result of group work, or a discussion based on teacher guidelines. Rules may include everyone tries, everyone is respectful, and everyone participates and helps.
- Aim for win–win situations. Cooperative learning facilitates this condition.
- Accept conflict as a natural consequence of group dynamics. Until a conflict arises, group health will not be tested—and strengthened.
- Recognize dysfunctional behavior: aggression, blocking communication, self-confessing or self-pitying, horsing around, withdrawing.
- Conflicts may arise for different reasons. If students are confused, it may mean that they lack information or interpret information differently. They need to get the facts—objectively.
- Competitive conflict may arise from students having different needs or goals. Students may feel they are not being heard, or they may put down others. In such groups, students need to define their individual needs and goals so everyone may be satisfied to some extent.
- Structural conflict may arise from power struggles or questions about procedures. Students may blame one another or have sudden outbursts. Clear goals and procedures minimize personal power struggles. Using heterogeneous groups with shared responsibilities also helps control such conflict. Changing specific social task roles may also change the group's dynamics.
- Conflicting values may lead to blocked decision making. Sometimes students may role-play the opposing value to gain insight. Sometimes groups may need to agree to disagree: "Can you live with differences of opinion?" Fortunately, having an activity task and project provides an overriding goal and common ground for coalition building.
- Time constraints may lead to conflict. Teach time management skills. Assign a timekeeper

for each group. Provide wind-down time for each session.

- Provide students with the skills to solve problems. Help them gather facts, identify and define the problem, brainstorm solutions, evaluate possible solutions, and make a plan based on the agreed-upon solution. As students use critical thinking and creative approaches, they strengthen their problem-solving skills as well as improve cooperative learning skills in general.

- Intervene when a group is absolutely stuck—or is in a high-risk situation. Support students' efforts. Give new ideas. Talk about feelings. Diffuse tension through humor. Temporarily remove a student who is out of control. Assign individual tasks until the group can discuss the problem calmly. And know that you can intervene for positive behavior, too!

How do I help mainstream students with disabilities into cooperative learning groups?

Some students with disabilities may have difficulty receiving information, processing information, or expressing information. They may also have low self-esteem or may exhibit mood shifts, poor coordination, different behavior in different subject areas or types of activities, or difficulty in accomplishing tasks. The following suggestions might be useful to teachers and librarians who work with such students.

- Provide a variety of instructional modes, materials, learning tasks, and assessment methods.

- Encourage groups to assign specific tasks to individuals, taking advantage of each person's particular skills and interests. The nature of cooperative learning reinforces peer tutoring and support.

- Assess the students' needs and the activity's goals to determine what specific modifications need to be made.

- Help students become aware of and sensitive to various disabilities by involving them in simulation activities that illustrate a variety of handicapping situations.

- *Hearing impairments* create a particularly difficult situation. Separate groups to cut down on competing noise. Use visual instructions, and encourage face-to-face discussion. Take advantage of e-mail and intranet chats. Use short sentences.

- For *emotionally disturbed* students, provide high structure and clear time reminders. Give immediate and specific feedback.

- For *visually impaired* students, provide a magnifying glass and large paper with markers. Use an overhead projector. Be sensitive to lighting and viewing angles. Show students how to enlarge the typeface on computer applications.

- For *educable mentally retarded* students, subdivide the activity into smaller tasks. Use concrete materials and emphasize kinesthetic tasks. Give brief directions.

- For *learning disabled* students, give one direction at a time. Divide worksheets or forms into segments. Help students stay organized.

- Even though they are not disabled, students with *little English knowledge* compose a significant group and require special attention. Often, cultural as well as language barriers must be overcome. As much as possible, allow these students to draw upon their prior experiences to share their unique insights with peers. As with other challenged students, these learners need extra instructional prompts and practice.

CHAPTER

2

Inclusive Ways of Learning

Cooperative learning emphasizes heterogeneous grouping, based on the belief that complex problem solving flourishes when a variety of perspectives and skills are involved. How can educators ensure that all students will have equitable chances to learn and to share their knowledge? This chapter examines the total learning process and offers a framework for constructing effective learning experiences for all middle and senior high school students.

LEARNING FROM THE INSIDE OUT

It all starts in the body with the brain; specifically 100 billion nerve cells, or neurons, in the brain. Each neuron contacts another neuron between 5,000 and 50,000 times. As the neurons connect, neurotransmitters are stimulated and affect bodily functions, including learning. The five senses pick up information; this action is largely dependent on attention—which is driven by emotions. The brain (the limbic system specifically) then determines if that information is important. That's when the neurons kick in. Cells are stimulated and produce more neurotransmitters; this process strengthens short-term memory. With repeated neuron activation, long-term memory improves and messages are sent more effectively.

Because the brain is comprised of different parts, neural transmission results in specialized bodily reactions. For instance, the base of the brain controls basic biological processes and facial movements. The midbrain moves the eye, while the forebrain (cerebrum) deals with vision, memory, and social behavior. Each hemisphere of the brain directs one side of arm and leg movement. In addition, the left brain works analytically, focusing on sequencing and abstraction. The right brain covers the holistic and verbal functions. Some of the other left-brain, right-brain dichotomies include:

Left	Right
digital	spatial
computational	visuo-spatial
practical	original
symbolic	concrete
sequential	random
logical	intuitive
abstract	sensory

Yet all parts work simultaneously and affect one another. Because each person's brain develops slightly differently, various types of intelligences and means of processing develop.

LEARNING

Arthur Costa defines a problem as "any stimulus of change, the response to which is not readily apparent" (1985, 62). If new information fits with existing mental models, then there is no problem (this would be called assimilation by

Piaget). However, if the new data does not fit into existing structures, or if it contradicts present knowledge, then a problem exists. Either the person accepts, or accommodates, the information or the person rejects the new information. Actual learning, however, does not occur until that resolution is internalized, the result of comparisons and neural connections. Information blindly accepted is like rote memorization, called *taxon* memory. *Locale* memory, on the other hand, relates to the learner on a personal level and is truly learned.

Learning is not strictly a yes–no situation, nor is it one-dimensional. The Centre for Language in Primary Education (Barrs 1993) posits five dimensions of learning that students develop in interconnected ways:

- Confidence and independence
- Use of prior and emerging experience
- Skills and strategies: know-how
- Knowledge and understanding: content
- Reflection and metacognition

Cognitive Learning Elements

Benjamin Bloom's hierarchies of learning remain the classic model for looking at ways that persons use and apply knowledge. At the knowledge level, the learner defines and recalls data. With comprehension, the learner translates and interprets data. As the learner applies data, he or she can solve problems and predict results. On the analytical level, the learner connects and compares information. At the evaluative level, the learner appraises and critically views data. In this model, critical thinking is included in the highest cognitive mode of learning (Bloom and Krathwol 1956).

Interestingly, recent discussion on thinking notes that Bloom's taxonomy is not strictly hierarchically sequential. For example, in order to do a higher level of thinking, a student may have to draw upon what may be considered a lower form of thinking. It is the repertoire of cognitive responses that allows the student to display critical thinking consistently.

Several factors besides mode of intelligence are factors under this umbrella of learning.

Conceptual tempo refers to the timing mechanism of the brain. Girls tend to approach a problem cautiously, using a reflective approach. Boys are more apt to think impulsively. While children usually become more reflective with age, educators tend to pay more attention to the impulsive learners. Reflective students need more time to think through their responses, and impulsive students need ways to channel their energy.

Psychological differentiation deals with field dependence–independence. The field-independent learner is able to abstract stimuli and isolate them. The field-dependent learner takes context into consideration when making critical judgments. Traditional education favors the field-independent learner; cooperative learning favors the field-dependent learner.

Mindstyles is a construct (Reiff 1992, 16) that maintains that people are either abstract or concrete thinkers, and that they organize information either sequentially or randomly. Most people favor one or two combinations of learning styles: concrete sequential (step-by-step, hands-on learning), concrete random (trial and error), abstract sequential (decoding), or abstract random (holistic, emotional reflection). It should be noted that people change their modalities as they develop and as they react to different contexts.

Affective Learning Elements

Many educators forget about Bloom's other hierarchies: the affective domain and the psychomotor. The affective domain emphasizes feeling and emotion, while psychomotor deals with motor skills. Bloom considered affective categories to be hierarchical: from receiving (attention) to responding to value, to organizing values, up to the generalized characterization of a value complex. With respect to brain research, Bloom's taxonomy makes sense, because attention is one of the first necessary factors for learning, and emotion (or affect) accompanies attention.

Other manifestations of learning through the affective domain include:

Multidimensional thought: Students may construct meaning through multidimensional intellectual investigation.

Dynamic/changing knowledge: Students may consider knowledge as an evolving notion; information is seen as a gradual gathering and sifting of data that comes under constant scrutiny.

Decision making as clarified consensus: Students may emphasize understanding each person's perspective and promote a win–win situation that recognizes individual needs as well as institutional requirements.

PROCESSING

Many theories besides Bloom's focus on the concept of intellectual functioning. Most can be divided into three phases: data input (through the senses or from memory), data processing, and data output or application. In all cases, the term *information* refers to all kinds of data with which the learner comes into contact. Information itself exists independently of the learning and manifests itself in many forms. But until that contact point, any specific piece of information has no meaning to the learner.

At the input stage, learners often have preferred ways of sensing information. As they come into contact with stimuli, some learners prefer to observe, while others would rather actively experiment with the information. Input of data involves these skills:

- Being attentive to the environment
- Gathering data through the senses
- Recalling prior knowledge

The processing phase includes these skills:

- Internalizing information
- Setting new information in context of existing knowledge and beliefs
- Interpreting information
- Evaluating information
- Responding to the information
- Comparing information

The output phase includes these skills:

- Applying information
- Recreating information
- Disseminating information
- Acting upon the information
- Making predictions about the information

Multiple Intelligences

Howard Gardner's theory of multiple intelligences has become a mainstay in educational circles. The basic premise is that individuals relate to their surroundings in different ways. They may experience an affinity to certain subjects or may approach several subjects in the same manner. Most people use a variety of ways to learn but prefer two or three methods (particularly when under stress). Educators have the responsibility of teaching for different modalities and encouraging students to experience learning in a variety of ways. Yet it is also useful for students to identify their intelligence strengths and improve their weaker modes. Gardner's intelligences can be described as:

Word smart (linguistic): These students think in words and love reading and writing. Educators can give lectures and written assignments.

Picture smart (spatial): These students learn through images. Educators can use videos, visuals, games, and graphs.

Music smart (musical): These students learn through rhythms and melodies and by listening. Educators can use songs, raps, instruments, "super learning," and body rhythms.

Body smart (kinesthetic): These students learn through hands-on experiences, such as drama, sports, dance, manipulatives, and other sensations. Educators can use games, equipment, drama, movement, and other tactile experiences.

Logic smart (mathematical and scientific): These students use reason, logic, and symbols to form abstract connections and solve problems. Educators can provide experiments, puzzles, and calculators.

People smart (social sense): These students bounce ideas off people. Educators can offer learning teams, peer coaching, simulations, games, and clubs.

Self-smart (intrapersonal): These students reflect on their inner workings. Educators can suggest goal setting, journals, meditation, and self-paced projects.

Nature smart (naturalist): These students are sensitive to the natural world and can classify it in detail. Educators can encourage observation and link material to the environment.

Critical Thinking

As academic and lifelong needs change, the need for ways to assimilate information for decision making and problem solving becomes evident. This ability to appraise and critically view data in order to synthesize and apply it, planning and producing new information, comprises critical thinking. Bloom would consider these skills examples of the highest cognitive mode of learning.

Costa (1985, 45) identifies four complex thinking processes. Problem solving requires the ability to transform information in order to solve a problem or to generalize. Decision making looks for best alternatives through classification. Critical thinking aims for understanding and meaning through transforming and relating information. Creative thinking results in a novel product based on creating and transforming information.

Gallagher, Aschner, and Jenné (1967) categorize thinking modes along these lines: cognitive memory, which involves rote and recall; convergent thinking, which is analytic and integrated; divergent thinking, which is creative; and evaluative thinking, which is judgmental and value laden (Costa 1985).

Presseisen suggests five thinking processes: classification, which identifies and sorts information; qualification, which defines facts and problems; relationship, which analyzes and synthesizes; causation, which evaluates and predicts consequences; and transformation, which creates meanings through analogies and other logical induction (Costa 1985, 45).

Regardless of the models used to describe critical thinking, effective critical thinkers tend to have certain characteristics in common (Costa 1985, 24). They are perceptive, associative, conceptual, problem solving, critical, creative, and adventurous. They usually are goal-oriented, have a good repertoire of past knowledge and skills on which to overlay new information, have a good repertoire of processing strategies with which to manipulate new information, and can self-monitor their critical thinking processing. Some cognitive behaviors include good listening, checking for accuracy, posing questions, thinking and communicating precisely, and using all senses. In terms of the affective domain, they are persistent, deliberate, flexible, and curious (Costa and Kallick 1994). In short, effective critical thinkers know why to learn, what to learn, and how to learn.

Metacognition: Thinking about Thinking

A fourth dimension of thinking is metacognition: the conscious examination of the critical thinking process. Throughout learning, students should take time to reflect on the processes they use. In a way, research provides an abstract simulation of problem-solving strategies that people use throughout life. Students encounter obstacles and the unknown, and they must overcome or incorporate those issues through conscious decision making and reflection. This thinking about thinking, or metacognition, helps students transfer one experience or set of skills to other situations and problems.

Students can concretize metacognition in several ways. They can write learning journals about their efforts. They can think out loud and share their findings and frustrations. They can construct timelines that show their progress and forecast their next steps. Using a variety of metacognitive approaches affirms the differences among student learning strategies. Sharing those stylistic differences also provides all students a broader range of ways to respond to problems.

VARIABLES INFLUENCING LEARNING

The Learner

The most complex component in the learning process is probably the learner. Even the youngest learner has preferential ways of receiving, processing, and using information.

In terms of receiving or inputting information, learners may favor different sensory modes: vision, hearing, touch. As they come into contact with information, some learners prefer to observe, while others prefer to actively experiment with the information. The point of contact does not exist in a vacuum. Learners have different cognitive and affective styles of receiving information. Even physiological factors affect the reception of information: health, gender-linked factors, need for movement, inner-time rhythms.

At the processing stage, learners differ in the ways they manipulate information. Sternberg (1985) proposes a triarchic theory of information processing styles: (1) computational or analytical, in which the learner examines information step-wise; (2) experiential or creative, in which the learner intuitively processes information convergently; and (3) contextual, in which the learner relates to information by manipulating its environment.

At the output stage, too, learners usually have preferred ways of expressing their findings or restructuring information. Because the output information also becomes the basis for the new acquisition of knowledge and skills, output style often leads to input style. However, it should be noted that the preferred form of information for learner reception may well differ from the preferred form of learner expression. For example, an avid reader may not like to write. Although reading is certainly related to writing, the two activities require different skills.

In addition, students vary with respect to the extent that they can—and wish to—share information. They may lack specific expressive skills or interpersonal skills. They may have a disability that makes it difficult for them to use their preferred form of expression. And they may have varying psychological needs for sharing.

To further complicate the picture, the developmental stages of the learner must be taken into consideration. Jean Piaget noted the concrete stage of older children, who understand logic and rules. He asserted that the formal stage of learning occurs during the teen years or later. At that point, abstract thought, deductive reasoning, and idealism come to the forefront (Sund 1976). Erik Erikson (1950) provided a social/emotional counterpart to Piaget's cognitive stages, asserting that older children concentrate on industry: developing skills and achieving tasks. Teenagers must work out the task of identity: Who am I? These affective tasks color the learner's processing.

Blocks to Learning. At any processing point, internal dysfunction may occur. Lumped together as learning disabilities, these obstacles to learning require compensatory action. Students with learning disabilities live with some kind of disorder and may seem disoriented in terms of time or space.

The learning process may also be psychologically blocked by the student. Individuals may not be able to perceive the information or task at hand because they cannot isolate the problem, they cannot define terms, they do not use all their senses, or they cannot see the obvious. Their prior experiences and preconceptions may distort their perception and their ability to assimilate new information. Culturally, students may shape information to fit prior patterns, they may overgeneralize, they may not think independently of their background, or they may block out ideas that don't agree with prior ones. Emotionally, students may stop with the first solution to gain immediate success, they may want secure and nonthreatening answers, or they may fear or distrust the new information.

The Environment

Beyond the innate characteristics of the learner are the experiences that affect new learning contacts. The environment plays a significant role, be it the family and immediate social peers or the larger social climate or culture. In each case, variances exist in learning expectation and academic preparation.

Different cultures use a variety of learning modes and organize information in different ways. For example, some cultures use a spiral approach rather than outline form; others work in counterpoints. Teaching styles and resources available vary from country to country; in some countries, books are scarce and teachers may encourage rote learning or recitation to compensate for lack of materials. Attitudes toward competition and cooperation vary. In some cultures, what teachers in the United States would call plagiarism would be considered reverence for other minds. By the year 2000, more than half of the students in 53 American cities will be from minority ethnic groups. In addition, countries are developing more interdependence, which will require more Americans to learn about other cultures.

Even within the U.S. mainstream culture, current social trends are affecting learning and instruction. For example, a majority of students born in 1983 will live at some point in time with only one parent. With more parents working outside the home, the issue of latchkey children grows. Family stereotypes in books need to be re-examined, and extended hours for after-school education is becoming a norm. The labor force demand has shifted to service and information sectors, and job stability has steadily decreased. And, of course, as technology's role has increased, schools are mandated to integrate technical skills into the curriculum.

Educational Structure

Though the traditional school with "sage on the stage" lectures exists, many schools support more self-directed teaching. Teachers and students are given more freedom, and more responsibility, for structuring activities to foster authentic, powerful learning. Though the context for learning remains important, inquiry-centered learning predominates. In this scenario, the teacher acts as a coach and manager, rather than a boss. Students self-monitor their learning, and the teacher modifies lessons in response to student needs. A variety of thinking processes are valued, and whole-child development is encouraged. The school believes in partnerships for learning and carries that belief out in team-teaching and community involvement.

These practices mirror the development of student learning from an authoritarian, black-and-white approach to an open-minded commitment to exploring issues responsively. The student and the educator are working in tandem to solve meaningful problems together.

Educational Technology

Technology has helped change the way educators teach and students learn. More than ever, the preset lesson, in which the teacher controls the class and the resources, is an anomaly. Instead, the teacher and librarian structure a learning environment and use technology as a structuring and resource tool. In fact, particularly with the advent of the Internet, students have access to a world of teachers and other experts. Students then can control their learning to a greater degree. And, quite frankly, the lure of new technology attracts students and holds their attention.

Technology also allows students to demonstrate their learning in a variety of ways. Tests can vary from workstation to workstation. Students can use a content-neutral software program, such as a multimedia authoring program, to construct an original presentation. In fact, technology facilitates interdisciplinary projects so students may gather information and manipulate it in several ways simultaneously.

Diverse students can be accommodated more easily because of technology. Programs can be self-paced; students may be able to approach the content at different levels or at different points. Multimedia programs, in particular, combine text, graphics, and sound so students are given more cues in order to grasp concepts. Some technology is available in bilingual versions, and students can search the Internet for information in their first language. Adaptive technology can compensate for physical disabilities. For students to take full advantage of technology, though, the teacher has to feel comfortable with it—and needs to show students how to use the equipment.

HOW CAN EDUCATORS MAXIMIZE LEARNING?

In an academic setting, the linchpin in the learning process is the specific task or assignment. Taking into account the variety of learner characteristics and prior experiences, the educator can provide a planned learning activity or task that can guide students in their learning development.

The U.S. Department of Education has summarized research about teaching and learning in the publication *What Works* (1986): "How much time students are actively engaged in learning contributes strongly to their achievement. The amount of time available for learning is determined by the instruction and management skills of the teacher" (34). Educators need to plan class work, communicate goals, and regulate the learning activity. "When teachers explain exactly what students are expected to learn, and demonstrate the steps needed to accomplish a particular academic task, students learn more" (*What Works* 1986, 35).

Thus, educators determine what information students will come into contact with. They provide the goals and activity structure to guide the learning process. As expectations and procedures are clarified, students develop thinking skills more effectively. Educators can offer realistic challenges and relevant constraints, particularly as they ask probing questions. On their part, students should also use their own background knowledge to formulate questions that demand critical thinking.

With a guided task structure, the learning process can begin on a conscious level much earlier. Rather than dealing with incoming information haphazardly, the learner can plan ahead for an efficient point of contact with preselected information. Throughout the information process educators can facilitate student learning by:

- Creating a classroom climate conducive to critical thinking (e.g., respecting student efforts and encouraging risk taking)
- Structuring learning experiences that make skills meaningful
- Providing access to resources that enable students to accomplish the learning task
- Providing adequate time for processing and evaluation
- Modeling and demonstrating critical thinking strategies
- Verbalizing the critical thinking process while enacting it
- Posing open-ended inquiry questions about critical thinking
- Encouraging students to clarify their statements and justify their conclusions
- Providing feedback and other reinforcement to students about their learning processes
- Encouraging students to express and self-monitor their learning processes through verbalization or journal writing

How do educators deal with a potentially wide spectrum of learning differences? Obviously, a variety of instructional methods and activities must be used to help students connect with information. The more aware educators are of their students' predispositions for information processing and possible blocks to learning, the more effectively they can teach skills that can link the known to the unknown. Differences in learning styles justify the use of small-group work as a means to incorporate and take advantage of unique approaches to information. Educators must also be sensitive to differing cultural attitudes and expectations and promote pluralism. Finally, social upheaval demands instruction on problem solving and critical thinking so students can deal with family and occupational instability.

TIPS

What learning strategies correspond to left- and right-brain thinking?

Left-brainers respond well to clear, step-by-step directions; verbal instruction; logic-based problem solving; activities that emphasize facts and details; and standards-based assessment.

Right-brainers respond well to visual and kinesthetic instruction, open-ended assignments, emotional responses, intuitive problem solving, activities that emphasize main ideas and visualization, and descriptive, concrete rubrics.

How can I use problem solving to encourage critical thinking?

One approach to critical thinking and information processing is problem solving. Here are some questions the educator can pose to students to help guide them along the thinking route (Krapp 1988, 33):

Planning: What is the problem to solve? What is its nature? Can you break down the problem into smaller steps? What keywords are associated with the problem?

Preselecting information: What information is needed to solve the problem? What do you know already?

Evaluating information: What are the main ideas? Which information is relevant? What details are irrelevant? Is the information accurate? What is its bias? How is a stance justified? How current are the data? How complex or profound is the information?

Organizing information: Can you sort the information? Can you sequence the information alphabetically, chronologically, along a continuum, graphically? Can you connect the different pieces of information by outline, mapping, flowchart, or hypermedia stack?

Expanding information: Can you transform the information by analogy or metaphor, by visualization or imagery, by adaptation?

Synthesizing information: What conclusions can you make based on the information? What predictions can you make?

Using information: How does the information solve the problem? Can the information be used in another situation?

Sharing information: How should the information be restructured for sharing? What is an effective way to communicate the information and your conclusions?

How can I help students think more creatively and develop their neuron connections?

Critical thinking skills require creative manipulation of information. One needs to examine information from various perspectives, comparing it to different data or turning it inside out. Just as athletes warm up their muscles before performing, so too should learners warm up their mental muscles. Here are some mental warm-ups to do in groups or individually:

Transformation patterns: To change information, try these approaches:

- Change the size of proportion
- Change the characteristics or properties to make them thicker, softer, stronger
- Change the time frame
- Change the perspective to that of an ant, an airplane, a sea coral
- Examine from the inside out
- Divide it or combine it with other things
- Alter it: add, subtract, replace, relocate, redesign
- Make it simpler or more complex

Cross-system thinking: Have students develop mathematical formulas for social situations. Have them compose music to explain a scientific phenomenon.

Repeated shape: Give students a sheet filled with a repeated shape, say, small triangles. Students incorporate designs that creatively reveal concepts using the shapes.

New and improved: Students think of unusual uses for an object, such as a flower pot, a trashed car, a ruined diskette. Students think of improvements for an existing item, such as a toaster or pinball machine.

I am a camera: Students imagine being a camera, a doorknob, a turtle, a piece of masking tape, a peach pit.

Just suppose: Pose an improbable situation and have students explain the consequences, for example, "Just suppose that dogs could talk…"

Combos: Each student writes a word. In groups of three, students find a relationship among their words and develop a research hypothesis based on the relationship. For example, the three words might be *cow, leprechaun,* and *sweatshirt.* The connection could be "cows wearing leprechaun sweatshirts." A possible research hypothesis could be: "Cows wearing sweatshirts with leprechaun motifs are more common than leprechauns wearing sweatshirts with cow motifs." This exercise could be extended to include group brainstorming of possible research strategies to test the hypothesis.

Working backward: Students start with a result or end product and work backward to find the source, for example, Where does a mirror come from? Why are some butterflies colorful and others not?

Abbreviations: Students create new meanings for abbreviations. For example, MBA could mean Multiple-Backed Ant. Students may create abbreviations from proverbs or numerical equivalencies for other students to decode, for example, ARSGNM = a rolling stone gathers no moss; 7D in a W = seven days in a week.

Word play: Students find or create word plays and decode them. As examples, "ecnalg" means backward glance; "milonelion" means one in a million. Note that this exercise is more difficult for students who know little idiomatic English.

Mnemonics: Students create mnemonics to help them memorize lists. For example, HOMES indicates the initials of the five Great Lakes.

Brainstorming structures: As a class, students brainstorm possible information resources, topical experts, and ways to transform and present information.

Many logic, work, math, and game puzzle books include riddles and puzzles to solve. Students can locate resources and present mental warm-ups of their own choosing.

What strategies help ensure gender-equitable learning?

- Provide a wide variety of resources, both in terms of perspective and format.
- Encourage students to explore alternative ways to gather information: interview, observe, survey.
- Allow students to choose how to present their findings: written report, multimedia stack, slide–tape show, skit, game.
- Have students respond to an activity both intellectually and emotionally.
- Provide extra training or background explanation for students whose prior experiences put them at a disadvantage (e.g., Internet training for girls or students without home computers; reference sheet of literary allusions and their origins).
- Suggest various ways to organize information: outline, webbing, graphical organizers.
- Ensure that all students have equitable opportunities for physical access to information (e.g., everyone has time on computers).
- Ensure that students feel that they control their own learning.

CHAPTER 3

Outcomes-Based Education

What do schools want students to know and do when they graduate? What outcomes are expected? That's education's bottom line. In looking at this issue, schools have often planned a scope and sequence of courses to provide the information and experiences needed in order to graduate an educated person. If the student attended these courses and passed the required tests, then he or she was awarded a diploma.

This approach no longer suffices. The cry for standards, by both local and national constituents, signals the need for student and school accountability. Parents and the community demand that a diploma, or other certificate, mean more than a paper of completion of a certain number of hours. They want to be assured that the graduate is prepared to enter the world as a contributing citizen. This national movement points to the need for equitable education throughout the nation; today's highly mobile population requires a similar knowledge base from area to area.

How can learning become authentic and yet standard in schools in very different regions serving very different students? One possible solution is outcomes-based education. This chapter explores this concept and its implications for cooperative learning activities.

WHAT IS OUTCOMES-BASED EDUCATION?

Outcomes-based education embraces the concept of setting measurable goals as the intended result of a learning experience. When developed and stated clearly, outcomes specify what schools want students to accomplish. With the surge toward educational reform, outcomes serve as a way to define competencies needed for graduates and to align instruction with those competencies. Farmington, Minnesota, Public Schools lists four levels of outcomes:

Exit Outcomes: "Those things students should know, be able to do, be like, and feel when they graduate."

Program Outcomes: "Specific tools students need in each subject area; the purpose or justification for the subject."

Course and Grade Level Outcomes: "Specific tools students need in each course or grade level."

Performance Indicators: "Specific criteria for each outcome. They tell everyone exactly what is involved in learning that outcome, what things are to be taught and learned." (Parrott 1989, 1)

Costa distinguishes between *content* outcomes and *process* outcomes, the latter being more authentic because they apply the knowledge base to experience.

This may sound suspiciously like instructional objectives, in which the standard phrase is: "*XXX* number of students will do *YYY* to *ZZZ* level of ability within *AAA* conditions (e.g., time, space)." Both describe standards that the students will meet or exceed. Both are set within a framework of performance. Both are criterion-referenced; that is, performance is measured against an objective standard rather than in relationship to the abilities of other students. Both use an assessment tool to determine whether or not a student achieves the standard.

Some terms used in discussing outcomes and instructional objectives are comparable:

Outcomes	Instructional objectives
outcome	objective
descriptor	main intent performance
indicator	indicator behavior
benchmark	criterion test item

While instructional objectives are usually associated with specific units or activities, outcomes tend to be global. Typically, 1–10 outcomes describe a course. In the Tamalpais Union High School District, 14 student performance outcomes encompass the essential concepts and skills that graduating seniors must demonstrate. On the other hand, the performance indicators more resemble the instructional objectives; they are detailed and specific.

Here is an example from the Education Task Force (ETF), a consortium of K-14 public schools in Marin County, California. ETF has been developing a series of outcomes to drive education and provide seamless articulation between school levels. One of the outcomes identified by ETF is: "Using technology as a tool to access information, analyze and solve problems, and communicate ideas." To concretize the outcome, each is given a descriptor: "The student demonstrates competence in the use of authoring tools, graphic applications, and telecommunications. Uses technology in many disciplines to solve problems. Selects and employs a variety of electronic technology resources for research and communication. Creates products using technologies. Uses technology responsibly, legally, and ethically" (Tamalpais 1995).

A third step specifies the performance indicators that will be accepted as demonstrating that the student has achieved a particular outcome. For high school graduates, technology indicators include: "Within a curricular context the student will produce a solo project which exhibits mastery of the following technologies: authoring tools, graphics, telecommunications plus items from at least two different technology categories. Students may propose projects that encompass such processes as design, construction, and modeling. Or, the student will develop a portfolio that incorporates the use of three or more technologies with sample works from at least four subject areas." Two other indicators fill out the list. Additionally, benchmark indicators are identified for second, fifth, and eighth graders. For instance, the fifth-grade benchmark includes: "cross-curricular project presented by a small group, utilizing at least two authoring tools plus two other technologies" (Tamalpais 1995).

STANDARDS

Though it is not the intent of this book to focus on standards, certainly standards play a role in outcomes-based education and in examining student work in particular. Standards can be analogous to setting the bar: a high jumper is expected to clear (outcome) a 5-foot bar (standard). Schools and other educational entities are busy creating standards, from class level to national level. Such groups describe the level of acceptable or desired competence, but they vary widely in their perspective.

The Mid-continent Regional Educational Laboratory (McREL) has been developing a database of the national standards and benchmarks and has clarified the variation in definitions and approaches. First, McREL distinguishes between *content* and *curriculum* standards; the former states what students should know and do, and the latter states what should happen in the classroom. For example, "a student should be able to manipulate fractions" (content) contrasts to "a student should be able to draw, describe, or diagram fractions" (curriculum). McREL also distinguishes between *content* and *performance* standards. The critical difference is that a performance standard describes a task that a student is supposed to accomplish in order to demonstrate his/her knowledge or skill. In terms of fractions, a performance standard might be "a student should be able to accurately calculate how to share two pies among seven people equally" (Kendall and Marzano 1995).

In practice, standards are usually general statements. Content standards most closely resemble outcomes. Performance standards correlate to outcome indicators. Subcomponent standards refer to benchmarks, just as with outcomes-based educational terms.

In the context of standards, cooperative learning activities may be used as benchmarks. The products created by small groups demonstrate students' ability to synthesize and apply content skills and concepts. Educators set the standard and then assess the students' level of competence.

AUTHENTIC ASSESSMENT

Assessment, in general, refers to "the process of synthesizing information about individuals in order to understand and describe them better" (Brown 1985). Assessment is a basic part of education because it enables one to determine whether students "get it," whether they meet the standard. Authentic assessment ties assessment to real life. Not surprisingly, outcomes are more directly associated with authentic assessment than are instructional objectives. The underlying theory is that outcomes need to be authentic: that is, true-to-life and reflecting lifelong learning skills. Outcomes should also answer essential questions and use high-order thinking skills. Thus, to measure outcomes, authentic assessment is usually called for, referring to a complex set of performances. It is the difference between describing how to ride a bike and actually putting the foot to the pedal and pumping down the street. Thus, a Scantron bubble test would be an unlikely authentic assessment tool; a student-directed play would more closely correlate with real life, and a Junior Achievement business venture would constitute a still more authentic assessment, especially as students count their profits.

Authentic assessments can assume many forms. In their book on assessing classroom learning, McTighe and Ferrara categorize assessment items as follows:

Product: lab report, story, poem, art exhibit, model, videotape, spreadsheet

Performance: dance, demonstration, athletic competition, debate, recital

Process: conference, interview, journal

The assessment task itself should have these characteristics:

- Multidimensional and complex in nature
- Incorporated modalities of learning
- Demonstrated progress over time
- Learned with practice rather than based on native talent
- Built on practice and feedback
- Aligned with school outcomes and goals

This approach to accountability not only helps students see the relevance of their learning, but it also reflects the demand that education prepare students for the world of work. The 1991 SCANS report noted misalignments between education and employment: writing reports is useful, but literary criticism is not; topology has limited value in comparison with discrete mathematics, such as statistics and accounting.

Authentic assessment helps bridge the two worlds. By designing substantive projects, students concretely demonstrate their ability to work with peers and accomplish specific tasks. They show that they can apply theoretical concepts to solving lifelike problems. As a result, education doesn't seem to operate in a vacuum;

Outstanding: 4	Highly Competent: 3	Competent: 2	Not Yet Proficient: 1
Complexity in defining problem and stating thesis	Clearly defines problem or states thesis	Defines problem or states thesis	Does not define problem or state thesis
Accesses relevant information from a wide variety of sources	Accesses relevant information from diverse sources	Accesses relevant information	Does not access relevant information
Shows thorough understanding of the problem, concepts, and processes	Shows good understanding of the problem, concepts, and processes	Shows general understanding of the problem, concepts, and processes	Shows little or no understanding of the problem, concepts, and processes
Provides an exceptionally clear, coherent, complete, and organized explanation	Provides a clear, coherent, complete, and organized explanation	Provides a reasonably clear, coherent, complete, and organized explanation	Provides an unclear or incomplete explanation
Rarely contains technical errors	Contains few technical errors	Contains some technical errors	Contains many technical errors
Contains relevant information	Contains relevant information	Contains relevant information	Contains very little information
Uses correct language mechanics and usage	Uses correct language mechanics and usage	Uses correct language mechanics and usage	Contains many errors in language mechanics and usage
Production and composition are excellent	Production and composition are good	Production and composition are fair	Production and composition are poor
Integrates diverse technologies effectively	Integrates technologies effectively	Integrates technologies	Does not integrate technologies

Figure 3.1   Technology and product rubric.

it truly prepares students for the rest of their lives. It provides real learning for real results.

It should be noted that authentic assessment is not a one-time event. Just as in the world of work, assessment is an ongoing activity. As a person creates a draft or a model, that effort is analyzed and feedback is given so the ultimate product will be the best possible. So too in education, as students make a first attempt in a project, teachers should provide meaningful feedback—and students should assess their own work and their peers' to ensure the best final results.

RUBRICS

How does one assess projects objectively? Unlike instructional objectives, outcomes-based education typically involves rubrics that describe performance at various levels of competencies. These rubrics are developed at the same time as the outcomes so that everyone involved in the outcome has a clear understanding of what is being measured and the degree of competency required at each level. Building on the technology above, fig. 3.1 represents a technology and product rubric (Derich 1996).

As the chart shows, the difference between levels of competence often lies in degree or thoroughness, such as "wide variety" versus "diverse" or "some" versus "many." These keywords act as critical features to distinguish one level of competency from another. As educators and students develop rubrics, they identify what is "good" by identifying these critical differences. Concurrently, rubrics are anchored in actual products or performances, so everyone knows what a 4 looks like in comparison to a 3 or 2 or 1. How different is this approach to learning from the practice where a teacher gives an abstract goal or assignment and doesn't show any examples of the desired product at the beginning!

ALIGNING INSTRUCTION

Another critical feature of outcomes-based education is that outcomes represent essential learnings and shape instruction more thoroughly. Basically, once outcomes and specific indicators are determined, then the instruction can be aligned to them. Say that students will develop a stock market portfolio. To do so, students need to know key definitions, how the stock market operates, and how to invest. Knowing this, the teacher can then decide how to help students gain those prerequisite component skills. Perhaps a brief lecture and a reference sheet will provide the definitions, maybe a video about the stock market will give an idea of its operations. The teacher might use a Web site to allow students to follow the market and create individual investment portfolios. The assessment, then, is easy: to view student stock portfolios.

With such a lesson, it may be assumed that most students will have the same prerequisite component skills. However, some students may have little experience with the Internet, and they will need added instruction in its use. In fact, a few students might not know how to type in the required information or know how to read English. Teachers need to check their assumptions about students' prior learning experiences and modify their instruction to ensure that all students will "start on the same page" of learning so they can take the next critical learning step together.

In effect, this aspect of outcomes-based education is the most powerful one because it acknowledges the different experiences that each student brings to the classroom. In one sense, by the time students enter middle school, they should be able to read and work in groups; they have had opportunities to learn certain concepts along the way. However, in another sense, students become more divergent by the time they reach middle school because of the way they respond to school and to life experiences in general. That is why cooperative learning is a boon to teachers. Students do not have to master every prerequisite component skill in order to accomplish a project; they can learn from their peers or depend on them to take command of a particular aspect of the project. While some educators may wince at the prospect that a student is off the hook for learning a specific skill or concept, at least the student is seeing that skill or idea being modeled by a peer. Moreover, if that skill is considered essential for every student, then the assessment or the project itself can be designed to make sure that every student exhibits it. Taking the stock market example again, if each student has to know how to develop a portfolio, then the teacher makes sure that each student has a separate stock market account and keeps a running personal record of how she or he chose each stock and how each stock fared.

In aligning instruction to the outcome, the teacher breaks down instruction into manageable steps to the point that all students can achieve the desired outcome. Continuing with the stock market lesson, the teacher may have students create a Truth Table; students determine whether certain characteristics or terms are relevant to the stock market and enter them in the appropriate column of the chart (see fig. 3.2).

After students show they know the terms, they progress to the next piece of instruction. Those who do not understand the terms are remediated if that learning is considered essential, or with cooperative groups, the teacher might decide that students can pick up the jargon at the next step. The teacher works in partnership with students to control the conditions of assessment and learning.

The gaps between learning steps might be called the critical features, that is, the differences between *step n* and *step n + 1*. Those differences were noted when examining performance rubrics: "good" versus "fair," for instance. The difference between defining stock market terms and knowing how the stock market operates is a big step; students must identify each process or operation (both in terms of definition and function) and must also sequence these processes.

Yes	No
Securities and Exchange	Bureau of Labor
New York	Knoxville
brokers	sales clerks
bull	tiger
shares	slices
bond	diploma
commodity	package
mutual fund	adversary fund

Figure 3.2 Stock market truth table.

Looking at this jump, a teacher might well include a step that defines and demonstrates various stock market functions before explaining the entire organizational process.

IMPLICATIONS FOR COOPERATIVE LEARNING ACTIVITIES

Teachers must determine the prerequisite component skills of cooperation as well as content knowledge. When information literacy becomes a third factor, the prerequisite component skills in that area must be assessed as well. Instructional design can become quite complex because a student may be at different stages for each of these learning aspects. Heterogeneous groupings in cooperative learning help to level the playing or learning field so students have a better chance of gaining experience from each other in each of these modes and thus are able to achieve the desired benchmark performance. Everyone gains. Most teachers cannot afford the time to develop an individual program of instruction for each student based on his or her prerequisite skills; cooperative learning provides a learning environment that facilitates each student's ability to create his or her own individualized diagnosis and learning program.

Thus, a key to significant learning and achievement of outcomes-based education is the design of meaningful benchmark projects that demonstrate authentic student learning aligned with the desired skills and knowledge as well as the instruction. The project also needs to be open-ended enough to allow the strengths of cooperative learning to function so that each student can bring to it individual gifts and so the group can shape it to maximize their learning.

TIPS

How is outcomes-based education related to project-based learning?

Project-based learning uses the design and development of a product or presentation as the contextual vehicle for learning key concepts and skills. Typically, project-based learning spans several lesson units and crosses subject disciplines. Because of the amount of research and synthesis involved, projects may demand an extended period of time. Projects are often conducted by a group of students, and the teacher acts as a facilitator.

Outcomes-based education frequently utilizes projects as an effective way to authentically assess student learning. However, outcomes need not be cooperatively based, nor are projects a necessary way to measure outcomes. For example, developing and following a process might form the basis for the assessment; a formal report, such as a white paper, might be used to assess a student's applied knowledge.

Moreover, projects might not be based on a desired outcome. A teacher could assign students an open-ended project that has little to do with essential concepts or complex learning; an example might be the construction of a California mission model out of sugar cubes.

In this book, benchmark projects are intended to provide a learning experience that lends itself to authentic assessment of meaningful educational outcomes. In the final analysis, outcomes lie within the control of the learning community.

How does constructivist teaching fit into outcomes-based education?

Constructivism asserts that students learn by constructing their own knowledge. In this approach, teachers act as guides and consultants rather than directors of learning. The emphasis is on student conjecture and discovery rather than on conventional knowledge passed down from teacher to student.

Outcomes stated at the beginning may seem antithetical to constructivist theory, but the two can work together. Students should help determine outcomes, to have a say in what they think is important to learn. Within each outcome, students can construct meaning as they pursue ways to demonstrate their competence. Benchmark projects lend themselves to constructivist learning because they pose questions or scenarios that students must solve; students can develop individual or collaborative strategies.

How do I write a rubric?

1. Start with the purpose of the rubric. What is being assessed? Why is it being assessed? How is the rubric aligned with the outcome or specific benchmark?
2. Set the scoring criteria and descriptors. What features of the product are critical? How can those features be described?
3. Determine levels of achievement or competence. How many degrees of difference are needed? Usually, four to six levels provide enough of a range to discriminate between two products. How will those levels be defined? "Exemplary / competent / satisfactory / nearly satisfactory / beginning / no attempt" is one set of ratings that describe quality. Degrees of frequency might be represented by "frequently / sometimes / rarely / never." Degrees of competency could be listed as "expert / advanced / intermediate / beginner."
4. Create descriptors for each level. Use sample work to help anchor the descriptions. Differentiate levels through the use of the critical features identified earlier. Use concrete behaviors and evidence rather than abstract terms such as *understand* or *know*.
5. Develop a procedure and train assessors so scoring will be consistent and reliable. Find sample work that exemplifies each level, and have assessors determine why each sample fits the description.

What are some ways to introduce authentic assessments?

- Collect examples of authentic assessments.
- Build on existing teaching strategies; incorporate an activity that fosters student transfer of knowledge to the real world. An easy method is to structure a simulation: Students reenact a Senate proceeding, for example, instead of writing a paper about a Senate bill.
- Collaborate with another teacher to design an interdisciplinary unit that weaves in authentic assessment.
- Brainstorm with students about ways that they *know* that they can do something, i.e., drive a car, bake a cake, write a computer program, sing in a musical production.
- Brainstorm with students about possible culminating activities that would demonstrate deep learning that applies concepts to daily life.
- Use phrases such as "What does it look like?" "What do you feel when…" "How do you know?" as you think about and discuss assessment.
- Have students look at existing projects and identify critical features that distinguish various levels of accomplishment. From that exercise, have the class develop a rubric.
- Start with a clear-cut presentation, such as a lab procedure or a step-by-step demonstration, and develop two rubrics, one that

describes competence of the content and another that describes the presentation itself.

- Have students develop portfolios of their work that show progress over time as well as their best efforts. Then have students write reflective letters explaining their choices and assessing their own progress.

CHAPTER

4
Information Literacy

The U.S. Department of Labor's Secretary's Commission on Achieving Necessary Skills (SCANS) identified a three-part foundation of skills and personal qualities needed for employment: basic skills (three Rs), thinking skills, and personal qualities. They also identified five competencies, based on the first skills, that students need to exhibit: the ability to productively use resources, interpersonal skills, information, technology, and systems. The 1991 SCANS report, which asked industry what skills employees need as they enter a particular field, stated that the ability to process and communicate information was crucial.

Today's students have lived their whole lives in an age where information doubles every two years. The question is, How well do these young people understand, interpret, and use such information? Though basic facts and concepts (such as simple arithmetic and rules of grammar) need to be memorized in order to access them quickly, there is no way students can hope to master all the knowledge in the world. They *can*, however, learn how to find and examine information and decide how to deal with it.

The American Association of School Librarians asserts that information literacy includes three standards: accessing information efficiently and effectively, evaluating information critically and competently, and using information effectively and creatively. This set of learning processes constitutes information literacy and figures as a major component of cooperative learning activities in the library media center.

MODELS OF INFORMATION LITERACY

Several paradigms describe information literacy. None is definitive. Each proposes unique characteristics.

Probably the most fashionable model is familiarly called The Big Six, which was proposed by Michael Eisenberg and Robert Berkowitz in 1990. Their approach was to provide a strategy that would meet information needs or assist in decision making. The six skills include:

- Task Definition: framing the information question and identifying the information needed to answer it
- Information Seeking Strategies: brainstorming and selecting sources
- Location and Access: locating sources and information within them
- Use of Information: engagement and extraction
- Synthesis: organizing information from multiple sources and presenting it
- Evaluation: judging the process and product

The American Association of School Libraries is part of a National Forum on Information Literacy. To make sure that library resource centers help students and staff become effective users of information and ideas, AASL has identified the following information problem-solving skills:

- Defining the need for information: framing the need and relating information to prior knowledge
- Initiating the search strategy: organizing ideas, selecting key terms, identifying multiple sources
- Locating resources: accessing sources and specific information
- Assessing and comprehending the information: identifying and assessing relevant information, comparing sources
- Interpreting the information: using the sources to solve the information problem
- Communicating the information: determining purpose for communication and developing product
- Evaluating the product and process: How could it be done better?

AASL emphasizes the cooperative instructional efforts of classroom teachers and librarians as they instruct students in these skills. As Judy Pitts noted in her 1994 dissertation: "Students learn best when units of study emphasize both subject and information seeking and use; these units are best planned and implemented by teacher and teacher-librarian together" (*Emergency Librarian* 1995, 34).

Michael Marland (1981), of the British National Book League on Books for Schools, has examined this issue of helping students learn how to find out information. His thinking, which still has currency in Britain, is that students encounter nine question steps when doing assignments:

1. What do I need to do? (formulate and analyze need)
2. Where could I go? (identify and appraise likely sources)
3. How do I get to the information? (trace and locate individual resources)
4. Which resources shall I use? (examine and reject/select individual resources)
5. How shall I use the resources? (interrogate resources)
6. What should I make a record of? (record and store information)
7. Have I got the information I need? (interpret, analyze, synthesize, evaluate)
8. How should I present it? (present, communicate)
9. What have I achieved? (evaluate)

Marjorie Pappas and A. Tepe (1995) helped to develop a nonlinear information skills model. They contend students should have a repertoire of options as they gather and use information. One unique feature of their schematic is the inclusion of "appreciation and enjoyment." It brings up the point that research can be rewarding and satisfying. The other concepts are:

- Presearch: using prior knowledge and building background information
- Search: identifying key concepts and selecting information resources, tools, and providers
- Interpretation: assessing usefulness of the information and developing meaning
- Communication: organizing and formatting information in order to share it
- Evaluation: assessing product and process

In terms of research strategies, I have developed my own 12-step research process with two general directives: (1) document your steps and (2) periodically review and revise your question and keywords. The other strategies are:

1. Get background information.
2. Clarify definitions.
3. Use access tools, such as indexes.
4. Find in-depth information.
5. Find facts in specialized reference sources.
6. Find current facts in periodicals, databases, and the Internet.
7. Try alternative sources such as video, pamphlets, interviews, etc.

Table 4.1 Research Process Stages and Corresponding Instructional Strategies

Research Stage	Instructional Strategies
1. Identify information need.	Brainstorm/cluster/map; journal/Quickwrite.
2. Formulate search question.	Develop questioning processes.
3. Identify key concepts.	Use general sources for background information.
4. Identify possible sources.	Brainstorm; classify sources; critique sources.
5. Develop research strategy.	Use keyword and Boolean strategies; use research steps.
6. Locate/examine resources.	Interview; use other sites; collect resources; critique.
7. Select resources.	Develop search strategies; use research skills.
8. Search for information in sources.	Read; view.
9. Evaluate and organize information.	Cluster/map/outline; take notes.
10. Analyze/interpret information.	Review information in light of original needs.
11. Present information.	Determine presentation options; develop product.
12. Evaluate product and process.	Review; modify strategies for next project.

From California School Library Association, *From Library Skills to Information Literacy: A Handbook for the 21st Century* (Castle Rock, Colo., Hi Willow Research & Publishing, 1994).

8. Alternate between general information and specific facts.
9. Evaluate the citations listed in each source as a possible new direction to pursue.
10. Research other subject fields related to the question.

Obviously, information skills models overlap. James Herring (1997), from the United Kingdom, categorizes information literacy skills into four issues: purpose, location, use, and self-evaluation. One underlying tenet is that the user brings prior knowledge to the information experience and shapes the process. It is with the user's perspective that information is located, evaluated, interpreted, and shared. Reviewing the most common skills models, it is obvious that the emphasis on information skills has become constructivist in nature.

INSTRUCTIONAL STRATEGIES AND INFORMATION LITERACY

The California School Library Association, giving credence to the role of the student researcher, has developed a three prong information literacy model (1994, 2–9) that looks at the researcher's thinking, the research process stages, and instructional strategies. At each point in the research process, instruction may be provided, as shown in Table 4.1.

How does that instruction occur? Too often, not at all. Sometimes educators forget that information literacy is a highly complex set of skills that do not evolve automatically. Though some skills may be developed intuitively, students need to recognize them on a conscious level and generalize those skills so they can transfer their learning to other research efforts. Only then can those competencies be truly internalized to become part of their repertoire of learning tools.

The most effective instruction seems to be couched in meaningful context at the point of need. For example, when students need to identify current trends on a social issue, that's when they realize that periodicals would be good sources—and also realize that they need help locating useful articles. *That's* the time to teach how to use magazine indexes.

One related issue is the method of delivery of instruction. While most librarians still gravitate to the oral tradition, many incorporate visual aids. Person-to-person remains the most effective means, but stand-alone instructional aids can help. Reference sheets and signs, audiocassette guides, video demonstrations, and computer-aided instruction all provide means for students to learn. Ideally, the library could offer an array of instructional materials from which students could choose, based on their interests and learning styles.

Another issue is the audience of instruction. At times, most librarians teach students one-on-one at the point of need. However, group instruction is much more time-efficient. Typically, the librarian addresses the entire class. Though this approach takes less time, theoretically, the large group arrangement may also foster less personal student engagement and may result in follow-up re-instruction. With the incorporation of cooperative group learning, more options exist. The librarian can teach a small group of students, say, one representative from each small cooperative team, and those representatives can then teach their peers. The benefit of this approach is two-fold: instruction can intensify, and student instructors can learn the skill doubly well. Alternatively, the librarian can meet with each small group and personalize instruction to meet the specific needs of each group.

CURRENT TRENDS IN INFORMATION LITERACY

Decades ago information literacy implied the ability to read a straightforward text. Now that skill involves being able to apply for a job, use the Internet, draw inferences, and develop products that demonstrate information synthesis and original organization.

A major change in information literacy lies in constructivist educational theory. Basically, in a constructivist classroom or library, students use their own repertoire of literacy tools to shape information into a personally meaningful product. As a result, information literacy emphasis is placed on process rather than "the right answer," and on student-centered issues rather than teacher-driven abstractions.

Even the type of information has changed over the years. In the past, a significant part of information literacy dealt with a core set of reference resources: encyclopedias, dictionaries, atlases, and the like. While these secondary sources remain, more emphasis has been placed on primary sources, including people and artifacts. Where students once could rely on library materials, they are now encouraged to question their sources and determine the materials' perspectives. Particularly with the advent of the Internet and its sometimes questionable informational offerings, librarians need to pass on their professional skills in review and selection processes.

Information literacy has also expanded to include visual literacy, which encompasses the interpretation, often culturally based, of sophisticated imagery and icons. Implicit in this literacy is the ability to ascertain the contextual connotations of the image.

At the end of the research process, the possibilities for communicating findings and conclusions have also expanded incredibly. The five-page report, though still favored by many educators, has been supplemented by a variety of formats, including the following:

Written: list, story, poem, newspaper, magazine

Visual: collage, illustration, cartoon, chart, map, graph, bulletin board, list, calendar, photograph, brochure

Multimedia: display, model, slide–tape, videotape, hypermedia

Kinesthetic: demonstration, skit, simulation

As a result, information literacy must now encompass significant instruction in these presentation modes.

To a certain extent, the use of equipment has become a subset of information literacy because the user must be able to use the necessary equipment to access information and manipulate it. Just as students traditionally had to learn how to open and turn the pages of a book, now they have to know how to open and navigate through an electronic source. Moreover, the search engines on these systems require knowledge about Boolean strategies and formal questioning protocols.

Technology has broadened the possibilities of information literacy. Matthew Soska, in his article on technology and learning (1994), mentions several benefits:

- Students can use a variety of learning modalities: audio, visual, kinesthetic.
- Students can work more independently, engaging actively with the resource.
- Students can connect with resources from around the world.
- Students can communicate in more ways, with a larger audience.
- Students can have more opportunities to work cooperatively.

One problem with these developments is that a large gap exists between technology-savvy and technology-ignorant students. The same situation could be said of print resources in that some families have few print materials; however, the economics of technology render the inequalities even more wrenching. Schools, and libraries in particular, often provide the only access to technology for these students. Even these institutions may provide varying degrees of access to technology, depending on local support. As a result, the need for information literacy, including the use of technology, becomes even more crucial.

THE IMPACT OF INFORMATION LITERACY ON COOPERATIVE LEARNING

Because information comes in so many formats and is often contextually based, the use of cooperative learning structures facilitates student comprehension of various sources. Regardless of the model used, the basic tenet that research involves a variety of steps demanding constant revision and evaluation reinforces the usefulness of multiple perspectives—and the need to divide a significant project into manageable pieces.

Just as cooperative learning structures necessitate formal training in those processes, so information literacy requires extensive training and focused activities on single aspects of the research process. The classroom teacher and the librarian determine which skills to emphasize and how they will be taught. By and large, the projects outlined in this book require that the group follow an entire research model. However, individual members of the cooperative group may concentrate on certain steps. For instance, one student may focus on locating sources while another may concentrate on taking notes from those sources.

Each research step has its cooperative learning component:

Identify the information need. Students in small groups brainstorm ways to define the task or problem. Then they help each other determine what kind of information they need, based on what they already know and what they don't know. When students have prior experiences with resources, they can focus on the present project more easily. Establishing cooperative groups increases the likelihood that at least one student in the group will know something about the topic and relevant information resources.

Develop a research strategy. At this point, students need to figure out how to pursue their topic. Because both sequential and holistic research strategies may be useful, having a mix of students in a group broadens the search options and directions. To maximize results, at least two students in each group should pursue separate paths to information resources. Throughout this stage, groups should share their strategies so they can advise each other and redirect their efforts more efficiently.

Locate and access information. Several opportunities for cooperation arise during this stage. The group can brainstorm keywords and concepts to maximize possible meaningful hits. A variety of information formats can be accessed, depending on each student's learning style preferences. This flexibility is especially valuable when students face intellectual barriers to accessing or processing the information.

Use information. Because each student brings unique experiences to the research table, evaluation and interpretation of resources comes under greater and more realistic scrutiny in cooperative groups. Additionally, students can teach each other different ways to engage with the source material. Possible conflicting interpretations actually facilitate student learning because they help students appreciate information from a variety of perspectives.

Synthesize information. This step may be the most challenging for cooperative groups because at some point one conclusion needs to be reached. One way to delegate responsibility is for the group to assign one aspect of the topic to each member. In preparation for the presentation process, the group may want to develop a template or storyboard to ensure that each person will document their findings in a consistent manner.

Present information. This task requires translating the findings into terms that others can understand. By having a diversified group, a final product should be able to more accurately represent the findings of the group. The issue is how to resolve the different perspectives of the group members.

Evaluate product and process. How well do students present information and process their strategies? Cooperative learning allows students in each group to accurately assess their peers, because they have experienced the entire activity together. In addition, all of the groups can compare their experiences and products, which provides a broader perspective. The evaluation should also assess social task skills of individuals and the group as a whole. This approach reinforces the team approach as well as the usefulness of support groups. Finally, assessment should also signal the next direction, just as solving one problem uncovers another problem. The more students and teachers plan the learning journey together, the more meaningful the ensuing activities will be.

TIPS

How can technology be used throughout the research process?

Mike Eisenberg and Doug Johnson (1996) note several ways that technology can facilitate information literacy:

- Defining the issue: Use e-mail, online discussion groups, idea generating software.
- Developing strategies: Assess data-gathering resources, use project management software.
- Locating information: Use computer resources (online, CD-ROM), conduct online surveys.
- Using information: Download computer information, use spreadsheet and database software to organize information, use statistical software to analyze information, use word processing software to record and organize information.
- Presenting information: Use graphics and desktop publishing software to create documents, use database and spreadsheet software to create charts, use authorware and presentation software to create "shows," use video and audio equipment to produce a program, use telecommunications to share information.
- Evaluating: Use word processing utilities to edit work, use e-mail and online discussion groups to share assessments.

What criteria can students use to evaluate sources, especially on the Internet?

Fitzgerald (1997) offers a beginning list of electronic information evaluation skills:

- Consciously approach all electronic information critically. Don't assume anything.

- Browse the Net widely to develop a contextual framework for evaluation. Compare findings from various sources.
- Determine the intended audience.
- Evaluate the source's reliability and authority. Understand Internet conventions, such as URL syntax and acronyms.
- Distinguish between fact and opinion. Some clues that can tip the reader include faulty logic, oversimplification, inconsistencies, emotional language, and writing or mathematical errors.
- Determine bias and perspective.

How can students organize their research strategies or findings?

- Use a Venn diagram to show differences and likenesses.
- Create a chart to list concepts or features, such as fact versus opinion.
- Develop a timeline.
- Make a flowchart.
- Create a chain-of-events diagram.
- Create a web of connections on a topic.
- Write a research process journal. For each question in a particular research project, students write about "what I did," "what I found," and "what I learned or felt" (see fig. 4.1).

Name _____

Topic, Issue, or Problem _____

My Question:

_____

What I did:

_____

What I found:

_____

What I learned:

From *Cooperative Learning Activities in the Library Media Center.* © 1999 Lesley S. J. Farmer. Libraries Unlimited (800) 237-6124.

Figure 4.1   Template for a page from a research process journal.

CHAPTER 5

Building a Learning Community

Cooperative learning makes a difference. Lessons reflect meaningful interactivity and interdependence. The power of cooperative learning, though, really shines when it is embraced schoolwide. Teaching practice and philosophy, as well as school climate, can be strengthened by using cooperative learning as a catalyst for change—for improved education.

THE COOPERATIVE SCHOOL

The school community acts as a microcosm of society, and, as such, should reflect those behaviors that are valued in the real world. The SCANS report emphasizes cooperative work, and the basic reality of group existence underlies the importance of developing this skill. Thus, the entire school should affirm and model learning as a cooperative venture. What does this model look like?

- A sense of *inclusion:* Everyone is respected, and everyone participates.
- A sense of *cohesion:* Everyone plays an important role and is interdependent; everyone feels safe and supported.
- A sense of *authenticity:* Assessment and teaching relate to multifaceted performance; learning connects each person meaningfully with the world.

The administration sets the tone for cooperative learning through its priorities and decision-making process. Do administrators work in isolation? Do they focus on competition? These actions exemplify an individualistic approach to schooling. Even the term *team player* can be misleading, because it may apply to an exclusive group. On the other hand, when teachers and students help hire all staff, when decisions are broad-based, students see those practices as validations and extensions of their classroom cooperative learning experiences.

RESOURCE-BASED LEARNING

Cooperative learning goes hand-in-hand with resource-based learning, where students grapple with concepts by researching and analyzing a variety of resources. The traditional library, with its rich collection of print materials, offers a range of perspectives and depth to meet the varying needs of students. Now educators value other types of resources as well: audiovisual, human, realia (e.g., places and artifacts), and electronic.

Of course, each type of resource requires a unique set of skills, which can be facilitated through cooperative learning. Analyzing a scientific article differs from interpreting a poem. Interviewing an expert differs from extrapolating meaning from a television biography. Examining a Native American weaving differs from examining a Web site. Different students are attracted to various media and content. Each student has a unique combination of processing and analytical skills. Thus, resource-based learning affirms the need for cooperative learning activities so students can help each other become competent in those skills and take the greatest advantage of the richness of available resources.

FOSTERING COOPERATIVE LEARNING IN THE LIBRARY

As the center of educational resources, the library is the obvious hub of cooperative learning. Its collection of materials should reflect the various needs of students in support of the entire curriculum. Resources should represent a variety of views and approaches. Not only should the library stock a rich collection of magazines and newspapers, but it should offer access to periodicals through CD-ROMs, the Internet, and interlibrary loan (preferably through a fax service). Does the library provide videos and CDs? Can students listen to or view audiovisual materials in the library? Does the library maintain a list of local speakers or other experts for students to interview? Is equipment adequate for all students to access the resources they need? (Do computers have video cards and sound capabilities?)

Intellectual access is as important as physical access. Does library instruction take into account students' various learning styles? Does it foster a cooperative approach to resource access? One simple model of instruction that facilitates cooperation incorporates learning stations. Four types of electronic sources may be introduced at once, as a library staff person or student aide stands by each resource stand (say, CD-ROM magazine index, CD-ROM encyclopedia, the Internet, and news digest). One representative from each cooperative group learns how to use that particular resource, and then incorporates it into the group's project—and teaches the rest of the group how to access the information using that resource.

Even the library's facilities can encourage or discourage cooperation. Does the library have tables for group work? Are there group cubicles or partitioned areas for group discussion? Do acoustics permit group work without distracting other library users? Does the overall library climate invite students to interact with resources, with peers, and with the library staff?

Indeed, the most concrete evidence of cooperative learning is the partnership between student and librarian. They can form an investigative team to uncover the wealth of ideas in the library!

COOPERATIVE PLANNING

As educators design and facilitate cooperative learning, they model the behavior expected of their students. Their own planning should serve as a mega-lesson about cooperation. Moreover, the resultant student projects should be richer because the activity reflects the planners' unique perspectives and insights.

The basic framework for learning activities involves three functions: (1) structuring the learning environment, (2) facilitating learning, and (3) tracking and assessing learning. In addition, cooperative learning activities factor in these other tasks: clear definition of the specific cooperative tasks, group assignment, and instruction on group processing.

Each function involves all of the key stakeholders: classroom teacher, library media teacher, the computer specialist (as needed), and students. The librarian brings knowledge of resources and information literacy. The classroom teacher brings knowledge of the content area and of group dynamics. The computer specialist brings knowledge of computer skills and specialized training techniques. Students bring a wide range of personal experience, capabilities, needs, and interests. Of course, support for collaboration should come from the school district or board, the principals, and all staff. However, even working on ground level with one teacher at a time provides the foundation for effective coordination between librarians and other educators.

First, the roles of librarians and classroom teachers must be clarified and accepted. The

American Association of School Librarians and Association for Educational Communications and Technology document on school library media programs (1988) clearly defines the library media program mission "to ensure that students and staff are effective users of ideas and information" (1). Specifically, the mission is implemented through intellectual and physical access to information, "learning experiences that encourage users to become discriminating consumers and skilled creators of information," and "leadership, instruction and consulting assistance." A revision of that document, which is now published, strengthens the concept of collaboration and expands the role of librarian to that of instructional *partner*. In fact, the concept of the educator *team* best captures the spirit of working together to plan and implement a meaningful learning activity.

To establish that team, both librarians and classroom teachers must proactively discover what the other professional actually does. Both parties must communicate their own professional needs and methods of satisfying the other's needs. Both benefit by pooling their resources and efforts. They can learn new ways of solving old problems and can sometimes eliminate duplication of work. After *one* need is satisfied, such as a bibliography of hi-lo reading or an instructional unit on comparative magazine articles, the planning team will likely want to continue and expand their professional relationship.

Only then can meaningful action follow communication. Part of the reason more cooperation doesn't occur is a lack of mutual planning at the start. It takes time and effort to coordinate activities, just as it takes time for cooperative groups to manage effectively. In sum, the process of mutual staff planning and implementation mirrors student effort—and can serve as a significant model of success for young people. The process, as well as the group dynamics modeling, leads to more authentic and more engaged student learning.

STRUCTURING THE LEARNING ENVIRONMENT

As with all learning activities, a positive learning environment provides a healthy background for effective group work. Particularly in cooperative learning, a balance must be struck between content and process, lecture and interaction (Meyers 1986, 59). Class expectations must be made clear through rules and consistent modeling.

Planning should be set within the context of content and informational skill objectives or outcomes. What should students learn? The specific objectives must fit into the context of the curricula scope and sequence as well as the capacities of students. What do students already know? What information skills do they already possess? For cooperative learning, a social task objective must also be determined. In addition, the objectives should contribute to lifelong learning.

Levels of accomplishments for each outcome should be delineated. A rubric offers specific descriptions that characterize the desired product and process. Both the educators and the students should have clear expectations in terms of the outcomes. Only then can they accurately assess their efforts.

Next, the appropriate *resources* must be determined by asking several questions:

- What resources are available in the school library media center, locally, through interlibrary loan, via remote access (e.g., the Internet)?
- How available should resources be: preselected and placed in the classroom, based on the library media center's access for students to select, cited in accessed sources, dependent on student access off-site?
- What appropriate media are available? Do resources take into account the variety of student learning styles and processes?
- What resources or instructional materials need to be prepared or modified, particularly as guidelines for student activity?

As the activity is designed, the outcomes, characteristics of students, and types of available resources shape the *teaching methodology*. Again, pedagogical questions arise:

- Will both content knowledge and information skills be taught, or will one of these concepts be reviewed to facilitate the learning of the other concept? For example, the main outcome may be student identification of distinguishing characteristics of various schools of art. Relevant informational skills would be locating resources and classifying images, but these may require only modest review rather than emphasis.

- What prerequisite skills are needed to learn the next concept? For example, if students are to learn opposing viewpoints about a controversial topic by evaluating appropriate articles after locating them, then students must know how to locate magazine articles before starting the activity.

- What kind of introductory instruction will be given: a problem to solve through class discussion, probing questions accompanying a stimulating videotape, a role–play enactment of a current topic?

- Who will provide instruction? Ideally, team instruction blends content and information processing. However, the spectrum varies from the classroom teacher dumping the class into the librarian's lap to the librarian coaching individual students during the specific activity period. With the incorporation of technology, the computer specialist enters the scene and may provide training about specific computer tools. Team instruction requires a delicate negotiating process, which improves with time as successful activities pave the way.

- What is the time frame? How much time is needed for instruction, for guided practice, for the cooperative learning activity (including research and production), for assessment? Do students need extra time for training in production skills? Furthermore, additional time is needed at the beginning as students learn how to work cooperatively in small groups. Shortchanging this step results in lengthier, less efficient work throughout the year.

- Where will the activity take place? While the library media center may be considered an ideal learning laboratory, a typical cooperative learning activity project utilizes a variety of spaces. Students may begin planning in the classroom. They may begin locating resources in the library media center. Then they may use a media lab in order to produce their final project. The three centers of learning may be augmented by off-site visits, explorations in science labs, and investigations of school grounds. In some cases, an academic commons may include the library, adjacent seminar rooms for group work, a multimedia computer lab, and a production center. Otherwise, the choice of room may depend on the accessibility of resources.

- What is the exact assignment or cooperative group activity? Because an assignment includes a content area, information processing skills, and group task, an effective way to meld various types of outcomes is through benchmark projects. These concrete products provide meaningful application of information acquired and processes. They are also substantial enough to require several tasks by several people.

FACILITATING LEARNING

A major trend in education is the switch from "sage on the stage" to "guide on the side." The trend builds on the concept of student-focused learning. Basically, the teacher sets the stage for learning, but the students play the major roles. To extend the drama analogy, the teacher no longer hands out the script but describes the main theme and plot and works with the students to create the script, find the appropriate props, and produce the play. The school might be considered the producer and the educators as light-handed directors or specialty consultants.

Typically, the classroom teacher guides students to *identify their own needs*. Say that students will develop a mock Senate, debating a set of controversial issues. The teacher would conduct a preresearch brainstorming session with the class to determine what information students need in order to portray senators accurately. Points generated might include information about the state or region and background information about senators and about the issue to be debated. At this point, the librarian may step in as students determine what kinds of literacy skills are needed in order to extract that information (e.g., locating congressional voting records, finding lobbyist sources, gathering state data). The computer specialist may work in tandem with the other teachers to help students identify specific computer resources or skills needed to access government data. The educational team can help individual students throughout the process as students come to certain points where they discover other conceptual or literacy needs.

The educator team also *stimulates student thinking* throughout the learning activity. At the onset, the teacher provides the context for learning and helps students tackle the new issue. If the activity is constructed as a problem, the teacher then sets up the challenge and the parameters for solving the problem. Perhaps students get bogged down in the middle, they reach a research dead-end, or they are stymied on ways to present their findings. The educator team intervenes, offering a new direction or perspective so students can get back on track. Sometimes students work on an activity on a surface level. The educator team encourages students to dig deeper, to ask new questions that extend the experience. Particularly when a class includes a wide variety of abilities, this kind of intellectual prodding and extension ensures that all students remain challenged so they can advance according to their ability.

Hand-in-hand with stimulating thinking is the educator team's task of *facilitating understanding*. Perhaps a student group is recreating a newspaper of Dickens' time, but has difficulty because the members haven't seen a sample newspaper of the times or don't know about important issues of the period. The librarian, in particular, can lead the group to sources that provide that information. Perhaps a student is having difficulty searching the Internet; a simple clarification about the difference between an Internet browser and a search engine can help a student understand the Net's workings and locate the sources needed.

Students may not have the prerequisite skills or background experience to deal with a concept. For example, students may understand the idea of perspective when reading an article, but they might not know the information skill of how to find two articles on the same subject but with differing views. The educator team *assists when necessary* so students can progress on their project. A cooperative group may be floundering because they misinterpreted directions or have a mismatch of personalities; the teacher typically provides the assistance needed to help the group past the obstacle.

TRACKING AND ASSESSING LEARNING

When assessment is established and outcomes are identified at the start of a project, monitoring becomes naturally integrated in the process itself. As educators simultaneously work with student groups, they can check with each other about the groups' progress and make necessary adjustments. What cognitive processes are students using? How is their information literacy developing? The team may notice that only boys are using the Internet; perhaps one girl representative from each cooperative group should come together for targeted Net training. The educator team can evaluate the resources being used—or not used. Perhaps specialized reference books are being overlooked; the librarian can call for a representative from each group and point out the usefulness of key resources. Likewise, the teacher may notice that the students aren't finding good details in encyclopedias because they don't use the index volume; a quick reminder can alert students to more possibilities. Summative assessment also improves the learning experience as the educator team examines how well students achieve their outcomes of content, literacy, and cooperation. Based on student achievement, the team can modify future activities to maximize results or design ones that build on the skills learned during current efforts. Likewise, the processes used by students and educators also bear examining in order to build on that experience.

USING BENCHMARK PROJECTS

A benchmark project is a concrete application of knowledge and skill. Usually a culminating activity, a benchmark project enables students to locate and evaluate content and then transform it. The context for benchmark projects thus transcends a specific lesson and typically requires several days to accomplish. An exciting blend of skills, information, and product motivates students and provides an authentic context for learning. Examples of benchmark projects include a reenactment of a major event, a multimedia stack on the brain, a trivia facts game on Africa. Several tasks are involved, which demand the efforts of several people. Benchmark projects require active involvement and creativity, which facilitates meaningful learning. For some benchmark projects, each group may design one section, and the components can be joined among the class groups to form a significant package of information.

Ideas for benchmark projects constitute the second half of this book. However, additional inspiration can come from any direction: nature, television, overheard conversations. Some effective ideas for formats follow:

Written: database, newspaper, magazine, cipher, code, poem, lyric, short story, play, anthology, white paper

Visual: photograph, illustration, cartoon, collage, chart, diagram, poster, bulletin board, display, timeline, flowchart, map, calendar, computer-assisted design, brochure, blueprint, advertisement, banner

Aural: audiocassette, radio program, speech, interview, debate

Multimedia: film, videotape, slide–tape, hypermedia, CD, drama

Kinesthetic: demonstration, drama, dance, scavenger hunt, mechanism, fair

Game: observation, relay, puzzle, categories, card, board, physical challenge, role–play, wide game

To choose an appropriate benchmark product, teachers and librarians must look at the content and literacy outcomes first. A good way to approach the activity is to think of realistic applications of the skills learned. How might this information be used in daily life? The more closely a project imitates life, the easier it is to interest students and facilitate the transfer of learning. For example, students can use the principles of physics to construct a model bridge.

Natural associations are made between certain concepts and forms of presentation: people concepts suggest speech and drama; sports concepts connote games; history concepts relate to documentaries and primary sources; biased information concepts connote propaganda posters. These natural associations are not the only ones that can be made, however; cross-linking concepts and forms of presentation yields a wealth of rich possibilities for benchmark projects.

Games, in particular, offer wonderful opportunities for all types of cooperative learning-based benchmark projects. Their format increases motivation and interest, provides immediate and active feedback, gives information, facilitates decision making and problem solving, and simulates reality (Bell and Wieckert

1985, xxii). Middle schoolers especially like this learning format.

In designing a game, several factors must be determined:

- Model: type of board game, relay
- Objective of the game: the basis for winning
- Rules of the game: the method of playing
- Roles of the players
- Time frame
- Resources and materials needed

More generally, for any benchmark project, students need to know how to create the product (in this case, the game) and how to use it.

Games should be pilot tested before being played. In a cooperative learning environment, groups may exchange games to test their validity and to provide an effective assessment of the activity. Again, this same process of testing and assessing should be applied to any benchmark project.

Some popular game formats are:

Categories: The object of this game is to fill a chart with words related to selected topics. Students begin by drawing a grid with five columns and five rows. The box in the upper right corner is left blank. In the remaining rows of the left-hand column, students list several aspects, or categories, related to their topic. The four columns to the right are labeled with letters chosen at random. Students fill in the chart with words that fit the topic and begin with the appropriate letter (see fig. 5.1).

Observation game: Several items (such as cards with terms written on them) are placed on a board. The players observe the objects for one minute. The board is covered, and one or more items are removed. The players must identify the missing items from memory.

Rummy: A special deck of cards is created, with 13 sets of four related cards. For example, in one set of four cards, each card might represent a unique part of a specific bird (i.e., find: beak, feather, foot, egg). Another set of four cards in the same deck might feature the same parts of a different bird. In a game about birds, 13 different birds would be represented, with four cards about each bird. Players try to gather complete sets of four cards for each bird.

The cards are shuffled, and each player is dealt the same number of cards. The remaining cards become the draw pile. Players ask each other in turn for cards belonging to a specific set ("Do you have the feet of a penguin?"); they draw from the pile if the other player does not have the desired card. When a player gathers a complete set of four cards about one bird, he or she places the cards face up on the table. The first player with an empty hand wins.

Snakes and ladders: Players advance along a board to reach the top. At various squares players encounter ladder shortcuts or snake detours, which are keyed to subject concepts.

Circle board game: Players move their pieces around the board several times until they acquire enough points (the number must be predetermined) to win. Question or chance cards along the route provide opportunities to answer questions and gain points.

	L	A	N	D
AFRICA	Libya	Algeria	Nigeria	Dahomey
ASIA	Laos	Afghanistan	Nepal	Diego, Garcia I.
EUROPE	Luxembourg	Austria	Norway	Denmark
AMERICA	Louisiana	Argentina	Nicaragua	Dominican Republic

Figure 5.1   Categories game using countries.

Path board game: Players advance along a path in order to reach a destination. Squares along the way may refer to question cards, similar to the circle board game.

Role–play game: Each student assumes a role and may be given detailed characteristics or properties. Students adopt their roles to generic situations, which may be supplemented by group-generated factors.

Wide game: This game consists of several learning stations with a different type of activity at each one. The object is to discover which groups can find or do all the activities called for in the game.

EXPANDING COOPERATIVE LEARNING

It is apparent that cooperative learning activities can open new doors of learning for the entire school learning community. After the beginning steps have been taken and positive results have been achieved, new horizons beckon.

Activity plans may be combined or adapted in unlimited ways to provide a rich repertoire of activities. For example, a database of scientists may be created as easily as a musician's database. Interview techniques may be applied to most content areas. Illustrations may be used in most contexts. Hypermedia stacks can be used to create presentations in any discipline. When the educator team develops a sensitivity for cooperative benchmark projects, it can see possibilities all around: adapting advertisements to content, noting how market displays can lead to creative projects, transforming a bike hike to a class simulation.

Cooperative learning activities lend themselves to interdisciplinary approaches. For example, aspects of the Middle Ages can be incorporated into all disciplines: alchemy in science, calligraphy in art, Gothic chants in music, courtly love poems in English, food in home economics, and the feudal system in social studies. A school could hold a Medieval Fair, with each department exhibiting products students have researched and created.

Cooperative learning blossoms in a community setting. Opportunities for business and cultural involvement are possible, for instance, students could explore cultural and artistic history in museums, or they could work with local businesses to gain insights about sociology and mathematics.

Telecommunications offers a world of cooperative learning opportunities. The stock market may be studied online. Area libraries may be contacted to provide additional resources. Students from several schools may produce regional newsletters or magazines, or they may work with a nationwide weather-reporting system. Students may access electronic newsgroups or online forums with international users.

Cooperative learning occurs on the professional level as well. Organization offerings and collegial networking are two directions that teachers and librarians may take. A successful educator team may share its experiences or plans with other staffs, either informally or during in-service workshops. Effective cooperative planners may present their findings at professional conferences or in professional journals. Cooperative activity is never-ending!

TIPS

How can I begin librarian-teacher cooperation?

- Get into the other person's frame of mind. What are the challenges of the job?
- Find common interests.
- Regularly demonstrate that librarians are teachers, too.
- Attend department or grade-level meetings.
- Volunteer to create booklists or subject guides for research in a content area.
- Provide workspace for teachers.
- Acquire professional reading material.
- Photocopy good cooperative learning activity articles and send them to teachers.

- Observe teacher classrooms.
- Offer to do booktalks in the classroom.
- Conduct in-service workshops for teachers.
- Display student work in the library.
- Grade or, at least, examine student work, especially research projects.
- Work with teachers to develop an information literacy scope and sequence curriculum.

In what ways can students be part of the planning process?

They can:

- Choose the specific topic
- Choose the specific approach
- Choose the presentation format
- Bookmark good Internet sites
- Develop guiding questions
- Help develop rubrics
- Suggest extension or next-step activities based on a current activity

What are some techniques for designing gender-equitable learning experiences?

- Personalize content to engage students more fully and to help them identify with it.
- Be aware of possible gender-sensitive content, such as day care or military tanks.
- Encourage use of nonprint and human resources.
- Provide a variety of ways to relate to the content and to share it.
- Encourage students to look at a topic from several perspectives.
- Encourage students to look at the context of the data found, not just the immediate facts.
- Encourage both sexes to take on various group roles, such as leader and recorder.

- Design the activity so that the culminating experience has a real call to action, so students can make a real difference.
- Make sure that assessment deals with process, for both the social and academic task, as well as the product.

What evidence demonstrates that collaborative planning is effective?

- Students perform better on assessments.
- Students express positive feelings about cooperative learning.
- Librarian-teacher relationships increase in frequency and intensity.
- Partners support each other and their plans.
- Librarians and teachers discuss instruction and curriculum regularly, both formally and informally.
- More cooperative learning activities are planned.
- Collection development is done more collaboratively.

What are some signs of a learning community?

- The entire school—staff, students, parents—are committed to long-term improvement.
- All staff believe that all students can learn.
- Learning is an ongoing activity for both students and staff.
- Staff and students assess work daily.
- Instructional resources are selected based on student needs.
- A cooperative problem-solving process is used to remove barriers to learning.
- There is ongoing communication among all staff.
- There is broad-based decision making.

CHAPTER 6

Activity Plans: An Explanatory Key

The following is a key to the structures of all the activities in the book. There are many cross-disciplinary ideas and possible adaptations for the units presented.

Activity description: a one-sentence general description of the group's activity.

Content outcomes: a list of student performances, products, or knowledge related to a specific curriculum area.

Information literacy outcomes: a list of student performances, products, or knowledge related to the processing of information. Most activities combine these skills: locating and selecting sources of information, critically evaluating them, organizing and synthesizing information, and sharing results with others.

Prerequisite skills: a list of those skills or concepts that the student should exhibit prior to beginning the activity. For example, if students are supposed to make energy maps, then they should be able to read map legends before they start.

Rationale for the process: This section answers the question, Why are we doing this? The issues and problems raised in this section are explored through the related activity.

Activity:

Grade level: Identifies the general academic level for the activity. Most activities include modifications that allow middle schoolers to participate as well as challenge the most advanced high-school students.

Time frame: A general guideline for predicting the amount of time required to accomplish the entire activity. Daily periods of 45–60 minutes are assumed. The amount of time depends on the students' prior knowledge, the intent of the activity (whether for introducing new skills or reviewing old concepts), the percentage of work to be done outside of class, and the modifications made (either to focus and simplify the activity or to expand it).

Resources: A general list of the types of resources students will use to complete the activity; also included is a list of materials needed to produce the benchmark project.

Grouping: A list of types of students to combine to maximize the diversity of groups, taking into account the type of learning involved in the specific activity. Such diversification acknowledges the unique experiences and skills of each student and encourages peer teaching. Based on their strengths (or weaknesses), group members may be encouraged to assume major responsibility for specific tasks. For example, one student might locate information, another might read the data, a third evaluate and interpret the findings, and another develop the presentation. Both individual accountability and group consensus are needed.

Group tasks: The specific steps that groups carry out independently. Occasionally included is a "prestep," a guided group activity to prepare students to work independently and a "post-step" to help groups independently evaluate their work.

Tips: In this section, helpful hints and ideas for modifying the activity guide the classroom and librarian teachers as they facilitate group learning.

Within each curriculum area, one activity is fully developed. The tips include ideas for introducing the concepts and skills; guided class preparatory activities to practice new skills and provide immediate feedback; suggestions on resources and ways to access information; guidelines for producing benchmark projects; evaluation checklists and forms; and ways to modify the activity (focus the activity, simplify it, make it more challenging, expand it).

Examples provide teachers and students with a concrete handle to understand a concept. To avoid the tendency to be constrained by the example, the class may agree that after an example is given, no one may use it for their project.

Assessment: Each activity is evaluated on several levels. As much as possible, the criteria for evaluation should be explained at the beginning of the activity. Several activities include sample evaluation forms or rubrics.

In all cases, both individual and group work should be evaluated. Groups may evaluate their own members. Students may take individual formal tests or document their individual learning. The benchmark project provides one basis for evaluating group effort.

When feasible, cross-group evaluation is included to encourage peer teaching and accountability. Both content and presentation are examined. The teacher evaluates the groups' evaluation processes to validate their judgment and provide feedback on evaluation techniques.

Class evaluation and closing discussion provide an opportunity to synthesize learning and extend the experience beyond the specific benchmark project.

Besides the academic task, a social task should be included for each activity. This task may be determined by the teachers or the students. This social task needs to be evaluated too. The chapter on cooperative learning provides appropriate social skills and evaluation techniques.

Activity Variations: A list of possible ways to modify the content, skill, focus, groups, and presentation format.

BASIC ACTIVITY PLAN FORMAT

Here is the basic format for your own benchmark project. You may modify an existing plan or cooperatively design an original one. Enjoy!

Activity plan

Activity description

Content outcomes

Information literacy outcomes

Prerequisite skills

Rationale for the process

Activity
  Grade level
  Time frame
  Resources
  Grouping
  Group tasks
  Tips

Assessment

Activity variations

CHAPTER 7

Activity Plans for Art

VIRTUAL ART MUSEUM TOUR

Activity Description
Each group creates a thematic virtual museum tour by combining multimedia and other technologies.

Content Outcomes
Students will:

- Categorize artwork according to theme.
- Sequence artwork in a logical, artistically appropriate manner.
- Identify and describe critical artistic features.

Information Literacy Outcomes
Students will:

- Use laser discs to locate and select artwork that corresponds to a particular theme.
- Recognize and use a variety of media sources about artistic themes and artistic topics.
- Identify main ideas and details.
- Use a multimedia format to organize and present information.

Prerequisite Skills

- Word process.
- Perform basic computer operations.
- Develop a classification system.
- Operate laser discs (optional).
- Use multimedia (optional)

Rationale for the Process
Not only does all artwork possess patterns (e.g., light/dark, related shapes, composition), but artistic patterns exist *between* pieces of art as well. Artists may gravitate to general subjects (e.g., landscapes, still life, portrait) or specific subjects (e.g., street scenes, flowers, Madonnas). Sometimes artists build on their predecessors' work: Picasso, Dali, and Cezanne are three such artists.

By examining common themes, students can discover how different artistic schools or movements approach their subjects. There may not be anything new under the sun, but each person puts a personal spin on each object.

Art museums are well acquainted with artistic patterns as they create thematic exhibits. Now students can create their own virtual museums of thematic art.

Activity
Grade level: middle school and up

Time frame: five to seven days

Resources: art laser discs (e.g., *Louvre*). CD-ROMs (e.g., *National Gallery of Art*), Internet, art print sources in combination with a scanner, multimedia authoring program, storage peripherals, references on art (i.e., themes, styles, art movements, techniques, artists)

Grouping: visual and kinesthetic learners, analytical and creative thinkers, concrete and abstract thinkers, technological novices and experts, sequential and holistic learners

Group tasks:

1. Determine an art theme.
2. Locate artwork that exemplifies the theme.
3. Locate information about each art piece.
4. Import and sequence art into a multimedia authoring program.
5. Incorporate textual information into the hyperstack.

Tips: To introduce this activity, show examples of art according to one theme, such as portraits. Lead a class discussion on their stylistic differences (e.g., degree of abstraction, composition, painter quality). Students then brainstorm possible thematic patterns and generate critical facts. Books on thematic art may also be shared and analyzed. Younger students may focus on concrete examples such as sports, music, family; older students may try more abstract themes such as patriotism, vanity, fortune.

Students may locate appropriate pictures using several types of resources. Emphasize the use of key term searching techniques to access art in electronic resources. For example, many CD-ROMs and laser discs include search engines.

Students may subdivide their work by locating and researching one piece of art each. Alternatively, one student may locate all pieces of art, another locate information about each piece, one write, and one oversee the authoring process. To prevent down time, students need to work closely. As soon as one piece of art is chosen, information about it can be located. The authoring expert can also begin planning the look of the presentation.

Creating the museum tour varies according to the resources used. Laser discs that work with multimedia programs may have built-in sequencing and presentation routines. Students can also extract text from the laser disc to create a dialogue box for the selected artwork. This approach works well for middle schoolers.

Authoring programs such as HyperCard and HyperStudio can actively access CD-ROM and laser disc sources. However, all the players must be connected during the presentation. Another approach is to export the image onto a disk. Because images take up so much room, classes typically use high-density storage peripherals such as Zip drives or rewritable CD-ROMs. The image is then imported into the authoring program at any time. Of course, students need to find out in what form those image files should be stored as to be compatible with the authoring program. Sample extension names include GIF, PIC, TIFF, and PDF. Pictures for art books can also be incorporated by using a scanner. Again, the graphic file must be saved in a compatible format.

Students may word process their textual information separately from the authoring tool as well. The easiest approach is to create a separate file for each piece of art, and then import it when convenient into the group's authoring stack.

Assessment

Groups exchange stacks, assessing them in terms of:

- Choice of pictures
- Accuracy and thoroughness of textual information
- Stack structure and sequence
- Overall stack appearance

As a closing assessment activity, the class may discuss patterns across themes:

- Do different themes seem to be accentuated during different eras?
- Does artistic style influence the choice of theme?
- What commonalities exist within or between themes?

Activity Variations

1. Students focus on one form of art (e.g., painting, sculpture, printmaking).
2. Students focus on one period of time or one artistic movement.
3. Students focus on one culture or examine one period of time across cultures.

4. Students develop slide–tape shows for the museum tour.
5. Students develop Web-based virtual museum tours.
6. Students do a jigsaw activity: one theme is followed within one art movement or one period of time, and then compared with another theme or another art movement.

PERSUASIVE ART

Activity Description

Each group presents two pieces of artwork that represent two different attitudes toward the same subject or issue. They then identify the artistic principles that connote different attitudes. (This activity could be used in social studies and psychology as well as in art.)

Content Outcomes

Students will:

- Identify the attitude or philosophical stance presented in a piece of art.
- Identify what artistic principles underlie the attitudinal differences between two art pieces.
- Create a piece of artwork that demonstrates a specific attitude or philosophical stance.

Information Literacy Outcomes

Students will:

- Locate and evaluate examples of persuasive art.
- Locate information about propaganda and connotation in art.
- Apply general principles of propaganda and connotation to analyze forms of bias in artwork.
- Create an original work of persuasive art.

Prerequisite Skills

- Use library catalogs and indexes to locate relevant information.
- Identify artistic principles.
- Create artwork.

Rationale for the Process

Art does not live in a vacuum, nor is it value-neutral. Art with a message often tries to persuade the viewer. The most obvious example of such persuasion is advertising illustration. The most potent examples relate to war propaganda. It should be noted that, while persuasive art is often credited to a political entity (such as the Communist Party) or big business, the art of persuasion or social criticism lies just as strongly with the individual. Of particular interest is the political art done by Third World artists reaching out to their fellow citizens as well as to the outside world.

In completing this activity, students become more aware of the overt and covert messages embedded in art. They understand art's social influence, which is possible through the manipulation of visual/artistic principles.

Activity

Grade level: middle school and up
Time frame: two to five days (depending on sophistication of created artwork)
Resources: resources on art, visual literacy, advertising, and propaganda; media for presentation
Grouping: concrete and abstract learners, creative and analytical processors
Group tasks:

1. Locate and select two pieces of artwork about the same subject or issue.
2. Determine the attitude or philosophical stance of each work.
3. Locate and examine information about propaganda and connotative art.
4. Identify the artistic principles or visual connotations that convey that attitude or stance.
5. Create a persuasive piece of art.

Tips: To introduce the activity, discuss advertising illustration. If needed, the class may share examples from magazines. Leading questions include:

- What have you ever bought because of an advertisement? Why?

- What images come to mind when you think of car ads? Perfume ads? Alcohol ads?
- Have you seen advertisements that condemn some stance? Were you convinced? If so, on what ground: facts or feelings?
- What other kinds of illustrations are persuasive in tone (e.g., political cartoons and posters)?

Next, students may brainstorm ideas about issues that spark strong controversy, such as war or economic equality. These words may be added to their keywords or subject headings list. Students may also brainstorm synonyms for "persuasion" or be reminded to use a thesaurus to look up such words. These keywords become the subject headings to use when locating persuasive art.

Some students may need guidance in determining what artistic features evoke emotion or persuade the viewer. You may want to focus the activity by having the groups find evocative pictures and then leading a class discussion to intuitively determine the artistic principles by asking questions such as:

- How do the colors in the picture highlight or downplay ideas?
- How are the figures or objects placed on the page? Do some stand out or seem superior?
- How does the line quality or use of space evoke a response?

To expand the activity, students may research how propaganda works, based on visual clues. Because of its ungoverned nature, many examples of propaganda (including art) are available on the Internet.

Students may create their own persuasive pictures, either inductively learning about the artistic principles involved or deductively applying the formal "rules." A single piece of art created by a group can be very challenging. As an alternative, each person in the group can create one piece, or the group may divide the project up into subtasks: one person to locate art, one to research propaganda, one to create the artwork—and all critiquing the art.

Assessment
The class develops a set of artistic principles that relate to persuasive art. Groups may create their own persuasive pictures, which are evaluated by another group according to the class set of principles.

Activity Variations
1. The entire class may concentrate on one issue, such as political freedom.
2. Half of the groups may concentrate on "pro" art and the other on "con" art.
3. Students may concentrate on one medium, such as sculpture or film.
4. Students may research propaganda art more formally.
5. Students may create persuasive advertisements.
6. Students may create an anthology of art and writing on a specific issue.
7. Students may explore other communication media, such as music or poetry.
8. Students may concentrate on one time period or one geographic region.
9. Each group may choose a different time period or geographic region.

ARTISTIC BROCHURE

Activity Description
Each group chooses an artistic movement and designs an exhibit brochure describing the style.

Content Outcomes
Students will:
- Identify the significance of a particular artistic movement, including its artists, achievements, and influence.

Information Literacy Outcomes
Students will:
- Recognize and use a variety of media as sources of information about an artistic movement.
- Identify main ideas and details.

- Assess information by verifying facts, recognizing forms of bias, and determining adequacy of data.
- Use classification techniques and patterns to organize information.
- Use visual skills to research and organize information.
- Use a brochure format to organize and present information.

Prerequisite Skills

- Use library catalogs and indexes to locate relevant information.
- Employ desktop publishing techniques (optional).
- Cite sources accurately.

Rationale for the Process

When studying art history, students may identify artistic trends more easily when they can link information to a period or individual artist. Furthermore, by examining one movement, such as Realism or Expressionism, in depth, students learn a process that can be used to compare other artists or schools. Yet, too often the resulting report seems lifeless; copying facts provides little insight.

By producing a brochure, students accomplish several tasks:

- Synthesizing facts rather than copying them
- Developing an aesthetic product, perhaps reflecting the movement itself
- Providing information to other students for comparative analysis.

Activity

Grade level: high school
Time frame: three days to one week
Resources: art reference books, other art resources, graphic materials for product, desktop publishing resources (optional)
Grouping: visual and verbal processors, creative and analytical thinkers

Group tasks:
1. Choose an artistic movement, such as Impressionism or Neoclassicism (within teacher parameters).
2. Locate and select visual and written information about the movement.
3. Evaluate information for significance and categorize it.
4. Create a brochure with written and visual information describing the movement.

Tips: Begin the activity by discussing artist brochures and museum promotions. Students may want to collect artist brochures as examples. They may examine museum catalogs or visit a museum. Discuss possible reasons for producing these brochures: quick information, attractive reminder, guide for further study.

Students may need help determining what is meant by an artistic movement. You may share examples of artistically different treatments of the same subject; for example, compare horse paintings by Delacroix and Marc (see also "Virtual Art Museum Tour" activity). To help each group determine which facts about an artistic movement are important, you may provide a checklist of ideas, such as vital dates, nations represented, typical media used, subject matter, characteristics of style, representative artists of the movement, most important works, main achievements, and influence. More effective, though, would be a class discussion about the factors that make an artistic style unique, then students may develop their own lists of significant points.

Students may need instruction or guidance in locating different art resources. Specialized art reference books are important, as well as monographs, periodicals, and nonprint sources (slides, videotape, films, CD-ROMs, laser discs, Internet). Students should also be reminded to maintain bibliographic citations for possible further reference. By requiring these citations to be included in the brochure, you reinforce the "for further reading" aspect of brochures as well as emphasize the need to verify information.

> **BROCHURE ASSESSMENT FORM**
>
> **Content**
> - Kind of information
> - Depth of information
> - Information included—and omitted
> - Bibliography and further research
> - Use of quotations
> - Writing style
> - Intended audience
>
> **Visual**
> - Type of visuals (illustrations, photographs)
> - Number of visuals
> - Dimension of visuals
> - Source of visuals (artist, brochure producer)
> - Charts, diagrams
> - Use of color
>
> **Layout**
> - Brochure dimension
> - Balance between visuals and written material
> - Organization and arrangement
> - Style
> - Use of types and fonts (including boldface, italics)
> - Use of headings and subheadings
> - Paper quality
>
> From *Cooperative Learning Activities in the Library Media Center.* © 1999 Lesley S. J. Farmer. Libraries Unlimited (800) 237-6124.

To help students understand the components of a brochure, you may have each group analyze an example, following the Brochure Assessment Form above.

In developing the brochure, students will need to analyze the most effective layout format to fit their information. You may want to provide them with more structure by defining the size and look of the brochure, such as one two-sided legal sheet of paper folded twice. The form used to evaluate existing brochures may be given to students as a checklist for the format. Some students may use desktop publishing programs to produce their brochures by computer.

Assessment

The class shares its brochures, analyzing each artistic movement and assessing each group's brochure. For example, groups may exchange their brochures and use the Brochure Assessment Form to analyze results. Partners may compare two artistic movements in terms of artistic principles (e.g., use of color and space, composition) and compare the resultant brochures in terms of communication effectiveness.

As a closing assessment, the class discusses artistic styles in general:

- What constitutes an artistic school or movement?
- Who determines the movement or name?
- What stylistic trends do you see in contemporary art?
- How can artistic style be conveyed in a brochure?

Activity Variations

1. The entire class may concentrate on one artistic period or movement such as realism, and vary the country or medium.
2. The entire class may concentrate on one particular medium.
3. The entire class may concentrate on one artist, each group choosing a different medium or time period. Picasso and Leonardo da Vinci exemplify artists with good stature and work for this approach.
4. Students may interview local, living artists.
5. Students may compare how different sources treat the artist.
6. The brochures may be written as recruitment pieces to attract emerging artists to a particular art movement.
7. Students may present information on the artist or movement in other forms: a poster, a slide–tape show, a video, a multimedia stack.

MASKING ART

Activity Description

Using a CAD program, each group designs a series of masks that reflect a specific culture.

Content Outcomes

Students will:

- Recreate identifying cultural motifs and styles shown on masks.
- Use a computer-aided design program to create mask variations.

Information Literacy Outcomes

Students will:

- Use a variety of sources, especially visual, to locate and select mask images.
- Analyze cultural masks according to artistic motifs.
- Determine critical features that identify specific cultural motifs and styles.
- Transform analysis into visual CAD form.

Prerequisite Skills

- Use a computer-aided design program (optional).
- Create a classification scheme.

Rationale for the Process

Most cultures use masks for creative or ritualistic activities, some since the dawn of time. While some designs are common to several groups, each culture puts its own artistic "stamp" on its masks. Masks have been considered sociological artifacts or second-class craft projects. However, fine artists such as Picasso have been inspired by native masks. The form transcends function.

This activity helps students analyze artistic motifs and styles and realize the cultural context of artistic principles. With the recent artistic recognition and acceptance of crafts and other folk creations as valid art forms, this activity helps students pull out those design elements. The CAD program facilitates the creation of stylistic variations and allows students to build an artistic "toolkit."

Activity

Grade level: high school
Time frame: three to four days
Resources: visual art resources, CAD program (and required hardware/peripherals)
Grouping: creative and analytical thinkers, technological experts and novices, visual and kinesthetic learners
Group tasks:

1. Choose a culture to research (e.g., Aztec, Japanese).
2. Locate and select visual images of that culture's masks. If possible, locate critical analyses of that culture's artistic motifs and styles.
3. Identify critical stylistic features and motifs by analyzing the masks.
4. Design original masks in the style of that culture.

Tips: To begin the activity, share some examples of traditional masks. An easy way to help students determine unique features is to show a representative mask from two different cultures and have students compare and contrast them. If possible, have students generate a list of possible criterion upon which to guide their visual analysis. Some artistic properties would include angularity, color, complexity, degree of abstraction, geometric shapes, textures, composition, symmetry, pattern, size, degree of dimension. Motifs might include animals, humans, fantasy, plants, and sections of each of these (e.g., hand, wing, leaf). Two excellent books that model such analysis are:

Stewart, Hilary. *Looking at Indian Art of the Northwest Coast.* Seattle, Wash.: University of Washington Press, 1979.
Holm, Bill. *Northwest Coast Indian Art; An Analysis of Form.* Seattle, Wash.: University of Washington Press, 1965.

As students begin their CAD work, they can develop "templates" or basic shapes for their masks based on their analysis. The CAD program then allows the user to repeat or modify those shapes. Each student can create his/her own mask based on the common templates, thus reinforcing the idea of variation within a visual vocabulary (like an artistic authority file). The final presentation should include examples of the cultural masks, the identified motifs and templates, and the generated student masks.

Assessment

Groups assess each other's set of mask images, evaluating them in terms of congruence and accuracy of elements. Alternatively, groups exchange their original images and templates/motifs and have the evaluators create a mask based on the given information; then that generated mask is compared to the masks developed by the original group.

As a closing assessment, the class as a whole compares the different cultural masks and determines common elements. This analysis can be displayed as a criterion grid. In looking at the general principles, the following questions can be posed:

- Do elements vary geographically?
- Do primitive masks from different cultures resemble each other more than masks from the same culture but from different periods of time?
- Do masks reflect societal values or norms?
- How do artistic elements of masks transfer to other art forms within the culture?

Activity Variations

1. Groups may concentrate on primitive masks.
2. Groups may concentrate on masks from one continent, or each group may focus on a different continent.
3. Half of the groups may concentrate on primitive masks and half on modern masks.
4. Groups may study the function of masks.
5. Groups may create actual 3-D masks.
6. Groups may study other traditional art forms (e.g., pottery, jewelry, basketry, weaving) from the same culture.
7. Groups may study one other art form from several cultures.

MORE IDEA STARTERS

1. Morph paintings from one style to another.
2. Analyze weather through paintings with clouds and other weather signs.
3. Develop history through art.
4. Determine social status through art.
5. Find quotations about art.
6. Match poetry or lyrics and art.
7. Create artist timelines. Develop transparencies of separate timelines for each culture or country, drawing them to the same scale. Overlay them, and analyze the findings.
8. Analyze art created in wartime. Each group may choose a different war.
9. Compare other art forms (e.g., cartoons, posters, architecture) throughout history.
10. Compare landscape paintings with photographs of the same area.
11. Compare portraits of one person done over time by different painters.
12. Determine artistic influences on fashion (e.g., folk costumes, primitive art motifs, optical illusions).
13. Locate glossaries for different art techniques (e.g., etching, ceramics, ironwork). Create a game using these technical words.
14. Identify blueprint symbols and conventions. Create a blueprint for a sandwich or outfit.
15. Research the methods used to make paint or ink.
16. Design a poster or advertisement in the style of another era.
17. Compare geometric patterns in primitive art. Each group may choose a different culture.
18. Trace the techniques and materials used to make fabric.
19. Explore different art techniques done on computer.
20. Compare techniques, composition, and functions of tattooing.

CHAPTER 8

Activity Plans for Domestic Sciences

HOUSING A.D. 2020

Activity Description
Each group designs a model home or shelter for the year 2020.

Content Outcomes
Students will:
- Determine aspects of effective shelter.
- Recognize relationships between housing and technology and social trends.
- Predict housing patterns for the year 2020.
- Develop a model shelter using a CAD program or other modeling method.

Information Literacy Outcomes
Students will:
- Use a variety of media as sources of information about housing and housing trends.
- Recognize relationships and patterns among data about housing trends and technical/societal factors.
- Analyze and interpret statistical and graphic forms of data.
- Extrapolate data to a future context.
- Transform their findings into three-dimensional form.

Prerequisite Skills
- Ability to use a CAD program or other construction tool (e.g., cardboard, clay) to model the shelter.
- Use catalogs and indexes to locate sources about housing.

Rationale for the Process
As students examine living styles, they need to look at housing. Some basic aspects of housing remain constant, but others change. Moreover, the arrangements and combinations of these factors vary by human need and material availability.

By constructing a shelter of the future, students discover the necessary aspects to consider. General factors will be useful for them in the near future and will provide them a broader perspective about future issues in housing.

Activity
Grade level: middle school and up
Time frame: one to two weeks
Resources: sources on architecture, housing, construction, environment, social patterns, demographics, and futures studies; materials to construct a model or blueprint
Grouping: students who present information in different ways (visual, concrete, written), concrete and abstract learners, analytical and creative thinkers

---

HOUSING A.D. 2020 ASSESSMENT FORM

Locale
- Place
- Climate
- Natural environment and resources
- Community demographics

Building
- Dimensions
- Materials
- Style

Inhabitants
- Quantity
- Configuration (single adults, extended families, etc.)
- Lifestyle

Justification statement
Assessment factors (Exemplary, Commendable, Satisfactory, Fair, Limited, Minimal)
- Shelter appropriate to locale
- Shelter appropriate to community/inhabitants
- Shelter appropriate to time period (is it credible?)
- Valid justification statement
- Technical quality of model

From *Cooperative Learning Activities in the Library Media Center.* © 1999 Lesley S. J. Farmer. Libraries Unlimited (800) 237-6124.

Group tasks:

1. Determine living style and environmental factors that affect housing tasks.
2. Locate and evaluate information about housing and housing trends, especially in light of human needs and technical capabilities.
3. Extrapolate findings to project housing needs and possibilities for the year 2020.
4. Design a three-dimensional model of the shelter, as imagined for the year 2020.

Tips: To help groups clarify their tasks, introduce the activity by asking questions such as:

- What is the difference between a house and a home?
- What different possible housing/shelter arrangements exist (e.g., apartment, detached single home, duplex, tent, communal home, condominium, townhouse, vehicle, sidewalk)?
- What details do you need to consider when renting an apartment or choosing a house (e.g., location, maintenance, utilities, comfort)?
- How does living style affect your choice (e.g., income, family size, occupation(s), expenses, recreation, transportation)?
- How does the environment affect your choice (e.g., climate, geography, population density, pollution)?
- How do you prioritize these factors?
- What trends in housing have you seen in the last ten years? What trends do you predict for the next ten to twenty years?

You may also want to lead a brainstorming session on feasible information sources: environmental studies, historical treatments, business, studies about the future, architecture, government agencies. Students should examine historical charts and statistical sources to build a foundation for extrapolating trends. The added task of predicting the future may be omitted; the class may design shelters based on present-day factors instead.

Groups may present their ideas in various forms: scale model, blueprint, collage, computer-aided design. Examples of different presentations may be shared in class. Note that some formats will entail further instruction (e.g., how to read and create a blueprint). This added skill will require more time for the activity.

Because so many factors are involved in developing a model, you may want to keep all factors but one constant. For example, the entire class could use the same setting but each group could vary the economic condition of the inhabitants. Likewise, the class could assume the same living style and each group could vary the environmental factors.

Assessment

Each group exchanges its future shelter model. To facilitate assessment, the class may use a standardized form or develop its own. Use the Housing A.D. 2020 Assessment Form.

The model may complete the first section of the form, which the assessment can verify. The entire class discusses general housing needs, details, issues, and trends.

- What comparisons may be made about trends across groups?
- What different assumptions and attitudes about the future are implied in the models?
- How has the past affected the future?
- How will you need to adjust your lifestyles or expectations in light of possible future trends?

Activity Variations

1. The entire class may present their homes using the same modeling tools.
2. Each group may select a different modeling tool for presentation.
3. Each group may develop a scenario (i.e., details about the lifestyle and environment), which is given to another group as the basis for its housing project.
4. Each group may follow the building's construction from the ground up (e.g., building codes and permits, installation of utilities, house plans, etc.).
5. The class may take a historical perspective, with each group examining housing trends for a specific decade or century.

RAISING KIDS, RAISING MONEY

Activity Description

Each group develops a yearly financial plan for a family.

Content Outcomes

Students will:

- Identify economic factors in raising a family.
- Calculate yearly costs for raising a family.

Information Literacy Outcomes

Students will:

- Identify and use a variety of sources on family economics.
- Use primary resources as sources of information.
- Draw conclusions from raw data and primary sources.
- Determine correlation and cause–effect relationships relative to family economics.
- Transform information into a spreadsheet format.

Prerequisite Skills

- Use library catalogs and indexes to locate relevant information.
- Interview effectively (optional).
- Produce a spreadsheet.
- Calculate accurately.

Rationale for the Process

A surprising number of teenagers have children. This activity shows students the overt and covert costs of raising a child. The goal is for young people to make reasonable decisions about having and raising children.

Even without children, financially managing independent living can be burdensome, especially when one is caught short when bills or unexpected expenses arise. This activity provides an economic perspective on living on one's own.

The spreadsheet aspect of the activity allows students to predict expenses and use the program to explore the consequences of financial decisions.

Activity

Grade level: high school
Time frame: four to six days
Resources: child-rearing sources, financial planning sources, generic spreadsheet program or financial software (e.g., Quicken)
Grouping: concrete and abstract thinkers, extroverts and introverts, mixed genders, numerical and interpersonal intelligences

Group tasks:
1. Develop a family scenario
2. Choose one year to financially track expenses.
3. Research costs associated with family living.
4. Develop a financial plan for the year.
5. Present the plan using a spreadsheet program.

Tips: To begin the activity, have the class discuss the issues of raising a child. Brainstorm needs of children and the costs associated with those needs. Issues raised should include prenatal care, housing, clothing, food, safety, medical and health needs, insurance, care/supervision.

Have each group construct a family situation and include all relevant demographics. They should determine place, employment, age, health, and possible events. Based on that information, they then research the associated costs. As much as possible, encourage each group to represent a different year of the child. As a formative assessment, have groups present their scenarios *before* they begin their financial research and planning.

Encourage students to ask parents, child-care experts, and medical professionals for financial advice. Students should also consider looking at income tax forms, monthly bills, and other primary documents for relevant information.

To enrich the activity, have students react to an intervening issue (divorce, automobile accident, flood) and change the spreadsheet accordingly. Assessment then takes into account the original plan and the modified financial picture.

Assessment

Group pairs exchange financial plans and scenarios. Assessments should consider the alignment between scenarios and the plan, the numerical accuracy, thoroughness of the plan, and feasibility of economics.

Students may wish to complement their spreadsheets with a skit presentation.

The entire class compares the spreadsheets and explains differences according to the child's age and other family demographics. The relative financial impact of various events may also be analyzed.

Activity Variations

1. The entire class may focus on one family, with each group preparing a plan for each year.
2. The class may start with the same family, with each group researching differences by region.
3. The entire class may focus on one family, with each group responding to a different crisis.
4. Each group may develop a long-term financial picture.

A CLOTHES HORSE OF A DIFFERENT COLOR

Activity Description

Each group designs a clothing outfit and wardrobe based on fashion trends.

Content Outcomes

Students will:
- Categorize fashion elements.
- Link fashion trends to create an original outfit.
- Explore color and texture affects on clothing.
- Use a computer paint or graphics program.

Information Literacy Outcomes

Students will:
- Recognize and use a variety of media as sources of information about fashion styles.
- Categorize fashion elements.
- Analyze fashion styles using classification patterns.
- Synthesize their findings about fashion design elements by creating an original fashion wardrobe.

Prerequisite Skills

- Use library catalogs and indexes to locate relevant information.
- Use a classification schema.
- Use a computer design program.

Rationale for the Process

Fashion includes several elements: silhouette, cut, fabric and texture, detailing, accessories. Each historical time period and each ethnic group have combined these elements to create original clothing.

By examining one fashion trend, students learn to use these elements separately and together. By taking elements from different trends, students create new designs and see fashion's dependency on past trends. Designing a coordinated wardrobe enables students to see how clothing and accessory elements can be combined creatively.

This activity also heightens students' visual literacy and computer techniques.

Activity

Grade level: high school

Time frame: three to five days

Resources: sources on clothing, fashion, costumes, and history (particularly visual data); computer design program (e.g., SuperPaint, Photoshop), color printer, and scanner (optional)

Grouping: concrete and abstract learners, analytical and creative thinkers, computer experts and novices

Group tasks:

1. Choose a historical period.
2. Locate and select information about clothing and fashion for the period.
3. Categorize fashion elements.
4. Analyze fashion trends according to design and clothing element categories.
5. Create templates for each element.
6. Using a set of combined elements on a computer program, design an original fashion outfit.
7. Combine templates and elements to create a fashion wardrobe.

Tips: Fashion transcends simple functional clothing to evoke images of other times, of ideas, of traditions. To clarify group tasks, introduce the activity by asking questions such as:

- What fashion styles and trends are "in" and "out"?
- How would you distinguish one style from another? What elements are involved (e.g., fabric, color, cut, silhouette)?
- Do today's fashions reflect other fashion trends or images?

The class may need guidance finding sources in the library media center. They should consider looking in areas such as costumes, theater, sewing, art, and the historical period being analyzed. Also encourage groups to consult nonprint sources such as video, film, CD-ROMs, and the Internet.

Students may brainstorm the different elements of fashion, so they can have a standardized list of categories to examine (e.g., fabric, texture, color, cut, silhouette, accessories). Some categories may be subdivided (e.g., sleeves, neckline, length).

To provide enough variety and to demonstrate variations, each group should create and print out at least two templates (preferably on a computer design program) for each category. Each template should include the element diagram and explanation. They should also design at least one outfit that incorporates those elements. Ideally, each member in the group would design one, with the group developing a coordinated wardrobe.

Each group presents and describes their outfit/wardrobe and template set as a whole so that the concept of aesthetic combination is modeled. Afterward, templates for each category are collected separately, shuffled separately, and redistributed to groups separately.

Assessment

Each group presents its template set and outfits, explaining the fashion of the time. As an optional evaluation, group pairs may exchange template sets and assess the outfits to verify their accuracy and alignment.

After the templates are shuffled and redistributed, each group designs an outfit based on the templates received and presents its outfit to the class for evaluation. Each template should be saved as a separate file and named systematically. Ideally, all templates would be installed in a common networked folder so each student could have access to it.

As a closing assessment, the class compares trends across template sets and categories.

Activity Variations

1. Each group may choose a different ethnic group or "image" (e.g., western, intellectual, adventurer, antiestablishment).
2. Each group may locate contemporary fashions that reflect the fashion trend researched.
3. The entire class may create a database or multimedia stack of fashion trends.
4. Each group may concentrate on one aspect of fashion (e.g., shoes, jewelry, hats, coats).

DR. FIX-IT

Activity Description

Each group develops a set of instructions for a specific repair procedure.

Content Outcomes

Students will:

- Identify steps to make a repair.
- Sequence directions for a repair procedure.

Information Literacy Outcomes

Students will:

- Recognize and use a variety of media as sources of information about repairs.
- Evaluate repair instructions.
- Develop a set of clear, accurate, complete directions for a repair procedure.

Prerequisite Skills

- Sequence information.
- Follow directions.
- Draw clear and accurate diagrams (optional).
- Use a camcorder (optional).

Rationale for the Process

Students should be able to do simple repairs around the house. Yet, sometimes a direction may be difficult to follow, because the language is unclear or directions are incomplete or the student does not have the required tools or prerequisite skills.

By explaining the repair procedure to others, students learn how to clarify and sequence directions, as well as appreciate different modes of instruction and learning. Moreover, they realize that through teaching one learns.

Activity

Grade level: middle school and up
Time frame: two to three days
Resources: manuals and other sources on repairs; camcorder and videotape (optional)
Grouping: visual and kinesthetic learners, concrete and abstract processors, sequential and holistic learners, technologically adept and nonadept
Group tasks:

1. Choose a repair procedure.
2. Locate and select sources with instructions on how to make the repair.
3. Examine and evaluate the given instructions.
4. Create a set of clear, accurate, and complete directions for the repair procedure.
5. Communicate to another group how to make the repair.

Tips: To help groups clarify their tasks, brainstorm examples of simple repairs (e.g., changing a flat tire, replacing a fuse, clearing a stopped toilet, straightening a videotape).

A good exercise to raise student awareness about directions is to play "Muffin, Muffin." A few students act out how they would make a muffin. The rest of the class coaches or makes observations about the process. The following issues may arise:

- What assumptions were made (e.g., Were all ingredients and equipment out and available? Did the group know what equipment to use when?)?
- How complete were the directions (e.g., Was the oven preheated? Were the muffin tins prepared?)?

- What substitutions could have been made if an ingredient or tool had been unavailable?
- How effectively was the muffin made?

The class may also discuss different ways to give directions: in writing, pictorially, verbally, through demonstration, by video. Leading questions include:

- What are the characteristics of each medium?
- What are the advantages of each?
- How might the medium relate to the kind of repair being made?

Encourage groups to find two sets of directions for a given repair job, preferably using two different media. In that way, groups can compare the directions for completeness and clarity.

Because each group will direct another group in a repair procedure, students will probably want to practice the skill beforehand. They may pantomime the directions, coach each other, or independently perform the repair job at home.

Assessment

Groups pair off, taking turns giving the directions for the other group to pantomime. Alternatively, the actual repair may be done with the real equipment. The groups then evaluate the repairs and the instructions. Although more time-consuming, it is more effective for each group to pantomime a repair procedure for the entire class so the general procedures can be taught to all.

As a closing assessment, the class discusses directions and training in general.

Activity Variations

1. Each group may create a separate index card or HyperCard for each step in a set of directions. The cards are shuffled and given to another group to sequence correctly.
2. Each group may develop a set of cards similar to "Authors," which would include cards indicating the tools, resources, and steps required to carry out a specific repair. A class game would then be developed and played.
3. Each group may pantomime correct and incorrect ways to make a specific report. (Note that sometimes the wrong way is the one remembered.)
4. Each group may create a database for repairs.
5. The entire class may use the same format for stain removals or recipes.

MORE IDEA STARTERS

1. On a world map, mark the origin of foods and food dishes; make a journey map of food migration.
2. Create "daffynitions" for tools.
3. Invent a recipe.
4. Explore careers that use household skills.
5. Simulate dropping out of school and learning how to manage life.
6. Produce a skit on housing conditions.
7. Compare woods and finishes for different functions.
8. Trace laws and regulations dealing with housing or food.
9. Create a database or multimedia stack for vitamins and minerals.
10. Create a database of consumer protection agencies.
11. Trace the definitions and histories of trademarks.
12. Invent a cosmetic product.
13. Experiment with color in food, clothing, interior design.
14. Note differing images of homemakers in literature or television.
15. Produce a soap opera based on soap advertisements.
16. List the uses of different metals.

17. Use CAD programs for interior designs and furniture.
18. Trace the history of cottage industries.
19. Trace the history of prepackaged foods (e.g., cake mixes, pasta dishes, frozen dinners).
20. Compare costs for renovating or rebuilding.

CHAPTER

9

Activity Plans for English

LITERARY WALKABOUT

Activity Description

Each group develops a Web-based literary tour of a local area.

Content Outcomes

Students will:

- Identify major points of literary interest within a geographic area.
- Write accurate descriptions of the sights.

Information Literacy Outcomes

- Recognize and use a variety of sources to locate and select information about a geographic area.
- Use primary sources to research information.
- Determine main facts from sources.
- Sequence information logically.
- Transform information into a Web page.

Prerequisite Skills

- Use library catalogs and indexes to locate and select relevant information.
- Interview for facts and descriptions (optional).
- Design a Web page (optional).

Rationale for the Process

Just as it has been said that every person has a book inside him or her, so every town bespeaks a book. Furthermore, most towns have long-time residents who can relate interesting stories about the area. Buildings each tell a story as well.

This activity enables students to tell their local town's story and share it with others through the Internet. In some cases, it may the first time that students have looked at their community as literary inspiration. The activity also reinforces the idea that "a sense of place" plays an important part in stories.

Activity

Grade level: middle school and up

Time frame: five to seven days

Resources: resources about a geographical area, with emphasis on primary sources; pictorial sources or photographic equipment; Web development tools; scanner (optional)

Grouping: visual and kinesthetic learners, sequential and holistic learners, writers and illustrators or photographers, Web developers and novices

Group tasks:

1. Choose a geographic locale.
2. Research information about the locale. If possible, interview residents, locate primary sources, or photograph the area.
3. Sequence the information logically (e.g., chronologically, spatially).
4. Produce a Web page tour.

Tips: To begin the activity, lead a class discussion about the use of a setting or place to tell a story. Share brochures or Web sites about towns or tourist sites. Discuss the elements of a good tour. Then round out the discussion about using a tour to tell the story of a geographic region.

This activity can be done to foster community awareness, although any locale could be considered. With local access, though, students can discover a variety of information about their area. Have the students brainstorm possible sources; the list should include interviews, local periodicals and monographs, local museums or historical societies, oral history tapes, old school publications, local Chambers of Commerce, city hall records, church archives.

Photographs, both past and present, liven up the story. Students may locate pictures and scan them on the computer. They may also take regular or digital photos, importing them into the Web page.

In terms of dividing time and area, each group can take one street or section of town. The entire class can decide the Web page structure. For instance, a map of the area can be scanned in, with hot links to each part of the tour. Alternatively, each group could research a different time period with the final Web page taking a literary walk through time.

Assessment

Ideally, group pairs would take the actual tours using the literature created. The assessment, then, would determine the accuracy and thoroughness of the tour in light of the actual area. If the final Web page includes a way for users to respond, another assessment would be e-mail feedback.

Activity Variations

1. The class develops a tour composed entirely of local writing, both factual and fiction.
2. The class creates literary walkabouts for remote areas.
3. The class creates literary walkabouts for imaginary places.
4. The class videotapes their literary walkabout.
5. The class produces a literary walkabout brochure or book.
6. The class develops a series of local oral histories.

GUEST AUTHOR

Activity Description

Each group produces a videotape on an author, simulating an interview.

Content Outcomes

Students will:

- Identify significant facts about an author.
- Identify major works by an author.
- Analyze authors within the context of the author's historical period.

Information Literacy Outcomes

Students will:

- Use a variety of media as sources of information about an author and his or her works.
- Use primary resources as sources of information.
- Identify main facts and supporting details.
- Distinguish among fact, fiction, and opinion.
- Apply interviewing techniques to interpret and organize information.
- Synthesize information to develop a specific point of view.
- Integrate and translate findings into a role-playing model.
- Use videotaping techniques to document the interview.

Prerequisite Skills

- Use library catalogs and indexes to find information about authors and their works.
- Interview effectively.
- Ability to storyboard and videotape.

Rationale for the Process

Literature lives when students learn about the author and gains meaning when examined in light of the times during which it is written.

In this activity, each group "becomes" the author. Students ferret out personal and professional facts, read literary criticism about the author's works, and delve into the time period's nature. Primary documents become more meaningful through this process.

The interview format provides a simple structure for organizing information and makes it seem immediate. It also allows students to role-play and really "get into" their subject. On another level, interviewing and role-playing allow students to interpret findings to present a specific viewpoint.

The videotape provides a permanent record for future study, serving as an introductory lesson for future classes.

Activity

Grade level: high school

Time frame: one to two weeks

Resources: primary and other sources on literature, authors, interviewing, videotaping; videotaping equipment

Grouping: kinesthetic, auditory, and visual learners; creative and analytical processors; concrete and abstract learners; videotaping experts and novices

Group tasks:

1. Locate and select information, especially primary sources, about and by an author and the associated time period.
2. Read works by the author.
3. Determine the main significant facts and supporting details about the author and the times.
4. Translate the findings into interview form.
5. Produce a videotape about the author.

Tips: To help students begin this activity, lead a class discussion on gathering information about a person. The class may develop a checklist of questions to research, such as:

- What was your childhood like?
- Who were important people in your life?
- How did you get into writing?
- What kind of writing do you like best?
- What obstacles did you encounter? How did you overcome them?
- Do you consider yourself successful?
- What do you consider to be your greatest achievement?
- What regrets do you have, if any?
- What is your social life?
- What interest do you have in politics, religion, society?

Then lead a discussion on ways to find out about people:

- Interview them.
- Ask friends and neighbors about them.
- Read their writing or examine their creative work.
- Examine their setting: home, town, society.

Translate these approaches to information sources found in the library media center. Emphasize primary sources such as diaries, letters, their own work, contemporary documents, and literary criticism of the day. Encourage students to use nonprint sources such as illustrations and photographs, and audio and visual tapes. Remind students to look at information from several viewpoints to get a more objective perspective. You may make the analogy that different people (e.g., parents, peers, teachers) have different opinions and viewpoints about a student.

To help groups organize and present their findings, lead a brainstorming session on interview structure. You can discuss television interview programs and their contrasting treatments depending on the interviewer's objective. Barbara Walters interviews differ from exposés on "60 Minutes." You may help students look at different aspects of interviewing:

- Tone (supportive or attacking)
- Structure (single issue, life history)

- Setting (neutral place, "on location")
- Timing (significant points in an author's life—or after death)

Groups may simulate an interview at the time in history that an author lived, say, William Shakespeare at his Globe Theater in 1600.

The interview structure also helps groups organize their fact-finding strategy. If they develop a list of interview questions and objectives first, they can use that information to locate relevant answers. Alternatively, students may browse the collection for interesting facts about the author and times, and only afterward customize the interview approach to fit the findings.

Videotaping provides a permanent record of the interview and reinforces the format's immediacy. Students who have difficulty speaking in public may use this medium to improve speaking habits by watching their performance and retaping it until they are satisfied with the results.

Another approach to videotaping, particularly if most students are uncomfortable with the equipment, is to have an outside person videotape the "live" interviews in class. Students may take class time or independent time to view the productions in order to assess speech habits.

Assessment

The groups present their interviews. Time permitting, the rest of the class may ask the presenters additional questions about the author, similar to a question-and-answer period after a speech. When assessing the interviews, the class can use the Interview Assessment Form.

INTERVIEW ASSESSMENT FORM

- What is the objective? Is it clear? What is the tone?
- Who is the interviewer?
- What is the setting? Is it appropriate? Is it accurate?
- What is the time frame?
- Are author facts accurate and complete?
- Are interview questions appropriate and interesting?
- What bias exists?

From *Cooperative Learning Activities in the Library Media Center.* © 1999 Lesley S. J. Farmer. Libraries Unlimited (800) 237-6124.

Group pairs may also be utilized to structure an activity and assessment. Two groups may study the same author and interview each other. Alternatively, each group may study a unique author but be interviewed by different groups. In either case, the "expert" group will have less control over the interview—and may have to be more prepared!

As a closing assessment, the class discusses general issues about authors:

- What connection do authors have with their society or times?
- What patterns exist, if any, in authors' lives or works?
- How does the interviewing structure affect the presentation of information?

Activity Variations

1. Groups may choose the author, or the teacher may assign the person.
2. Groups may produce a skit or dramatic story about the author.
3. Groups may produce a slide–tape program about the author.
4. Groups may "interview" the author's contemporaries.
5. Groups may concentrate on one work by an author, perhaps translating the story into video form.
6. Groups may use a "press conference" format, whereby the rest of the class asks the author questions.
7. Groups may develop an interview simulation of a living author, and then actually interview the person via video conferencing or by e-mail.
8. The entire class may interview the same author but at different points in the author's life.
9. The entire class may interview authors of the same culture but of different historical periods.
10. Groups may hold a simulated panel of different authors: a literary feast!

WORD FAMILY TREES AND JOURNEYS

Activity Description
Each group finds the etymology and related terms for assigned words.

Content Outcomes
Students will:
- Identify and relate the etymologies of associated terms.
- Trace the historical and geographical development of words.

Information Literacy Outcomes
Students will:
- Locate and interpret word etymology.
- Locate and identify related words.
- Assess a variety of sources to verify information.
- Structure their findings by constructing word "family trees" and "word voyages."

Prerequisite Skills
- Use dictionaries.
- Read maps.

Activity
Grade level: middle school and up
Time frame: two to three days
Resources: dictionaries, language reference materials, maps
Group tasks:

1. Locate the assigned word.
2. Determine its etymology.
3. Locate related words and their etymologies.
4. Verify etymologies by consulting additional sources.
5. Create a family tree of the related words.
6. Draw the words' etymological journeys on a map.

Tips: You may introduce this activity as a word genealogy project or a detective search. Discuss how one word provides a clue for finding another, related word.

If possible, introduce students to the *Oxford English Dictionary* and etymological reference works. Remind students about keys to abbreviations used in these volumes. If needed, share a few examples of dictionary entries for the class to extract.

You may model the activity behavior. For example, the word "example" comes from the Latin word *exemplum,* which is composed of *ex* ("from") and *emere* ("to take or buy"). *Webster's Tenth New Collegiate Dictionary* refers the reader to the word "redeem" for more detail. The search may continue along that separate branch, as well as proceed to derivative words and their etymologies, such as "examine" and "examination" or to synonyms. Thus, students should verify their etymologies using difference sources since different etymological versions sometimes exist.

Also review the structure of a family tree. For the map, one approach is to have all groups use the same outline world map—on a transparency. The word voyages can be done in marker and then compared as they are overlaid.

Assessment

Group pairs exchange their family trees and maps, potentially building on each other's work.

The class discusses the family trees and maps, noting any links between them. They may also discuss the variations found among different word etymologies or different sources.

Activity Variations

1. The entire class may concentrate on words in one subject area.
2. The entire class may concentrate on one concept, such as "time." Each group would search a different aspect of time.
3. Students may create a family tree or map of languages as a whole.
4. The entire class may concentrate on one word or concept, such as "tree." Each group would create a family tree for a different language (e.g., "arbre," "baum," etc.).
5. Each group may create a list of English words that come directly from another country. For example, Australian words would include "boomerang" and "kangaroo." Scandinavian words would include "sky" and "skill." Native American words would include "papoose" and "wigwam."
6. Students knowing other languages may create parallel family trees.

I SAY...

Activity Description

Each group presents a dramatic scene from a different perspective.

Content Outcomes

Students will:

- Identify characteristics of historical dramatic structures (e.g., commedia dell'arte, Greek tragedy).
- Relate performance style to dramatic structure.

Information Literacy Outcomes

- Locate and evaluate information about different historical approaches to drama.
- Apply dramatic elements in analyzing a dramatic selection.
- Interpret a dramatic scene in terms of a specific historical dramatic approach.

Prerequisite Skills

- Use library catalogs and indexes to locate relevant information
- Interpret a passage dramatically.

Rationale for the Process

The word "no" can be interpreted in many ways, depending on the speaker's inflection and expression. So, too, can entire plays carry different meanings depending on the interpretation.

Although the words are key in drama, the interpretation of those words as well as the costuming and setting affect the message. Shakespeare's works, in particular, have been interpreted in many ways: as period pieces, as contemporary studies, as simulations of the Globe experience. Even the language has been modified in some productions.

Likewise, drama has been produced in different forms throughout the ages. Morality plays present a perspective different from that of realistic treatments. The formal Greek rite differs from commedia dell'arte, although both share the concept of archetypal presentation.

By providing a historical context for a dramatic scene, students synthesize the dramatic techniques and approaches used in different periods. They also realize the importance of interpretation and supporting elements of costuming, sets, and props.

Activity

Grade level: high school
Time frame: one to two weeks
Resources: drama material, props, and other dramatic devices
Grouping: mixture of kinesthetic, aural, and visual learners; analytical and creative thinkers; abstract and concrete processors
Group tasks:

1. Locate and select information about a specific historical school of thought in drama, such as Greek or Theater of the Absurd.
2. Identify the main dramatic elements of the dramatic school.
3. Interpret a dramatic scene in light of the chosen historical dramatic approach and related elements.
4. Present the dramatic scene incorporating the school's elements.

Tips: To begin the activity, lead a discussion about the different ways that people can interpret words. Then you might generalize about different interpretations of stories or characters, such as Superman or Batman. Students may have seen different movie versions of the same story, such as *Romeo and Juliet*. These experiences facilitate understanding about the significance of interpretation and changes over time and across cultures.

The easiest way to carry out the activity is to assign the same dramatic scene, or at least play, for the entire class. In this way, the groups may concentrate on the treatment rather than the location of appropriate dramatic material. The choice of material is important; the more universal the topic and the less constricted the stage directions and scenery, the easier it will be for the students to modify the scene. Using a play with an obvious motif, such as the Cinderella story, also makes it easier for students to apply the historical "spin."

The time element is flexible, depending on the elaborateness of the dramatic presentation. If costuming and scenery are involved, allow enough time for students to produce the proper effect. To help classmates visualize the scene without costuming or other props, each group may sketch the stage and illustrate the characters for spectators' reference. A simple trick is to make a color transparency of the background scene, and project it onto a white wall behind the actors using an overhead projector.

Assessment

Each group presents the scene according to the historical dramatic context. They are assessed according to their alignment to the particular dramatic approach. The class discusses the differences in presentations, drawing inferences about the dramatic schools of thought and their relationship to performance style. Discussion can also lead to questions about dramatic motifs.

Activity Variations

1. The entire class concentrates on the same scene. Each group chooses a different dramatic approach.
2. The entire class concentrates on the same dramatic approach. Each group chooses a different scene or different play.
3. Groups research different movie treatments of the same story.
4. Groups present the scene using videotape or puppets.
5. Students produce a script of the scene.

MORE IDEA STARTERS

1. List movies or plays made from books.
2. Develop a database of authors.
3. Examine different sections of the newspaper for vocabulary, sentence structure, and bias. Produce a prototype newspaper.
4. Compare three stories on the same subject.
5. Rewrite a poem as a work of prose or drama.
6. Rewrite a story as a special issue of a newspaper.
7. Locate artwork that would illustrate a story.
8. Locate different illustrations for the same literary work (e.g., *Alice in Wonderland* or Dante's *Divine Comedy*).
9. Hold a mock press conference for an author.
10. Hold a mock press conference for a literary character.
11. Research literary criticism about an author over a period of time.
12. Compare best-seller lists to contemporary lists of twentieth century classics.
13. Create a card game about literary characters.
14. Survey great literature of different decades across cultures.
15. Create a timeline for science fiction.
16. Compare utopia literature; produce displays or dioramas illustrating that genre.
17. Debate censorship issues.
18. Create a multimedia presentation about regional folk legends.
19. Link story lines to news headlines.
20. Research portrayals of women in literature.

CHAPTER 10

Activity Plans for Foreign Languages

SLICE OF LIFE

Activity Description
Each group describes a cross section continuum of a country.

Content Outcomes
Students will:

- Objectively examine a country through content analysis and sampling techniques.
- Develop a perspective, along a continuum, of one aspect of a country.
- Develop a composite picture of a country through shared expertise.
- Recognize forms of bias and stereotypes associated with a country.

Information Literacy Outcomes
Students will:

- Use a variety of sources, especially visual, to locate and select information about a country.
- Use content analysis to critique information.
- Use classification patterns and techniques to synthesize information.
- Sequence facts along a continuum.
- Translate information into a pictorial context.
- Use sampling techniques to access and verify information.
- Assess data from a variety of viewpoints to make inferences.
- Recognize forms of bias as they assess data.

Prerequisite Skills
- Use catalogs and indexes to locate relevant information.
- Identify main ideas and relevant facts.
- Locate, select, and transfer computer images (optional).

Rationale for the Process
As students examine the countries and cultures related to the foreign language being taught, they develop perspective on language and people. The picture they develop, though, will be biased because of the materials and people they encounter. In fact, it is very difficult to form an objective picture of any culture.

Each country may be examined from many viewpoints, beyond demographic statistics and national products. Each aspect, or slice, has its own spectrum of experience and quality. For example, a country's population may be viewed from young to old, from rich to poor, from single to extended family.

In effect, by pursuing a number of cross sections, students develop a more complete picture of the country and culture as manifested in its language. In addition, they discover possible gaps, biases, or stereotypes about a particular country as they analyze different sources and study the continuum for that slice of life.

Activity

Grade level: high school

Time frame: three days to a week

Resources: resources on the country, illustrations to cut out, computer

Grouping: students who receive information in different ways (visual, auditory, tactile), sequential and global learners, print and computer-based researchers

Group tasks:

1. Perform a content analysis of a familiar document to check for objectivity and accurate portrayal of the subject.
2. Choose one aspect/cross section of a country to explore.
3. Locate and select information, particularly in visual form, about that aspect.
4. Critique information for accuracy and objectivity.
5. Develop a category with a continuum along which to place the information.
6. Place appropriate information along the continuum.
7. Critique the continuum for accuracy, objectivity, and completeness.
8. Describe the cross section continuum using illustrations/pictures or graphs.
9. Describe the country in light of several continuums.

Tips: Begin the activity by discussing a setting or culture. Use the school's yearbook as a concrete example of a descriptive picture of a "culture," and lead a class discussion about its representation of the school.

Students may perform a content analysis of the yearbook. Each group selects one aspect or category to examine: male versus female, each grade/year, time of day, academic versus co-curricular. With book in hand, each group then notes how much space or how many pictures fall into the category. Once the actual numbers relative to a category are known, groups can compare their findings with the true figures to determine the yearbook's accuracy or representation. Sophisticated learners may explore statistical descriptions of the data.

The findings lead to a class discussion about biased descriptions. You may ask questions such as:

- How does the yearbook differ from each person's perception of the school?
- How does placement and arrangement affect the perception of the school?
- How might the yearbook be changed to give a more accurate picture of the school?
- Why might biases be introduced into a yearbook? To present a positive picture? To attract certain students?

The yearbook's editor could attend this discussion as an expert and answer class questions about how the yearbook was created.

From this kind of discussion about a local setting, students can progress to discussing the variety of settings found within a country. You may bring in examples of resources on a country, such as travelogues, side sets, books such as *A Day in the Life of...*. Each group may examine a different source in several ways:

- Topics or themes (e.g., categories of information)
- Categorical arrangement for resource (e.g., showing activities chronologically)
- Information left out
- Producer/creator (e.g., Chamber of Commerce, history teacher, political leader)
- Aim or intent of the resource (usually found in the preface or introduction) (e.g., tourist promotion, political stance)

Next, draw the cross section concept, using the analogy of cutting across a tree trunk or diagramming the human body. Note that along any cross section, a range of information exists. For example, the cross section of a map may range from sea level to a mountain peak (see fig. 10.1). As an additional activity, you or student groups may find examples of cross sections to analyze (e.g., frog dissection, child development, timelines). Groups may exchange cross sections to compare their analyses.

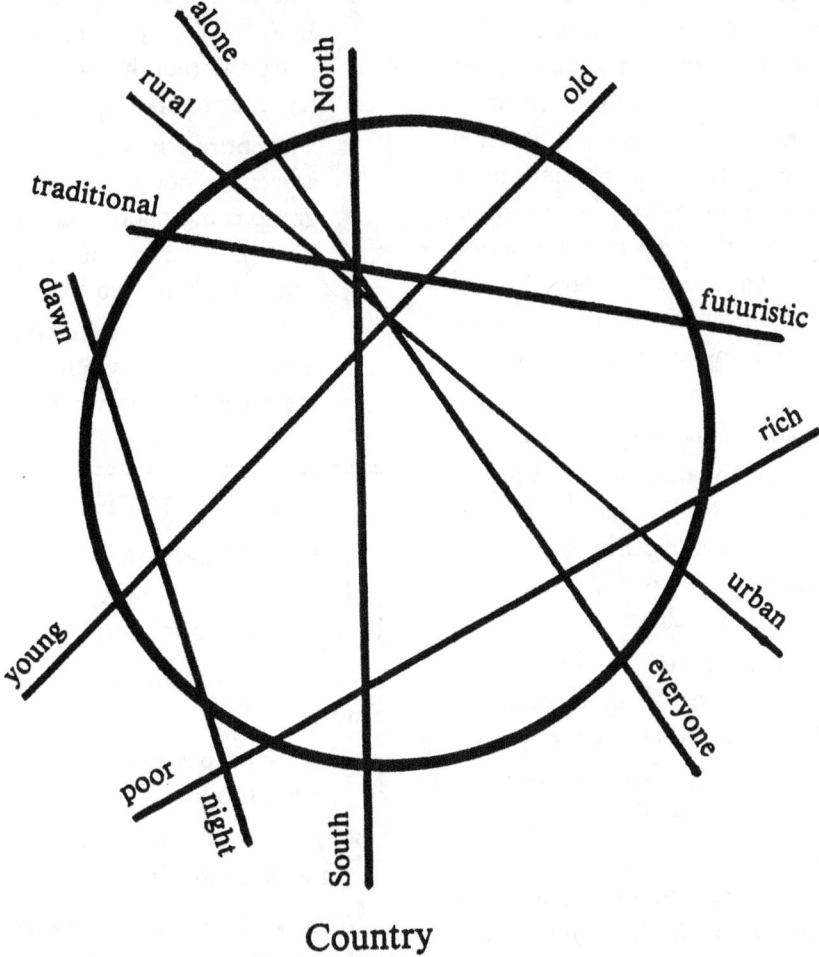

Figure 10.1 Cross section concepts.

Have students suggest cross section continuums that would describe a country. Examples may include rural to high-density, dawn to night, traditional to futuristic, north to south, young to old, natural to artificial, low to high, desert to jungle.

As an additional aid (particularly to less sophisticated learners or kinesthetic learners), students may arrange an existing set of slides or illustrations. They may see if a pattern or category seems to arise from the pictures. They may then sequence the pictures in some logical order within the classification.

Finally, examine the concept of sampling. You may use the analogy of a pizza. A half pizza may accurately describe the whole pizza, unless different toppings are placed on each half (it depends on how you cut the half, too). A slice of pizza may exclude some ingredient, and a crust sample gives little indication of the pizza flavor. So, too, does a sampling of a country give a limited picture of the whole. Note that the more cross sections that are used, taken from varied points of view, the more representative the resulting picture of the entire country will be.

To maximize the variety of continuums, the class should know each group's choice of continuum. You may preassign the possible continuums to focus or limit the activity.

Students may need help in illustrating the continuum. They may use a timeline format, with pictures sequenced along the line. Some students may prefer graphic representations, noting percentages along the continuum line. Students may also note that gaps may appear along the continuum. They need to consult a variety of resources. They may find different results for the same part of the continuum, so they may find that certain parts of a continuum are truly missing, thus slanting the information. To verify information, students may also talk with experts or citizens of the country, recognizing that each person brings a personal bias.

Assessment

Groups exchange their cross sections for cross-evaluation. Content may be evaluated for accuracy and completeness. Format may be evaluated for appropriateness and clarity.

The class examines the cross sections as a whole, discussing aspects such as:

- How good is the sampling? Are different approaches exemplified? What other continuums would have been useful to see?
- What gaps exist in various continuums? Why? Do stereotypes arise from the given information?
- Why might a country want to present a biased picture of its land? How would the political or social status of the producer possibly affect the results?
- What kind of format was used to describe the continuum? Do different categories lend themselves to different presentations?

Activity Variations

1. Groups may be assigned a cross section or may determine their own.
2. Groups may present their findings in other formats, such as video, slide–tape, multimedia presentation, poetry, or drama.
3. Each group may choose two cities and develop a description between the two points. The entire class may develop a cross-country trip, each group being assigned one portion of the journey.
4. The entire class may develop a "Day in the Life of…." Each group could be assigned one portion of the day, one part of the country, one population group, or one century.
5. The entire class may concentrate on one aspect of a country, such as music. Each group could choose one continuum: one point in time to another, young to old, rural to urban, solo to symphonic.
6. Two groups may develop the same continuum for a country but choose and arrange examples that show a different bias.

FOOD ON THE INTERNET

Activity Description

Each group creates a typical meal of a country by accessing information from the Internet.

Content Outcomes

Students will:

- Locate recipes and other food information on the Internet.
- Translate food information from another language into English.

Information Literacy Outcomes

Students will:

- Locate and select sources from the Internet about food in countries using a foreign language.

Prerequisite Skills

- Read recipes.
- Use foreign language dictionaries.
- Convert metric measurements into English measurements.

Rationale for the Process

An army and a culture move on their stomachs. One important way to learn about a foreign language is to experience the foods of the countries that speak that language. Food is a significant ritualistic and social cultural phenomenon.

This activity allows students to explore cultural food preferences and translate recipes.

Activity

Grade level: middle school and up
Time frame: three days
Resources: Internet sites and other sources on foods and recipes, kitchen and equipment to prepare food (optional)
Groupings: kinesthetic and visual learners
Groups tasks:

1. Choose a country in which another language is spoken.
2. Use the Internet to locate recipes from the country and in the language spoken there.
3. Translate the recipe from the foreign language into English.
4. Research information about foods or recipes in the foreign country.
5. Prepare the recipe.
6. Present the food and cultural background.

Tips: Begin the activity by discussing stereotypes about the foods eaten in the countries where the specified foreign language is spoken. Bring up the fact that the Internet is a global source of information, and that students can often find recipes in the foreign language.

The research on foods provides the context for the recipes and shows how cultures choose foods that are indigenous to their area or religious beliefs.

Assessment

Each group's dish is assessed according to how well it represents the culture and how accurate it is in translation of ingredients and measurements. The degree to which groups can tie their recipes to the country's culture should also be assessed.

The class as a whole discusses the foods, recipes, and food-related customs of the countries that speak the foreign language. They can compare the customs among those countries and determine what common practices occur and why they exist.

Activity Variations

1. The entire class may concentrate on one country, and each group can choose one part of a meal.
2. Students can find recipes in non-Internet sources.
3. Students can create a cultural cookbook.
4. Groups exchange recipes in the foreign language and select another group to prepare the dish.

VISUAL DICTIONARY

Activity Description

Each group creates a hypermedia stack giving the foreign terms for each part of an illustration (e.g., airplane, tree, etc.).

Content Outcomes

Students will:

- List the accurate term in a foreign language for individual parts of a whole item or concept.

Information Literacy Outcomes

Students will:

- Locate and select the correct term in a foreign language for individual parts of a whole item or concept.
- Identify significant parts of a whole, translating them into chart form.

Prerequisite Skills

- Use dictionaries.
- Create hypermedia stacks (optional).

Rationale for the Process

Usually, students learn the general concepts of a foreign language, but they neglect the finer parts of the whole. By creating an illustration in detail, students learn technical terms associated with a specific subject. This visual structure also facilitates vocabulary building.

Activity

Grade level: middle school and up
Time frame: two to three days
Resources: foreign language dictionaries, hypermedia software, scanner (optional)
Grouping: analytical and creative thinkers, technological experts and novices

Group tasks:

1. Locate foreign language terms for technical terms.
2. Create a hypermedia stack displaying terms in a foreign language.
3. Verify validity of terms.

Tips: The students or teacher may choose the terms to define. Words should reflect fairly complex or varied terms, such as "zoo" or "school" or "shopping mall."

The most concrete way to show the definitions is for each group to create a diagram for the system and label each specific term. Students may import existing diagrams from the Internet, CD-ROMs, clip art, or scanned images. Hot links can provide the terms and definitions. Students can also record the sound of the terms and link them to the appropriate parts.

Part of the activity should include the verification of terms. Many students start with the English word to find the foreign term. However, few students check its validity by looking at the foreign word, especially in another reference source, to check its English equivalent. Students should also be reminded that some dictionaries have a British orientation rather than an American one, so the terms may not be equivalent.

Assessment

Each group assesses another's hypermedia stack. The groups verify the terms using different sources from the ones used by the originating group. The group stacks can be merged into one comprehensive stack.

The class and teacher assess the stacks for completeness and accuracy. Closing discussion issues may include:

- Ease or difficulty in finding technical terms for the specific subject or concept
- Difference among sources
- Usefulness of learning a group of related terms

Activity Variations

1. The entire class concentrates on one area of definitions, such as sports. Each group chooses an individual sport.
2. Groups may present the definitions through a diorama or display.

CARTOONS AND PHOTO NOVELLAS

Activity Description

Each group creates a cartoon strip or photo novella in a foreign language.

Content Outcomes

Students will:

- Demonstrate language competency to create humorous dialogue or captions.
- Recognize and use visual clues that help one understand a foreign language.

Information Literacy Outcomes

Students will:

- Recognize and use a variety of media as sources of information to help them create comic strips or photo novellas.
- Locate accurate words and idioms.
- Use visual techniques and patterns, especially cartooning and photography, to organize writing.
- Coordinate visual and written elements to create a comic strip or photo novella.

Prerequisite Skills

- Use library catalogs and indexes to locate information.
- Design a cartoon strip or photo novella.

Rationale for the Process

A humorous element can stimulate participation in learning, and students may express inner feelings through humorous strips. The sequencing found in strips also reinforces foreign language conversational style. In fact, comic books and photo novellas are very popular in many foreign countries. Additionally, as students search for idioms that translate humor, they gain appreciation for the differences in language quality.

Do visual elements constitute a language? How universal is visual literacy? How are feelings expressed in language? Are certain elements universal? On a philosophical level, these fascinating issues may be addressed as well.

Activity

Group level: middle school and up

Time frame: two to three days

Resources: foreign language dictionaries and grammar resources, cartoon and comic books, photo novellas

Grouping: visualizers and verbalizers, sequential and holistic processors, analytical and creative thinkers

Group tasks:

1. Write a comic strip or photo novella dialogue/sequence.
2. If the strip/novella is originally done in English, then translate it into the appropriate foreign language.
3. Design the strip/novella to complement the text.

Tips: Students should discuss cartoon strips and photo novellas before the activity. They may bring in these strips written in a foreign language.

As a warm-up activity, students may translate an English-language strip into the appropriate foreign language.

Some students may design the strip visually before putting in dialogue. Some students may begin with foreign language conversation and fit the strip to it.

Assessment

Each group shares its strip. The class and teacher assesses them for foreign language skill, humor, and creativity.

Activity Variations

1. Each group locates a strip and removes the dialogue. The blank strip becomes another group's basis for writing humorous text.
2. Each group designs a strip, without dialogue or captions. Two groups exchange strips and write the text in the foreign language.
3. Each group writes a humorous script, for which another group designs the strip.
4. After the strips are created, the panels are mixed up. The mixed version is given to another group to unscramble.

MORE IDEA STARTERS

1. Develop a database of famous people from a foreign country.
2. Develop a database of famous U.S. immigrants from a foreign country.
3. Explore careers that use foreign languages.
4. Compare advertisements or commercials in a foreign language to those in English. Create ads or commercials in a foreign language.
5. Create a brochure in a foreign language.
6. Develop a family tree in a foreign language.
7. Locate a foreign folktale and dramatize it, either in English or in the foreign language.
8. Gather foreign language poetry, songs, or folklore to create an anthology.
9. Celebrate a holiday of a foreign country, using that language.
10. Compare quotations or proverbs from a foreign language to those in English. Translate and illustrate them.
11. Compare periodicals in a foreign language to those in English. Note coverage and style.
12. Create crossword puzzles in foreign languages, either translating or using all foreign words.
13. List foreign words and phrases that have been adopted by English speakers.

14. Compare different aspects of life in the foreign country and the United States (e.g., education, dating, rites of passage, family life).
15. Translate into English foreign language stories for children.
16. Illustrate a foreign language folktale for a picture book.
17. Translate a board game into a foreign language (e.g., Monopoly, Pictionary, Clue).
18. Produce a soap opera or melodrama in a foreign language.
19. Hold a pretend press conference for a famous foreign person.
20. Interview foreign students.
21. Role-play a foreign student, demonstrating how he or she would react to immigrating to or visiting the United States.
22. Compare television programs or films in a foreign language to those in English.
23. Compare laws in foreign countries to those in the United States, either in terms of the judicial process or as applied to specific issues, such as marriage or child abuse.
24. Develop a database listing the typical foods, dress, rites of passage, holidays, sports, and activities for different foreign countries.
25. Develop a card game using a foreign language. Suits may be made of related terms.
26. Plan a trip to a foreign country. Consider passports, medicine, transportation, clothing, holidays, currency, customs, etc.
27. Plan a trip to the United States as a foreign visitor.
28. Explore the work of translators.
29. Produce a cross-cultural presentation through key-pal teams in the United States and a foreign country.

CHAPTER II

Activity Plans for Health and Physical Education

EMERGENCY PREPAREDNESS

Activity Description
Each group develops an emergency scenario, and each group carries out another group's scenario.

Content Outcomes
Students will:
- Analyze emergencies.
- Demonstrate appropriate safe behavior in emergency situations.

Information Literacy Outcomes
Students will:
- Recognize and use a variety of media as sources of information about appropriate safe behaviors in emergency situations.
- Analyze and evaluate information to determine its accuracy and adequacy.
- Create emergency scenarios.

Prerequisite Skills
- Create and follow directions.

Rationale for the Process
Emergency preparedness involves a repertoire of safety measures and a calm approach to situations. Both elements demand practice.

By creating emergency scenarios, students visualize and concretely deal with problems. By demonstrating how to handle emergencies, students apply classroom knowledge in a safe environment.

Activity
Grade level: middle school and up
Time frame: two to three days
Resources: first aid and safety sources
Grouping: concrete and abstract processors; visual, aural, and kinesthetic learners; analytical and creative thinkers
Group tasks:
1. Create an emergency scenario.
2. After exchanging scenarios with another group, locate and select information about coping with the given emergency.
3. Evaluate information for accuracy and appropriateness.
4. Decide what to do in the given emergency.
5. Act out the appropriate safe behavior for the given emergency.

Tips: This activity may be introduced at the beginning of a safety unit or used as a reinforcement/review at the end of the unit. In the former situation, the groups will spend more time locating information. In the latter, the emphasis will be on class evaluation of the groups' decision making.

To help the groups clarify their scenarios, you may lead a class discussion on details to include in an emergency situation, such as:

- Site (urban versus rural, geographic constraints, building)
- Time (day versus night, weekend versus weekday, season)
- Climate and weather conditions
- Material resources at hand
- Degree of emergency or injury
- People (number, age, physical capabilities, knowledge)
- Communication and transportation at hand

By having one group design the scenario and another group react to it, the class experiences a more realistic simulation. In addition, groups assess the designers' ability to describe and predict the factors involved in an emergency.

Assessment

Each group simulates the emergency scenario, demonstrating appropriate safe behavior. The other groups assess their behavior and their sources of information.

Activity Variations

1. Each group may develop a set of cards for a specific aspect of an emergency scenario (e.g., site specifications, weather conditions). A class set of cards is developed. Each group then receives one card for each factor and demonstrates appropriate safe behavior from the resultant combination of emergency facts.
2. Each group may demonstrate the wrong way to react and contrast that with the correct response.
3. The entire class may concentrate on the same kind of emergency (e.g., water safety, outdoor practice, earthquake preparedness). Each group designs a variation on the theme.
4. Each group may locate an article about an emergency and analyze how people reacted.
5. Each group may develop a multimedia stack training module with decision points and consequences for different reactions to an emergency.

NUTRITION SURVEY

Activity Description

Each group develops a nutrition-value menu based on restaurant or school cafeteria food.

Content Outcomes

Students will:

- Analyze and calculate the nutritional content of food.
- Combine food in terms of nutritional values to develop healthful menus.

Information Literacy Outcomes

Students will:

- Locate and select nutritional information about food.
- Analyze food according to a nutrition-based classification system.
- Synthesize and organize findings using a menu format.

Prerequisite Skills

- Interview for facts.
- Calculate accurately.
- Use classification schema.

Rationale for the Process

Sometimes the statements "If it's junk food, it's bad for you" and "If you don't like it, it's probably good for you" aren't true. Students may be surprised at the nutritional choices they have at restaurants and cafeterias.

Students are encouraged to eat nutritionally balanced meals, and they sometimes study the nutritional benefits of individual foods. But do they have a good choice of nutritious items when eating away from home?

By analyzing and developing institutional menus, students become more aware consumers.

Activity

Grade level: middle school and up
Time frame: two to three days

Resources: menus, nutrition charts (including those from fast food restaurants), and other sources on nutrition

Grouping: concrete and abstract thinkers, analytical and creative processors, mixed genders

Group tasks:

1. Locate and select a menu from a restaurant or school food service.
2. Locate and select nutritional information about the food on the menu.
3. Analyze the food nutritionally and calculate its nutritional value.
4. Determine the overall nutritional value of the menu's offerings.
5. Create a nutritionally balanced menu using the restaurant's or school's offerings.

Tips: Begin by leading a class discussion on perceptions about commercially prepared food by asking questions such as:

- How nutritious are "fast foods"?
- Is junk food junk?
- Can you eat well (nutritionally) at school?
- How do you know what ingredients are included in commercial food? Does such information make a difference?

Groups may find as they examine menus that they do not know what specific ingredients are included in an entree. For the purposes of the activity, they may interview the chef or make assumptions about the ingredients.

Students may need help finding nutrition tables. Remind them that cookbooks and almanacs sometimes include such information. Specialized computer programs and the Internet deal with such data. Student should also consider the nutritional information included on prepackaged food.

They will also have to remember serving sizes as they calculate nutritional values.

Assessment

Each group presents the nutritional evaluation of a specific menu. They compare the menus and develop nutritionally balanced menus using separate or combined sources. Instead of assessing a menu overall, groups may present two meal choices: one that is nutritionally sound and one that is nutritionally unsound.

As a closing assessment, the class discusses nutrition in general, considering questions such as:

- How healthy are commercial and institutional foods?
- How do different menus compare nutritionally?
- What specific factors affect the nutritional value of foods (e.g., preparation, prepackaging, serving size)?
- How can people become wiser consumers nutritionally?

Activity Variations

1. Each group may create a nutritionally sound menu for a hypothetical restaurant.
2. Each group may interview a specific restaurant chef to analyze his or her use of nutritional knowledge.
3. Each group may choose a different ethnic group and do a nutritional analysis of foods associated with that group (e.g., Chinese, Italian).

EXERCISES BY BODY PARTS

Activity Description

Each group develops and measures the physiological impact of a set of exercises for a specific part of the body.

Content Outcomes

Students will:

- Categorize exercises by their value for specific parts of the body.
- Create an exercise routine that uses different combinations of exercises.
- Measure physiological impact of exercises by manipulating scientific instruments.

Information Literacy Outcomes

Students will:

- Recognize and use a variety of media as sources of information about exercises for a specific part of the body.
- Use a classification system to analyze and categorize information.
- Interpret data from scientific instruments.
- Transform data into spreadsheet or chart format.
- Communicate clear and accurate directions.
- Develop a module-based presentation of information.

Prerequisite Skills

- Use library catalogs and indexes to locate a variety of sources.
- Interview for facts.
- Use science probes and other scientific measurement tools.
- Create spreadsheets or charts.

Rationale for the Process

Most exercise routines incorporate exercises that use different parts of the body. However, students may want to vary the routines or concentrate on exercises that condition one part of the body.

By locating multiple exercises relative to parts of the body, students are given a module-based repertoire with which to develop a variety of routines that best satisfy their own needs. They also learn how a specific exercise influences different parts of the body.

Incorporating scientific measurement tools enables students to verify the benefits that exercise brings. Organizing that data into spreadsheet format facilitates comparative analysis.

Activity

Grade level: high school
Time frame: four days
Resources: exercise and fitness sources, including human resources; card stock and writing/drawing instruments (or optional multimedia authoring program)
Grouping: concrete and abstract processors, kinesthetic and visual learners, analytical and creative thinkers
Group tasks:

1. Choose one part of the body.
2. Locate and select exercises that help that part of the body.
3. Categorize and evaluate the exercises, noting the specific benefit.
4. Measure the impact of exercise by using science probes and other measurement tools.
5. Develop a set of instruction sheets or cards, one per exercise.
6. Develop an exercise routine based on the class set of cards.

Tips: To help groups clarify their tasks, lead a discussion about exercise, asking questions such as:

- How do exercise routines benefit the body?
- How are routines developed?
- What is the difference between conditioning and toning?
- How would you exercise differently if you wanted to lose weight rather than develop muscles?
- How can you customize an exercise routine to focus on specific parts of the body?

Groups should brainstorm a variety of information sources, such as fitness books, training videos, and interviews with fitness instructors and coaches.

As groups locate exercises, they should note the specific goal of the exercise. They should note, if possible, different ways to perform the exercise, depending on the person's physical ability and goal (weight loss versus muscle tone).

Groups should be encouraged to share resources. If one group finds an exercise that helps more than one part of the body, it may pass that information on to the appropriate group.

As students examine the benefits of exercise, they can brainstorm ways to scientifically measure the physiological impact. An available computer or programmable calculator facilitates the use of scientific probes and other measurement tools. To provide a thorough analysis, each exercise should be carried out and measured using a variety of tools so groups can determine a variety of physiological effects.

To facilitate cross-comparisons of physiological measurements, the class can develop a spreadsheet template like this:

	Exer. 1	Exer. 2	Exer. 3	Exer. 4
Pulse rate				
Temperature				
Muscle contraction				
Blood pressure				

To help groups design their exercise cards, lead a discussion on how to develop lucid directions and illustrations, providing both clear and ambiguous examples. Students may choose how to explain their exercises. However, having a standard card size facilitates manipulation of the modules. Alternatively, if students use a multimedia authoring program, each card can show one exercise, and labels can be linked to create different combinations. Of course, the computer needs to be handy for it to benefit the class.

Have each group cite their sources, as well as include a measurement chart, for each card. As part of the assessment, other groups verify the information.

Assessment

Each group presents its set of exercises to develop a class set. Each group then creates an exercise routine for a specific physical health goal. Group pairs cross-assess the tables and routines for accuracy and optimal benefits.

Activity Variations

1. Each group may produce a videotape of exercises. Note that this format is more difficult to rearrange.
2. The class does only one part of the activity: either the cards or the scientific measurement.
3. Each group may be assigned a physical disability, for which it must choose appropriate exercises or exercise modifications.
4. Each group may be assigned a different age or gender group (e.g., pregnant women, infants), for which it must choose appropriate exercises or exercise modifications.
5. Each group may be assigned a different health goal (e.g., weight loss, muscle control, stress relief), for which it must choose appropriate exercises.
6. Each group researches the physics behind each exercise. Sets of exercises can demonstrate different physics or machine principles (e.g., lever, wedge).
7. Each group explores different exercise options (e.g., tai chi, yoga, aerobic), linking them by body-part specific exercises.

HIV/AIDS: FACT OR FICTION?

Activity Description
Each group explores an aspect of HIV/AIDS.

Content Outcomes
Students will:
- Describe the medical and physiological aspects of HIV/AIDS.
- Identify social and legal aspects of HIV/AIDS.

Information Literacy Outcomes
Students will:
- Use a variety of resources to locate and select information about HIV/AIDS.
- Recognize forms of bias as they assess and interpret information.
- Transform information into chart format.

Prerequisite Skills
- Use library catalogs and indexes to locate information.
- Distinguish between fact and opinion.

Rationale for the Process

It has been said that HIV/AIDS will be the social issue of students of the '90s. Certainly, this disease has affected the social lives of young people and has impacted medical research.

Even now, myths and misconceptions about HIV/AIDS exist. Students need accurate information about the different aspects of this disease so they can make reasoned decisions in the future.

Activity

Grade level: high school
Time frame: three days
Resources: a wide variety of sources on HIV/AIDS, materials for chart construction, index cards for writing game questions
Grouping: analytical and creative thinkers, concrete and abstract thinkers, mixed genders
Group tasks:

1. Choose one aspect of HIV/AIDS.
2. Locate and select information about that aspect.
3. Determine what is fact and what is opinion or myth.
4. Transform this information into chart format.
5. Develop a set of questions that can be used in a game format about HIV/AIDS.

Tips: Begin this activity by discussing preconceived notions about HIV/AIDS. Students can refer to this initial list as they research their topics. The class then identifies different aspects or the impact of HIV/AIDS: medical, physiological, social, legal, etc. Have the class talk about the sources of HIV/AIDS information, and then list ways to determine whether information is fact or opinion.

Because of its controversial nature, HIV/AIDS discussion may need to have prior clearance and parental permission. Additionally, students who choose to interview people with HIV/AIDS may need to get permission from the school or parents as well as the interviewees.

Assessment

Groups create fact/myth statements derived from their research. Those sets of statements are combined to form the basis of a game. Jigsaw teams are composed of one representative from each original group. In turn, teams guess whether each statement is a fact or an opinion or myth.

The group charts are assessed afterwards for their accuracy and thoroughness.

In closing, the class revisits their original notions about HIV/AIDS and discusses how the information gathered will affect their future decisions.

Activity Variations

1. Each group may study a different virus and compare findings.
2. The class may examine HIV/AIDS from an historical point of view.
3. The class may create a multimedia presentation about HIV/AIDS.
4. The class may research statistics about HIV/AIDS.

MORE IDEA STARTERS

1. Create a card game of do's and don'ts in safety.
2. List and compare games from around the world.
3. Develop a database of sports or sports personalities.
4. Play observation games using a first aid kit.
5. Develop an anthology of literature, lyrics, or quotations about sports.
6. Create a game using the nutrition labels on food products.
7. Create a card game based on food groups.
8. Create a card game based on aspects of different sports.
9. Recreate sports awards nights for historic achievements.
10. Determine good and bad treatments in sports medicine, and play "Simon Says" based on the findings.
11. Compare boys' and girls' rules in sports.
12. Compare amateur and professional rules in sports.

13. Present a skit on health or safety for younger children.
14. Use periodical articles to compare the same sport or athletic event.
15. Compare the newspaper sports page by sport, time of year, and amateur versus professional games.
16. Compare the newspaper sports page by men's and women's sports.
17. Develop a timeline for sports history.
18. Trace the Olympic games: by statistics, types of games played, types of participants, sites.
19. Examine sports figures as ideals: image versus reality, the notion of myth, historic importance.
20. Examine the careers of professional sports figures in terms of length of sports participation, salary, post-sports careers. Compare kinds of sports and gender differences.
21. Compare the Special Olympics to the Olympics.
22. Analyze sports writing in terms of action words, jargon, and bias.
23. Analyze sports statistics.
24. Trace laws and regulations related to sports or safety.
25. Compare the role of sports in different cultures or different historical periods.
26. Create new sports games, or start a new sports team.
27. Modify sports rules to accommodate different physical disabilities.
28. Explore careers that apply physical education knowledge or skill.
29. List sports or safety groups and organizations.
30. Explore health myths.

CHAPTER 12

Activity Plans for Mathematics

HOW DO YOU MEASURE UP?

Activity Description
Each group develops a set of body measurements and converts them.

Content Outcomes
Students will:
- Measure and convert units accurately.
- Identify and analyze physiological proportions.

Information Literacy Outcomes
Students will:
- Read and interpret numerical data.
- Classify and transform data into graph and table form.

Prerequisite Skills
- Calculate proportions and conversions.
- Read and produce graphs and tables.

Rationale for the Process
Students often "size" themselves and their peers. They also encounter different measurement units. This activity allows students to approach measurement from a personal point of view as well as examine some of the myths of ideal body proportions.

Activity
Grade level: middle school and up
Time frame: three to five days
Resources: measurement tape and other tools, conversion tables, resources on body measurements (particularly in the areas of fitness and nutrition)
Grouping: mixed genders, different body proportions, kinesthetic and visual learners, concrete and abstract thinkers
Group tasks:
1. Identify one type of body measurement.
2. Research that type of measurement, finding numerical data for variations of that measurement.
3. Convert measurements into another unit of measure (e.g., inches into centimeters), and produce a conversion table of the data.

Tips: Begin the activity by talking about body measurements. As a warm-up, have each student write down their best guess ideal measure for their age and gender. With that data, create a table and calculate accompanying description statistical concepts: mean, median, range, normal distribution, and variance. Then talk about the basis for normative and desirable body measurements.

The class also brainstorms different types of measurements related to the body: vital statistics, nutrition, fitness. They may also generate a list of factors that change measurements: age, health, culture, social norms.

Assessment
Groups cross-evaluate graphs and tables in terms of numerical accuracy and response. As an

activity extension, groups may meet in pairs (i.e., groups 1 and 2, groups 3 and 4, etc.) and compare their findings. The class as a whole may review their initial opinions, revising them accordingly. Individually, students may use their own measurements and compare them to a group's chart.

Activity Variations

1. Groups may gather information about body measurements from the community through interviews and observations.
2. Groups may explore body measurements of animals.
3. Groups may use other measurement tools, such as odometers or scientific probes, to research other physiological phenomena.
4. Groups may research clothing measurements.

EARTH TO MARS

Activity Description

Each group develops a trip to a planet, incorporating all of the relevant mathematics.

Content Outcomes

Students will:

- Identify mathematical tasks needed in order to travel to a planet.
- Calculate reasonable figures relative to space travel.

Information Literacy Outcomes

Students will:

- Locate and select mathematical information about space travel.
- Extract mathematical statistics and functions relative to space travel from selected information.
- Transform information into a narrative journey form.

Prerequisite Skills

- Use library catalogs and indexes to locate information.
- Calculate accurately.

Rationale for the Process

Mathematics in the real world is not a simple, course-specific situation. A variety of calculations are necessary in order to perform complex tasks, such as space travel.

This activity enables students to identify and explore mathematical concepts as they relate to space travel. While most students will not go to the moon or beyond, they will certainly need mathematics as they plan a major trip. And the complex calculations involved in space travel give students a greater appreciation for human efforts in space exploration.

Activity

Grade level: high school
Time frame: three to five days
Resources: information about space travel, planets, and mathematics; calculators (optional)
Grouping: analytical and creative thinkers, sequential and holistic thinkers, students with mathematical and verbal aptitude
Group tasks:

1. Choose a planet.
2. Locate mathematical information about traveling to that planet.
3. Calculate figures relative to space voyage and establishment of a colony there.
4. Present the information in a narrative journey form.

Tips: Begin the activity by leading a class discussion on the mathematics needed to travel to and colonize a planet. The generated list should include issues such as fuel, supplies, oxygen, trajectory, gravitational force, distance, weight, cost, etc.

While most information will vary from planet to planet, some functions, such as lift-off, will have some applicability among planet voyages. Encourage groups to share their information across the class.

Assessment

Groups present their voyage in mathematical terms. This information may be shared in the form of a game, where another group has to do the necessary calculations correctly to advance to the next mathematical function.

Groups cross-assess the voyages in terms of mathematical accuracy and thoroughness.

As a closing assessment, the class compares the tasks and figures across planets. They may also predict the feasibility of travel to each planet in terms of present-day technology and probable future technology.

Activity Variations

1. The entire class concentrates on the voyage and colonization of one planet. Each group researches the mathematics for one part of the exploration.
2. The entire class focuses on either the voyage or the colonization process.
3. The groups present their information in spreadsheet format.

MATHEMATICAL CROSSWORD PUZZLE

Activity Description

Each group creates a crossword puzzle that uses numbers instead of letters in the squares and equations instead of definitions (see sample puzzle).

Content Outcomes

Students will:

- Identify mathematical equations.
- Apply a variety of mathematical methods to generate numbers.
- Correctly calculate equations.

Information Literacy Outcomes

Students will:

- Use a variety of resources to locate and select mathematical equations and formulas.
- Use symbolic patterns and techniques to organize and generate numbers.
- Write accurate clues for a crossword puzzle.
- Design a crossword puzzle using mathematical equations, formulas, and definitions.

Prerequisite Skills

- Calculate accurately.
- Make crossword puzzles.

Rationale for the Process

Mathematical formulas and equations are often linked to a specific course rather than considered lifelong tools for problem solving. Taken outside their usual class context, such equations may seem foreign and unintelligible.

The familiar crossword puzzle format assumes a novel perspective when used to unify mathematical equations. Both word and numerical definitions help foster mathematical skill, and this puzzle format provides valuable clues in calculating the answers. The use of varied definitions also reinforces the many ways that numbers may be generated and derived.

Activity

Grade level: high school
Time frame: two to three days
Resources: mathematical references, computer crossword software program (optional)
Grouping: analytical and creative thinkers, students with verbal and numerical aptitudes
Group tasks:

1. Locate and select mathematical equations and formulas.
2. Generate and derive numbers based on the equations and formulas.
3. Provide definitions or values for equations and formulas, together with a correct numerical solution for each.
4. Produce the cross "word" puzzle, using the determined clues and numbers.
5. Provide a correct answer sheet for the puzzle.

Tips: To introduce the activity, lead a brainstorming session on methods of generating numbers by posing the question: "What are different ways to arrive at the number 9?" Some examples are arithmetical combinations, equations, formulas, functions, solutions to word problems, exponentials, and logarithms.

Mathematics Crossword Puzzle

Across
3. 5 in base 2
4. seconds in 12 hours
5. one gross
6. 3 cubed
8. kilo
9. 4 cubed
10. cubed root of 9 across
11. sine of 90 degrees
12. acres in a square mile
13. dozen
14. feet in a mile

Down
1. XC
2. 1000 – 26
3. 7 × 143
5. 42 squared
6. pounds in a ton
7. LXX
11. 5 cubed
12. 2 cubed times 3 to the fourth power

Next, apply the concept of number generation to definitions; that is, an equation defines a number. It is an easy step to interpret a crossword puzzle as a way to organize mathematical definitions. Because students probably have not seen such a crossword puzzle, it may help to design a sample one in class.

Crossword puzzles demand accuracy and clarity, both in numerical calculations and writing. By working in small groups, the puzzle clues are tested and refined. Each group should be reminded to provide a separate answer sheet.

Crossword puzzles may be generated with appropriate computer software. Encourage this method if the resource is available. In this instance, numbers will be handled as characters, so the computer puzzle should work as usual. Suggest to groups that they generate more numbers than necessary so the program can find an optimal crossword shape. Note that some programs may not accept numerical values. One creative solution is to assign a letter to represent a digit; the group substitutes the numerical value after the puzzle is generated.

Assessment

Groups exchange crossword puzzles and solve them. Then they should assess each other's puzzle in terms of the variety and quality of the definitions and equations used.

Puzzles may be reproduced as transparencies to share with the entire class for discussion. The following questions may be posed:

- What kinds of equations and formulas were used?
- What were the characteristics of word definitions?
- Were any new equations or formulas used?
- How did the crossword puzzle format affect problem solving techniques?
- What process did groups use to generate puzzles: from number to definition or vice versa?
- Was it easier to create a puzzle or to solve one made by another group? Why?

Activity Variations

1. Each group may choose a unique puzzle shape.
2. The entire class may concentrate on the same category of clues (e.g., geometry).
3. Each group may choose a different category of clues.
4. The entire class may use only word problem clues.
5. Each group may use a different number base.
6. The class may use a foreign language for word definitions.
7. The class may use Roman numerals.
8. The puzzle may consist of just one number used in different configurations, such as five's.
9. The class may use only certain types of numbers, such as odd numbers, proper fractions, decimals, primes.
10. The class may concentrate on formulas for measurement.

NUMBERS THROUGH LITERATURE

Activity Description

Each group analyzes a piece of writing in terms of its mathematical concepts and uses it as a model to create another piece of writing.

Content Outcomes

Students will:

- Identify mathematical concepts in a piece of writing.
- Create an original piece of writing incorporating mathematical concepts.

Information Literacy Outcomes

Students will:

- Locate and select a piece of writing that incorporates mathematical concepts.
- Abstract mathematical concepts from literature.
- Follow a literary model to present an original piece of writing that incorporates mathematical concepts.

Prerequisite Skills

- Write in the same style as a given example of writing.

Rationale for the Process

Usually mathematics is associated with numbers and problem solving. Yet, creative writers have successfully woven mathematical concepts into fictional works. By locating and analyzing literature with this new perspective, students develop aesthetic appreciation for mathematics as a mindset.

Activity

Grade level: middle school and up

Time frame: two to three days (less time may be allocated at school if more work is done at home)

Resources: literature with mathematical insights, bibliographies addressing this topic

Grouping: analytical and creative thinkers, students with number skills and students with verbal skills

Group tasks:

1. Locate and select literature that includes mathematical concepts.
2. Analyze the literature, noting instances of mathematical concepts.
3. Abstract the mathematical concepts.
4. Using the analyzed literature as a model, create an original piece of writing that incorporates mathematical concepts.

Tips: Introduce this activity by sharing the book (or film/video) *The Dot and the Line* by Norton Juster (Random House 1977).

To help each group clarify its task, lead a class discussion on mathematical concepts in literature by asking open-ended questions such as:

- What picture books or nursery rhymes use numbers or shapes?
- How do folktales and fairy tales make use of numbers?
- What are some examples of riddles or jokes that involve mathematical concepts?
- How might poetry make use of mathematical ideas?
- What science fiction or fantasy writing or film depicts mathematical ideas?
- What other mathematical concepts might arise in literature (e.g., logic, measurement, topology, consumer mathematics, probability)?

Students may also consult specialized indexes to locate applicable pieces of writing. Some examples are *Short Story Index,* poetry indexes, genre indexes.

To focus the activity, you may assign a piece of writing to each group. Or ask each group to identify the mathematical concepts rather than create an original piece of writing.

Groups may need to brainstorm ways to use a literary model to create their own written piece. Two major modifications or transformations are:

- Use the same mathematical concepts and change the literary form (e.g., to a fable, poem, play).
- Use the same literary form and change the mathematical concepts (e.g., write a new chapter or episode for the same characters).

Assessment

Group pairs exchange their analyses and original works. The combination of products allows each group to assess how the other groups processed the information.

As a closing assessment, the class discusses mathematics in literature and other forms of expression.

Activity Variations

1. Each group may choose a different type of literature (e.g., poetry, short story, fable, play).
2. Each group may locate movies or artwork manifesting mathematical concepts.
3. Each group may design a picture book or comic strip incorporating mathematical concepts. (Anno's work serves as an excellent example.)
4. Each group may create a secret code or cipher that incorporates mathematical concepts.
5. Each group researches numerical connotations according to a different culture.
6. The entire class may develop a bibliography of literature that involves mathematical concepts, using the following list as a starter.

Starting Bibliography of Literature Containing Mathematical Concepts

Abbott, Edwin. *Flatland.* New York, N.Y: Dover, 1950.

Fisher, John. *Magic of Lewis Carroll.* New York, N.Y.: Bramhill, 1973.

Gardner, Martin. *Mathematical Carnival.* New York, N.Y.: Knopf, 1979.

Hunter, J. *Mathematical Diversions.* New York, N.Y.: Dover, 1975.

Juster, Norton. *The Phantom Tollbooth*. New York, N.Y.: Random House, 1961.

Lathan, Jean. *Carry On, Mr. Bowditch*. Boston, Mass.: Houghton Mifflin, 1955.

Newman, James. *World of Mathematics*. New York, N.Y.: Simon and Schuster, 1956.

Raskin, Ellen. *Figgs & Phantoms*. New York, N.Y.: Dutton, 1974.

Shepard, Esther. *Paul Bunyan*. New York, N.Y.: Harcourt Brace, 1924.

Stoppard, Tom. *Arcadia*. New York, N.Y.: Faber & Faber, 1996.

Thurber, James. *Great Quillion*. New York, N.Y.: Harcourt Brace, 1944.

Twain, Mark. *Complete Humorous Sketches*. Garden City, N.Y.: Doubleday, 1961.

MORE IDEA STARTERS

1. Develop a database of mathematicians.
2. Create posters to illustrate different mathematical recreations (e.g., magic squares, Mobius strip).
3. Create *USA Today*-type charts for different statistics.
4. Compare mathematical systems by writing/drawing equations in Roman numerals, Mayan, Phoenician, etc.
5. Create riddle puns using mathematical terms (e.g., "What did the acorn say when he grew up?" "Geometry!").
6. Play card games, such as 21, in other number bases.
7. Survey students and develop statistics based on the findings.
8. Develop a timeline for mathematical discoveries.
9. Explore careers that apply mathematical skills.
10. Create an anthology of mathematical poetry or lyrics.
11. Examine advertisements for mathematical concepts.
12. Make statistics "lie."
13. Create a card game that matches mathematical forms and formulas with different mathematical topics.
14. Interview businesses and consumer advocacy groups about mathematical applications.
15. Define sports rules and playing fields in other numerical or measurement systems.
16. Develop an original measurement unit system based on group dimensions.
17. Use scientific measurement tools to calculate mathematics in movement and space.
18. Identify and apply mathematical principles throughout a store.
19. Research mathematical application in harmonics and other musical principles.
20. Develop a mathematical magic kit.

CHAPTER 13
Activity Plans for Music

G(ENDER) NOTES

Activity Description
Each group analyzes one musical genre in terms of gender issues.

Content Outcomes
Students will:
- Identify musical genres.
- Objectively examine gender issues relative to musical compositions.
- Recognize forms of bias and stereotypes associated with a musical genre.

Information Literacy Outcomes
Students will:
- Use a variety of sources to locate and select information about musical genres.
- Use content analysis to critique information.
- Develop a classification system or criteria to organize information.
- Recognize forms of bias as they assess data.
- Transform information findings into table format.

Prerequisite Skills
- Use library catalogs and indexes to find relevant information.
- Recognize gender connotations.

Rationale for the Process
Music plays an important role in society. Both sounds and lyrics move teenagers, in particular. Music also reflects or influences societal norms. Who writes and performs the music, as well as content itself, provide a sociological slice of life.

This activity raises students' consciousness about gender issues relative to music. It also helps students do close reading of lyrics from a different perspective than is usually experienced in daily life.

Activity
Grade level: middle school and up
Time frame: three to four days
Resources: print and nonprint resources on music, including audio, with an emphasis on lyrics
Grouping: mixed genders, musical and nonmusical learners, analytical and creative thinkers, sequential and holistic processors
Group tasks:
1. Choose a musical genre.
2. Locate and select musical compositions within the musical genre.
3. Develop contextual criteria by which to analyze musical compositions.
4. Analyze musical compositions according to the criteria.
5. Present content analysis findings in table form.

Tips: To focus the activity, lead a class discussion on contemporary music, asking questions such as:

- What kind of music is popular now? Why?
- What influence does music have in today's society?
- What images of males and females does music generate?

Then have the class brainstorm different musical genres: heavy metal, country, jazz, etc. They may also consider some of the more classic lyrical musical forms such as art songs, ballads, hymns, etc.

As students consider gender issues in music, they can create a set of criteria by which to analyze musical compositions. Points may include:

- Composer and lyricist's gender
- Proportion of lyrics centered on males, females, mixed genders
- Portrayals of males and females

Musical "demographics" should also be recorded: date of composition, possibly age of composer/lyricist, country or ethnic background of composer/lyricist.

If students analyze music videos, they can expand their criteria to include visual image perspectives and performer gender.

Assessment

Groups exchange musical compositions and resultant tables to assess them in terms of conclusions reached and their justification. The two groups also compare findings to determine possible patterns and pose feasible hypotheses. Their discussion forms the foundation for an all-class analysis of musical genres relative to gender issues.

Activity Variations

1. Advanced students may develop chi-square statistical analyses of the data.
2. Half of the class may focus on music videos while the other half focuses on textual data.
3. The entire class may concentrate on contemporary music.
4. The entire class may focus on one time period, with each group concentrating on a different musical genre.
5. The entire class may focus on one musical genre, with each group concentrating on a different time period.

COMPOSING A DATABASE

Activity Description

Each group enters a database set of records about a different group of musical compositions. The class develops a growing database which each group then analyzes relative to a working hypothesis.

Content Outcomes

Students will:

- Identify musical compositions.
- List significant facts about compositions.
- Draw conclusions about trends among compositions.

Information Literacy Outcomes

Students will:

- Locate and select information about compositions.
- Classify information about compositions.
- Summarize and organize facts into appropriate categories.
- Enter data accurately into a database.
- Manipulate data using a computer-based database management program.
- Critically analyze and verify facts using multiple sources.
- Develop and test working hypotheses.
- Search and sort information by appropriate categories.
- Analyze information in database form to determine relational facts.
- Chart or graph data.

Prerequisite Skills

- Use catalogs and indexes to locate relevant information.
- Determine main ideas.
- Use a computer-based database program.
- Develop a hypothesis.
- Design a graph or chart.

Rationale for the Process

Music is created by composers within a cultural context, based on a foundation of prior musical works. Not only is a class-produced database about compositions time-effective and cooperatively beneficial, but it also mirrors the concept of mutual support among musical composers.

As the database is created, hypotheses about compositions may arise. The computerized aspect of a database facilitates the testing of such hypotheses and builds knowledge about music and database management.

Activity

Grade level: high school (middle school and up for musicians' database)

Time frame: three days to one week

Resources: resources about musical compositions (e.g., dictionaries, encyclopedias, biographies, timetables, compositions, nonprint materials), computer database software

Grouping: detail-oriented and holistic learners, creative and methodical learners (each group member assuming major responsibility for each specific task [e.g., locating the information, reading the facts, analyzing music, inputting the data, testing the hypothesis])

Group tasks:

1. Locate and select information about assigned musical compositions.
2. Develop appropriate database fields/categories to organize information.
3. Classify information into appropriate fields.
4. Complete database record form for each entry.
5. Verify information in database.
6. Develop a working hypothesis about compositions.
7. Once the class database is established, analyze compositions to determine the validity of the group's hypothesis.
8. Graph or chart resulting data to justify conclusions.

Tips: You may start this activity by introducing the concept of a database. It may be defined as a list of items with specific information about each item. You may lead a quick review of information about databases that students already know: the library catalog, a story inventory, a telephone book.

Creating a database using a computer provides a time-efficient way to manipulate large amounts of data in several ways. Different aspects of compositions can be labeled as fields (e.g., date composed, musical form, composer, instrumentation, style). Based on these fields, students can search for specific information, such as all sonata compositions, or works composed between 1700 and 1800. Those compositions matching the specifications then can be sorted by another field, such as alphabetically by composer. The standardized structure allows students to make comparisons easily, regardless of who inputs the information. Having set fields also allows the data to be manipulated in many ways, depending on the students' hypotheses. If possible, use peer teaching to demonstrate computer manipulations.

To facilitate fact finding, lead a discussion on possible sources of information about compositions. Students should consider different headings such as music, instruments, country, time period, biography. They should also consider different information formats (e.g., monographs, periodicals, specialized reference books and CD-ROMs, concert programs, videotapes, audiocassettes, recordings [especially the jacket information]).

The class may also determine the entry format for the database by deciding what kind of information is important to include and what field names best capture the information. This step provides the students more "ownership" in the activity's outcome and reinforces decision making by consensus. This step may be done before or after the fact-finding stage. If done before, this step helps groups develop a deductive approach to fact-finding and organizing. If done after, this step helps groups develop an intuitive approach to these tasks. For less advanced students, the task of fitting facts to established fields may be enough challenge.

As groups enter data, members can cross-check facts for inputting accuracy. This task points out the need to look at more than one source of information. Students may find that two different authors have two different dates for the same composition, at which point students must find out the basis for the difference. Point out that incorrect typing may be another source of errors; misspelling may result in "lost" information at the search–sort stage. The concept of "garbage-in garbage-out" is easily illustrated. Particularly as the resulting class database determines the ability to test hypotheses, the need for cross-checked quality control becomes evident.

Hypothesis testing may be a new concept for students particularly within the context of music. Lead a class brainstorming about developing hypotheses, posing questions such as:

- Do major creative periods of composing exist, or are compositions equally distributed along a timeline?
- Do the birthdays of composers fall within a certain range?
- Do composers tend to write their best works at the end of their lives?
- Is the type of composition correlated to the composer's age or nationality?

You may need to help students search and sort with the class-constructed database. You should give an example of hypothesis testing as a model for the activity. For instance, compositions may be sorted in ascending chronological order to test the hypothesis that compositions tend to occur in time "clumps" rather than evenly throughout time. You may also introduce secondary searching fields, such as by country in the above example, as a way to test more sophisticated hypotheses. Some may use Boolean logic to combine fields (e.g., unmarried composers by century) or take advantage of delimited field (e.g., >7 instruments). You may need to point out to students that not all hypotheses may be answered on the basis of the chosen fields. The way information is structured determines how it may be searched.

You may need to lead a class discussion on ways to graphically represent the information. Share examples of pie charts, line graphs, and other styles of data representation. Then ask questions, such as:

- What kind of conclusions may be derived from the data?
- What kind of data best suit a continuous line representation? A drawing? A Venn diagram?

Because several information skills are combined in this activity, students should have prior knowledge about graphing unless time is extended for this project to cover this skill. Alternatively, the activity may be carried out without the graphing task.

Assessment

This activity underlines the benefits of ongoing assessment. With each step, assessment helps the group redirect or refine its efforts.

1. Within each group, members check the accuracy of data entry and verify facts and correct classification of information.
2. In group pairs, students check each other's data entry for accuracy and correct classification information.
3. Using the class-developed database, each group tests its hypothesis. To document their strategy, students may use the Composing a Database Search Strategy Form.

COMPOSING A DATABASE SEARCH STRATEGY FORM

Group Members' Names:

Working Hypothesis:

Fields to Search (note additional limitations within each):

1.

2.

3.

Combination of Fields (Boolean logic):

Findings:

Conclusions:

Graph/Chart of Data:

From *Cooperative Learning Activities in the Library Media Center.* © 1999 Lesley S. J. Farmer. Libraries Unlimited (800) 237-6124.

4. Groups exchange their forms, assessing each other's according to class-developed criteria. To facilitate testing hypotheses, provide each group with the criteria for assessment at the same time that they receive or develop their Composing a Database Assessment Form.

An alternative way to assess the groups' work is to exchange only the hypothesis and have each group develop and carry out its own strategy. The two strategies can then be compared. Likewise, group pairs can exchange only the graphic representation and then develop the hypothesis and search strategy that would logically fit the graph. The two strategies can then be compared.

> **COMPOSING A DATABASE ASSESSMENT FORM**
>
> **Hypothesis**
> - Is it logical?
> - Is it clearly stated?
> - Is it answerable using the data provided?
>
> **Fields**
> - Are they appropriate?
> - Are the Boolean sets or field limitations appropriate?
>
> **Findings**
> - Do they follow logically from the search?
> - Are they complete and accurate?
>
> **Conclusion**
> - Is it logical?
> - Does it tie into the beginning hypothesis?
> - Is it justified by the findings?
>
> **Graphic Representation**
> - Is it clear?
> - Is it accurate?
> - Does it illustrate the hypothesis, findings, and conclusion?
> - Is the format (e.g., bar graph, pie chart, etc.) appropriate for the data found?
>
> From *Cooperative Learning Activities in the Library Media Center.* © 1999 Lesley S. J. Farmer. Libraries Unlimited (800) 237-6124.

5. As a wrap-up activity, the class discusses databases in general, debating questions such as:
   - Did the information lend itself well to a database format? What kind of information in general can be structured in this form? What kind of information would be difficult to structure this way?
   - How well did the fields "capture" the information? What kind of information was left out or didn't fit? How would you change the fields, after having used the database?
   - How does the database affect the development and testing of a hypothesis? What questions cannot be answered by this database? Can the data be searched in different ways to derive different conclusions about the same hypothesis?

The next step is to develop a hypothesis about the data results. This extension of the activity illustrates the educational practice called the cycle of inquiry. Suppose a group finds that composing efforts seem to "clump" rather than be distributed evenly throughout time. A logical question to ask is: "Why?" The group might generate a number of hypotheses: composers are more productive when they form support networks; composers tend to be more productive in peacetime; a style of music becomes popular and everyone writes in that style until it becomes overdone—and then they wait until a new style emerges. Students would then test their hypotheses by gathering more data and discovering new patterns to support or refute their predictions. Such an extension to the project will probably involve two to four more days of work.

Activity Variations

1. The entire class may concentrate on one group of composers or type of composition.
2. One group may design a timeline instead of testing a hypothesis.
3. The class may create a database of musicians.

PLAYING MUSICAL INSTRUMENTS

Activity Description

Each group creates a set of cards about a specific musical instrument, each card representing a different aspect of the instrument. The class develops several sets of cards, and teams play a game like Authors.

Content Outcomes

Students will:

- Identify and describe aspects of musical instruments.
- Compare characteristics of different musical instruments.

Information Literacy Outcomes

Students will:

- Locate and select information about a musical instrument.
- Develop and use a classification system to evaluate and organize information.
- Use symbolic patterns and techniques to present their findings accurately in card game form.
- Share expertise to expand knowledge.

Prerequisite Skills

- Use library catalogs and indexes to locate information.
- Play Authors.

Rationale for the Process

Musical instruments may be described in several ways: method of generating sound, musical quality, tonal range, dimension. According to the particular aspect, different instruments may be classified together.

By creating a set of game cards, composed of characteristics about instruments, students learn to examine these instruments in different ways and to categorize them accordingly.

Activity

Grade level: middle school
Time frame: two to three days
Resources: music sources, paper and writing/drawing tools to make cards
Grouping: visual and kinesthetic learners, analytical and creative processors, musicians and nonmusicians
Group tasks:

1. Choose a musical instrument.
2. Locate and select information about the instrument.
3. Categorize information using a classification system.
4. Create a set of cards about different aspects of the instrument.
5. After the class card sets are developed, play the card game in new teams.

Tips: Lead a class discussion about ways to examine or describe musical instruments.

To focus the activity, provide a classification system for the students to use as a guide to categorize data. However, the learning experience is enriched if the class develops the system. Students may suggest tentative categories, which they may modify as they examine sources about musical instruments. Afterward, the class then decides which categories to include to develop a standardized set of cards for the game. Descriptions may be verbal or visual, or a combination.

All cards should be the same dimension and format. A good size is 2½ by 3 inches (half an index card). Each card gives the description and labels the instrument.

When playing the final version of the card game, redivide the class into different groups so that instrument expertise may be shared. Additionally, teams should aim for group consensus when playing the game. If the card game is played as Authors, each team tries to collect a set of cards about the same instrument. Alternatively, a team may also try to collect a set of cards about the same category.

Assessment

Each group includes a set of cards to develop a class set. The entire class plays the card game in teams. This activity may be used to introduce a unit on musical instruments or may be modified to use as a way to review concepts about musical instruments.

Activity Variations

1. The class may create a card game for other aspects of music, such as terminology or composers.
2. The class may create a database about instruments instead of a card game.
3. The format for the cards may vary, being either written or visual.
4. The class may create a different kind of game based on musical instruments, perhaps including only sound clues.
5. The class may modify the information cards to play a "trivial facts" card game.

MUSIC MEDIA

Activity Description

Each group produces a multimedia presentation to complement a musical composition.

Content Outcomes

Students will:

- Identify the stylistic qualities of a musical composition.
- Recognize connotations evoked by music.

Information Literacy Outcomes

Students will:

- Recognize and use a variety of visual sources.
- Evaluate visual images to determine those that complement a musical composition.
- Produce cards and sequence them to create a presentation that complements a musical composition.

Prerequisite Skills

- Create a storyboard.
- Use a multimedia authoring program (optional).

Rationale for the Process

Much music transcends notes to evoke images in the mind. These mental pictures are counterparts to the music's style. In fact, art songs are so called for precisely this characteristic.

By creating a visual show of the music, students share their mental images. Concurrently, students may discuss the influence of music upon the visual, as depicted in films.

Activity

Grade level: high school (advanced middle school)

Time frame: three to five days

Resources: music and players (tape or CDs), visual sources (magazines, art books, CD-ROMs, laser discs, Internet), cameras, multimedia presentation program, scanner (optional)

Grouping: concrete and abstract thinkers, kinesthetic/aural/visual learners, analytical and creative thinkers

Group tasks:

1. Choose a musical composition.
2. Play the music, analyzing it in terms of style and visual imagery.
3. Locate, select, and evaluate visual materials to determine those that reflect the musical style and imagery.

4. Create cards from the visual material.
5. Sequence and time the cards to complement the music.
6. Present the multimedia stack.

Tips: Begin by leading a class discussion relating music to visual images. One method is to play a movement from "Night on Bald Mountain," and ask the students to close their eyes and imagine what is happening while the music plays. The class may also discuss movies or rock videos, noting how music triggers emotions, such as love or terror.

To focus the activity on visual imagery, have groups use ready-made visuals such as CD-ROM or laser disc illustrations, which could be imported into the authoring software.

Note that one movement, or portion of a larger work, may suffice to produce the multimedia presentation.

Assessment

Each group presents its multimedia presentation. The class discusses the visual and musical imagery and connotations.

Activity Variations

1. The entire class may concentrate on the same musical piece.
2. Each group may videotape an advertisement or other television segment and choose music to complement or counteract the visual message.
3. Each group may create a commercial using a musical composition.
4. Each group may create a one-minute preview of a literary work using a musical piece as background.
5. Each group may create a video or slide–tape show to complement a musical composition.

MORE IDEA STARTERS

1. Create displays about the history of musical notation.
2. Develop "daffynitions" for musical terms.
3. Make a crossword puzzle or anagram about music.
4. Create family trees about musical instruments.
5. Group music thematically; trace stories that inspire music, such as the Orpheus legend.
6. Develop a timeline related to music.
7. "Interview" musical composers in history.
8. Compare musical themes worldwide.
9. Locate music that has been incorporated into movies, such as *Fantasia*.
10. Create a music calendar, locating musical facts for each day.
11. Play 20 Questions or charades about music.
12. On a world map, indicate musical instruments associated with specific countries (e.g., sitar in India).
13. Create a sound game or card game that mixes up the sequence of a musical composition.
14. Play "Name That Tune" in teams, using classical compositions.
15. List movies or plays about music.
16. Explore careers that apply musical skill or knowledge.
17. Develop an anthology of poetry or quotations about music.
18. Develop a database of music groups or organizations.
19. Predict the future of music or musical instruments.
20. Make a collage about music.
21. Create a multimedia presentation or video about musical tone poems.
22. Explore a set of musical forms (e.g., opera, musicals, ballet) that have related themes.
23. Explore synthetic music.
24. Relate music to psychology.

25. Research the role of music in different religions.
26. Trace the manufacture and selling of a CD.
27. Calculate the harmonics and other physics concepts of different musical instruments.
28. Use science probes to measure musical qualities.
29. Compare musical qualities, including physical, of humans and instruments.
30. Create a business plan for starting a band.

CHAPTER 14

Activity Plans for Psychology and Sociology

I'VE GOT A PROBLEM

Activity Description
Each group diagnoses a personal problem, described in a case study, according to a psychological school of thought.

Content Outcomes
Students will:
- Identify a psychological problem.
- Develop a case study about a psychological problem.
- Characterize a psychological school of thought.
- Correctly diagnose a personal problem, described in a case study, according to a psychological school of thought.

Information Literacy Outcomes
Students will:
- Locate and select information about a psychological school of thought.
- Locate and select information about a psychological problem.
- Develop a case study.
- Interpret a case study.
- Assess data for completeness and bias.
- Assess various interpretations of the same data.

Prerequisite Skills
- Use catalogs and indexes to locate relevant information.

Rationale for the Process
Psychological schools of thought provide a way to deal with personal problems. Depending on the specific diagnosis, relative to the psychological school, one will use different strategies to ameliorate a situation or response.

In addition, a psychological problem exists within a social climate. A case study provides the unique insights of several people connected with the person who has a psychological problem. The varying perspectives help the psychologist diagnose the situation more completely.

By examining case studies of personal problems from various psychological angles, students learn that no single, right perspective or answer exists; rather, an array of options are available.

Activity
Grade level: high school
Time frame: three days to a week
Resources: resources on psychology and related schools of thought, personal growth materials, psychological case studies
Grouping: analytical and creative processors, concrete and abstract learners, students with interpersonal and intrapersonal intelligences

Group tasks:

1. Define and describe a personal problem.
2. Develop a case study about the personal problem.
3. Identify a psychological school of thought.
4. Locate information about the school of thought, relative to the case study.
5. Diagnose the problem described in the case study in light of the specific school of thought.
6. Offer solutions or strategies relative to the personal problems, in light of the specific school of thought.

Tips: Begin the activity by leading a class discussion on the topic of personal problems. Ask questions such as:

- What kinds of personal problems do teens have?
- How are you affected if a friend or a family member has a personal problem? Do you have a unique perspective on the problem?
- What do you do if you have a problem?
- Do you tend to agree with the opinions expressed in advice columns?
- Do you agree with the way other people solve personal problems?

You and the students may bring in advice columns for discussion.

To introduce the concept of a case study, share examples with the class. Basically, a clinical case study is a portfolio of descriptions about a personal problem and its effects. A student's file, for instance, might contain observations by teachers, administrators, a nurse, a counselor, and parents. Test scores or homework examples might be included. The professional diagnosing the problem can examine these different documents in order to understand the background of the troubled child and thereby provide better help. The case study becomes a history of diagnoses, treatments, and further observations.

To ensure a working personal problem, you may want to preidentify the problem and situation. One group could assume this responsibility, in which case they could role-play the problem or write a case study for the rest of the class. To get ideas about feasible problems to describe, the group may examine sources such as videotape programs, magazine articles, advice columns, psychology books, and literature.

While one group develops the case study, each of the other groups researches a different psychological school of thought. The class may have an existing list or they may search for a list independently.

To help the diagnostic groups focus their research, the "problem" group should provide a general idea of the problem as quickly as possible. Even given a couple of symptoms, such as substance abuse or domestic abuse, helps the diagnosticians locate useful reference sources that deal with the problem from the assigned psychological school of thought. Groups should also have a case study model diagnosis to follow. They may research their own model, or the teacher/librarian may provide it.

With this informational foundation, diagnostic groups can design questions of clarification to ask the "problem" group at the next class session. Getting additional information may be structured in two ways: each group may be given a time limit to interview the "problem" group, or clarifying questions may be asked by anyone at anytime.

Next, each psychological school of thought group diagnoses the problem, documenting it in case study fashion. To keep them involved, assign each member of the "problem" group to a different diagnostic group. One person may act as a silent observer, assessing how well the diagnostic group is performing as a social structure.

The next step after diagnosis is treatment. Groups may extend the project to include prescribing appropriate strategies. Groups may continue with the same school of thought or exchange with another group, so that a Freudian diagnosis would be followed by a Rogerian treatment.

Assessment

Group pairs exchange their diagnoses for cross-evaluation. They should consider these issues:

- On what points do the two diagnoses agree and disagree?
- What assumptions are made in each diagnosis?
- On what basis is each diagnosis made? Are the reasons credible and consistent with the psychological school of thought?
- What would be a possible outcome of a treatment based on the diagnoses?

As a closing assessment activity, the class may discuss psychological approaches in general:

- What characterizes a psychological school of thought?
- What relationships exist between schools of thought?
- Do different schools of thought assume and seek different kinds of information?
- How do the perspectives of different people associated with a psychological problem affect a diagnosis?
- What would happen if a person switched treatments from one type of psychologist to another?
- How might different cultures value different psychological approaches?

Activity Variations

1. Each group may locate a different problem and diagnose each relative to the same psychological school of thought.
2. Each group may role-play or videotape the diagnosis or treatment.
3. Each group may locate existing diagnoses relative to a specific problem and rediagnose the problem in light of another school of thought.
4. Each group may create a different problem and diagnose or exchange it with another group.

MULTIMEDIA DATING GAME

Activity Description

Each group develops a multimedia decision-making program that helps teens examine consequences of their dating behavior.

Content Outcomes

Students will:

- Identify consequences of dating behavior.
- Sequence behavior options according to prior decisions.
- Choose potential dates and dating activities responsibly.

Information Literacy Outcomes

Students will:

- Use a variety of resources on dating.
- Determine cause-and-effect relationships.
- Storyboard and script dating scenarios.
- Transform dating behavior into multimedia format.

Prerequisite Skills

- Use library catalogs and indexes to locate relevant information.
- Videotape and edit dating scenarios.

Rationale for the Process

As teenagers develop friendships and physical relationships, they need to consider long-term consequences of their dating decisions. However, they do not have the experience to make reasoned judgments, and learn too late what happens when inappropriate behaviors lead to significant changes in lifestyle, such as getting pregnant or acquiring HIV.

This activity enables teens to make decisions in a safe environment, including taking risks (within the multimedia presentation) to see what might happen. The process of creating the program enables students to role-play different decisions, research social behavior concepts, and develop behavioral flowcharts of decision consequences.

Activity

Grade level: high school

Time frame: two weeks

Resources: sociology and dating resources, drama resources, materials on decision making, video equipment, multimedia software, CD-ROM or other high-density storage device

Grouping: sequential and holistic thinkers, analytical and creative thinkers, mixed learning styles, mix genders, computer/video experts and novices

Group tasks:

1. Identify potential dates, related behaviors, and potential consequences.
2. Research decision-making styles, sociology, dating practices, and consequences.
3. Storyboard or flowchart and script typical dating patterns, decisions, and subsequent behaviors and consequences.
4. Videotape role–playing of the dating behaviors and decisions.
5. Create a multimedia stack of "The Dating Game." Incorporate text, decision points, and graphics.
6. Edit video for stack, and incorporate it into the program.
7. Play the stack.

Tips: Begin the activity by leading a class discussion on dating behaviors and possible consequences. Be sure to get opinions from both genders.

Students may need help in developing a flowchart of consequences, so walking through an example decision path facilitates their work. Decision points may include whether one drinks, whether one necks, whether one dates in pairs or groups. For each point, different consequences ensue, which then lead to other decisions.

Assessment

Groups cross-assess the stacks, assessing them in terms of:

- Content: accuracy, appropriateness, credibility, correct sequencing
- Form: acting, taping, editing, programming

The class then discusses dating practices and consequences in general.

Activity Variations

1. Groups may develop skits with decision points that the audience can choose.
2. Groups may research other social situations.

AGE IS IN THE EYE OF THE BEHOLDER

Activity Description

Each group develops a chart presentation on one aspect of old age.

Content Outcomes

Students will:

- Describe stages of human development.
- Identify the social contributions of older people.

Information Literacy Outcomes

Students will:

- Use a variety of resources to research characteristics and contributions of older people.
- Determine main facts and concepts from resources.
- Distinguish between fact and opinion.
- Transform information into chart format.

Prerequisite Skills

- Use library catalogs and indexes to locate relevant information.
- Create charts.

Rationale for the Process

Senior citizens have a wealth of experience to pass on and a surplus of time in which to do it. Teenagers have the energy and fresh outlook to transform the insights of older people into viable programs. In addition, both adolescents and the aged are marginalized in society; their union provides strength to make a difference.

This activity identifies the skills of each generation, examines the reasons for possible disenfranchisement, and works to facilitate the awareness of each generation.

Activity

Grade level: high school
Time frame: three to four days
Resources: materials on aging and adolescence, multimedia software
Grouping: analytical and creative thinkers, intrapersonal and interpersonal skilled learners, technological experts and novices
Group tasks:

1. Choose one sociological factor.
2. Locate and select information about the factor for the aged.
3. Contrast the factor's impact on the aged and on adolescents.
4. Produce a comparison chart showing the impact of the factor on the aged and adolescents.

Tips: Begin the activity by asking the class leading questions, such as:

- What is your image of an older person?
- At what age do you consider people to be aged?
- What problems do you think older persons might have to deal with?
- What contributions do you think older persons might be able to make?
- What do you think you have in common with older persons?

The class then generates factors that might affect older persons, such as physiological changes, emotional changes, intellectual changes, sexuality changes, housing issues, employment issues, and social issues.

To help students in their research of these factors, the following framework may be used:

- Title of factor or issue
- Description of factor
- How older persons are affected
- What older persons can do about the factor
- What is beyond the older person's control
- What teenagers can do about the factor

As students chart their findings, they can structure it by listing points for the aged on one side and adolescent points on the other side.

Assessment

Each group presents its chart, which is assessed for accuracy and thoroughness. The class develops general implications about the aged including adolescent interaction. The class may develop a plan for a possible intergenerational activity.

Activity Variations

1. The class may research each stage in human development, with each group concentrating on one stage.
2. The class may concentrate on another stage of human development.
3. The class may present their findings in another format: videotape, slide–tape, multimedia.

FROM BARBIE TO BARBARELLA

Activity Description

Each group presents images of femininity for one time period.

Content Outcomes

Students will:

- Identify perceptions about females and femininity.
- Explain psychological and sociological aspects of femininity and women's images.

Information Literacy Outcomes

Students will:

- Use a variety of sources, especially visual, about females and femininity.
- Ascertain main facts about perceptions of femininity through content analysis.
- Determine correlational and cause–effect relationships.
- Transform information into a visual medium.

Prerequisite Skills

- Use library catalogs and indexes to locate relevant information.
- Produce concepts visually.

Rationale for the Process

The concept of femininity is much subtler than the biological reality of being female. Cultural depictions and expectations for femininity change, and those social norms influence female and male roles and actions.

This activity raises student awareness about social definitions of femininity, particularly through visual imagery: their origins, their manifestations, and their influence. In the final analysis, each person defines femininity and masculinity.

Activity

Grade level: middle school and up
Time frame: one week
Resources: print and nonprint (especially visual) on fashion, media, history; folklore books
Grouping: mixed genders, students with artistic and written skills, analytical and creative thinkers
Group tasks:

1. Choose one historical period.
2. Locate and critically analyze the content and underlying messages about females and femininity.
3. Create a visual representation of the parameters of femininity for the time period.

Tips: Begin the activity by asking students their impressions about femininity. Compare these statements with thoughts about being female. List and compare the characteristics associated with each term.

To help students find resources, have them brainstorm visual resources and discuss how to analyze visual images of femininity: body language, clothing and make-up, hair styles, action, setting, spatial relationships with other people. The class may develop a standard way of assessing images.

Assessment

Groups cross-evaluate their visual representations in terms of conclusions reached and their justifications. The class discusses images of femininity across time and develops a definition of femininity that they are comfortable with.

Activity Variations

1. Each group chooses a different culture.
2. Groups present their images using television clips or advertisements.

MORE IDEA STARTERS

1. Hold a mock debate between Skinner and Freud.
2. Complete several psychological tests that deal with the same subject (e.g., careers, interests, aptitudes, personality), and compare the process and results.
3. Investigate the psychology of advertisements, commercials, political campaigns, war.
4. Role–play psychological situations (family crisis, peer pressure, etc.), with each group representing a different age group or sociocultural group.
5. Develop a database on drugs.
6. Develop an anthology of poems reflecting psychological states.
7. Create a game based on true–false definitions of psychology terms.
8. Develop a list of artworks reflecting psychological states.
9. Write psychological conversations that reflect different schools of thought (e.g., Rogers, Jung).
10. Write conversations or develop skits that reflect different psychological states (e.g., schizophrenia, manic-depressive).
11. Research plays or short stories that reflect different psychological states.
12. Develop a list of famous quotations by psychologists.
13. Conduct content analyses of fictional works about different psychological states.

14. Describe a personality type (e.g., sanguine or melancholic) from the viewpoint of two different schools of psychological thought.
15. Produce a multimedia presentation that traces the treatment of the mentally insane.
16. Compare two psychological themes and treatments, such as *One Flew over the Cuckoo's Nest* and *Marat/Sade*.
17. Create a collage of psychological states of mind.
18. Develop a database of psychologists or psychological schools of thought.
19. Develop a comic strip reflecting a psychological school of thought.
20. Develop a database of laws pertaining to psychology, or aspects of it.
21. Role–play group dynamics of different kinds of groups (e.g., Congress, families, prison inmates).
22. Research dreams in different cultures.
23. Compare human and animal psychology.
24. Investigate how the brain works in terms of psychology and in terms of science.
25. Compare psychological tests.
26. Trace the history of brain research.
27. Compare how people learn in terms of human development stages.
28. Examine love in light of human development stages.
29. Do sociograms about school.
30. Develop a community yellow pages.

CHAPTER 15

Activity Plans for Science

TRAVEL AGENT

Activity Description
Each group develops a travel agency promotion for a specific climate.

Content Outcomes
Students will:
- Describe typical geographic and biological features associated with a specific climate.
- Differentiate among climates.

Information Literacy Outcomes
Students will:
- Recognize and use a wide variety of sources having information about geographic and biological features associated with a specific climate.
- Use topics and themes to interpret and organize data.
- Recognize a variety of interpretations of the same data.
- Distinguish between fact and opinion.
- Interpret and present information in visual and written form.
- Use assessment forms and consensus decision making to assess information.

Prerequisite Skills
- Use library catalogs and indexes to locate relevant information.
- Use desktop publishing or authoring program (optional).
- Use videotaping and editing equipment (optional).

Rationale for the Process
Usually one thinks of travel in terms of specific countries. Yet, even within a single state, the climate may differ, and the life in that area differs accordingly. California, for example, is sometimes presented as twelve states in one because of the variety of climate zones found within its boundaries.

The travel agency approach to climate makes the concept of climate more concrete. By promoting each climate as being attractive and unique, this activity also illustrates the effective use of perspective and propaganda.

Activity
Grade level: middle school and up

Time frame: three to five days

Resources: sources on climate, geography, biography, biology, and travel (including nonprint materials); sample travel brochures and posters; sources on creating displays; paper, writing tools; display materials; desktop publishing or multimedia authoring program

Grouping: creative and analytical thinkers, concrete and abstract thinkers, kinesthetic and visual learners

Group tasks:

1. Locate and select information about the assigned climate, including sample towns, geographic features, typical flora and fauna, and lifestyles.
2. Develop themes or topics to organize the findings.
3. Analyze sources on travel for content and style.
4. Analyze displays or booths for content and presentation format.
5. Incorporate findings to design a promotion to attract others to that climate.
6. Assess climate promotion using a criteria form.

Tips: To help groups clarify their tasks, lead a class discussion about climate by asking questions such as:

- What does the word "climate" bring to mind?
- How does "weather" differ from "climate"?
- How does climate affect geography, plant and animal life, and the way people live?
- What relationship exists between national boundaries and climate?

Lead a class discussion about travel promotions. The class may bring in travel brochures, advertisements, or posters. Students may watch television commercials or visit travel agencies. Ask questions such as:

- Why do people like to travel?
- What features make a destination attractive?
- How do travel agents "sell" different sights?

Students may need help brainstorming resources they might want to examine for information (e.g., biology, geography, travel). Students should examine magazines and nonprint sources such as maps, film, videotape, illustrations, and realia.

Help students distinguish between factual information and opinion by having them consider factors when interpreting information:

- Who wrote or produced this material? What is the person's background or affiliation?
- How is the information substantiated: examples, statistics, expert opinion, scientific methods?
- Is there an emotional appeal? Are value judgments involved?

As students organize their information to create a promotional piece, they may refer to the following checklist:

Planning Promotions

Themes

- Are they eye catching?
- Are they easy to follow?

Content

- Are the written and visual materials clear and accurate?
- Are opinions backed by factual information?
- Are suggestions for further information included?

Layout

- Are artistic elements of color, balance, contrast, and shape used?
- Are the advantages of three dimensions used through varying heights, foreground versus background, realia, and movements?
- Is there opportunity for the viewer to interact with the promotion, for example, by touching models, lifting panels, or choosing options?
- Is the promotion technically well done? Is it neat? Does it look good? Is it well constructed?

The format of the travel promotion may be determined by the teacher, but students have more ownership if they can decide what kind of presentation to create: display, travel booth, multimedia, videotape.

Assessment

Each group presents its travel promotion. The groups may be given the following assessment form while they develop their promotion. Before the formal assessment activity, the groups complete the "Climate" portion of the form, which establishes the basis for comparison. The other student assessors fully complete a blank form.

An effective way to assess the promotions is to mix the groups so that each group member assesses a different presentation and not their own. After each individual rates the promotion using the Travel Agent Promotion Assessment Form, all the students evaluating the same promotion must come to a consensus in one evaluation. (One way to expand the activity is to include a class-developed assessment form. This added task assumes prior knowledge of promotional elements.)

The class as a whole compares the assessment forms. First, each consensus-based form is compared to the originators' "Climate" section. Then all the assessment forms are examined together to form a composite picture of climate. As a visual aid, the completed forms may be reproduced as transparencies to be viewed on an overhead projector. The class discusses general issues about climate:

- What elements are common to all climates? Which are unique to each?
- Are climates evenly distributed throughout the world?
- What is the relationship between climate and geography?
- What is the relationship between climate and plant/animal life?
- How is opinion and bias reflected in the promotion? What are the effects of such promotions?
- To what extent and how is information interpreted in a variety of ways (differences between creators and assessors, between individual assessors)?

TRAVEL AGENT PROMOTION ASSESSMENT FORM

Climate
- Area/country included
- Geographical features
- Animals and plants represented
- Typical lifestyles
- Unique features

Content
- Accuracy
- Clarity
- Completeness
- Use of opinion/bias
- Sources of information/further reading
- Use of visual/3-D elements

Styles
- Visual impact
- Arrangement
- Use of space
- Technical quality

From *Cooperative Learning Activities in the Library Media Center.* © 1999 Lesley S. J. Farmer. Libraries Unlimited (800) 237-6124.

Activity Variations

1. Each group may present its findings in other formats: slides, collages, a skit.
2. The entire class may concentrate on one continent or country; each group promotes one climate.
3. The class may develop a card game (e.g., Authors) or a database on climates.

DINOSAUR FIELD GUIDE

Activity Description

Each group produces a packaged interactive dinosaur field guide.

Content Outcomes

Students will:

- Identify characteristics of specific dinosaurs.
- Categorize characteristics of dinosaurs.

Information Literacy Outcomes

Students will:

- Use a variety of sources to locate information about specific dinosaurs.
- Categorize information.
- Transform information into field guide form.
- Package information into interactive form.

Prerequisite Skills

- Use library catalogs and indexes to locate relevant information.
- Create interactive materials.

Rationale for the Process

Dinosaurs continue to captivate young people. Particularly with the new findings about dinosaurs and the current books and movies about them, studies about these prehistoric creatures help students learn about other animals.

This activity uses a field guide approach to help students identify and categorize unique and shared animal characteristics. The inclusion of interactive features and packaging of information mirrors contemporary science museum efforts at engaging young audiences. In this case, it is the students themselves who create the excitement about these evolutionary ancestors.

Activity

Group level: middle school and up
Time frame: four to six days
Resources: a variety of resources about dinosaurs, sample field guides, sample packages of interactive introductions to concepts, materials to create packaged field guides, desktop publishing programs
Grouping: analytical and creative thinkers, visual and kinesthetic learners, concrete and abstract thinkers
Group tasks:

1. Choose a dinosaur species.
2. Locate and select information about the dinosaur.
3. Categorize information about the dinosaur.
4. Create an interactive field guide about the dinosaur.
5. Package the field guide.

Tips: Students probably know several types of dinosaurs but may need help in identifying scientific species. Likewise, they may need help in developing a common set of characteristics for dinosaurs. Probably the easiest way to approach this task is to have groups begin their research and find feasible classification schema or categories for comparison. As a closing activity of that session, the class as a whole can agree upon the criteria set.

Students should examine field guides and interactive resources, particularly in science. As another all-class activity, students can brainstorm ways to make a field guide interactive. Some of the ideas may include:

- Scavenger hunts within the guide
- Games: crosswords, word searches, anagrams, dot-to-dot pictures, mini-board games
- Original stickers or postage-type stamps to place in the guide
- Choose-your-own-adventure format
- Flip-up pages and pop-ups
- Maps to trace migrations

Students should also consider ways to package the information. Encourage them to examine toys and workbooks, museum guides, activity kits, and commercial packaging or graphics/advertising resources.

Assessment

Groups exchange their field guides, assessing them for content accuracy and thoroughness, degree and quality of interactivity, and overall presentation quality.

As a general assessment and follow-up, the class develops a class field guide, incorporating the distinguishing characteristics of each dinosaur species. This activity can be developed into a jigsaw project where each major category (e.g., distinguishing features, habits, geographic dispersion, period of time) is the basis of new groups, each comprised of one representative from each original group. Each new group then develops a decision chart that identifies the specific dinosaur. For example: (1) Is the dinosaur a carnivore? (2) If yes, then: ... If no, then: ...

When the field guide is developed, then a game of 20 Questions can be played using the field guide to give the correct yes/no responses. Alternatively, an unknown dinosaur may be introduced for the class to determine, based on the field guide.

Activity Variations

1. The class may produce multimedia presentations about dinosaurs.
2. The class may create interactive field guides for other biological entities.
3. The class may concentrate on one era or one geographic area.

ENVIRONMENTAL SUMMIT

Activity Description

The class holds an environmental summit at which each group debates issues from a unique perspective.

Content Outcomes

Students will:

- Identify major environmental issues.
- Determine the stance of a specific country on major environmental issues.
- Identify the impact of environmental issues on a country.
- Compare the impact of environmental issues and stances between countries.

Information Literacy Outcomes

Students will:

- Locate and select a variety of resources on environmental issues.
- Interpret findings in light of political, economic, and social perspectives.
- Draw conclusions based on data.
- Distinguish between fact and opinion.
- Transform information into debate form.

Prerequisite Skills

- Use library catalogs and indexes to locate information.
- Make accurate inferences from information.
- Debate issues.

Rationale for the Process

The environment has become a high-profile and high-stakes issue in the global political arena. While no one wants to destroy the planet, countries have sometimes conflicting priorities as they try to develop themselves and help their people.

This activity sensitizes students to the political, economic, and social impact of environmental issues and demonstrates how interdependent the world has become in terms of environmental decisions. The debate format helps differentiate the perspectives of different countries. Hopefully, the simulated summit will generate policies that everyone can live with, literally.

Activity

Grade level: high school
Time frame: six to seven days
Resources: a variety of informational sources on environmental issues and countries, sample governmental resolutions

Grouping: analytical and creative thinkers, abstract and concrete learners, oral and written expressers, students with naturalistic and interpersonal intelligences

Group tasks:
1. Choose an environmental issue.
2. Locate and select information about the environmental issue.
3. Determine the political, economic, and social impact of the issue.
4. Regroup according to country.
5. Research and make inferences about the impact of environmental issues upon the country.
6. Develop a resolution on an environmental issue based on the country's perspective.
7. Hold an environmental summit, debating environmental issues as country representatives.

Tips: To focus the activity, have students list contemporary environmental issues. Then have them brainstorm the impact of environmental issues upon countries. Their discussion should raise factors such as:

- Political—regulations and their enforcement, governance and control
- Economic—trade, labor, use of natural resources
- Social—consumerism, religious beliefs, lifestyle impact

As groups research their issue, they should consider how each of these factors are influenced.

One representative from each environmental issue then becomes a member of a new group, in jigsaw fashion. Each new group is assigned to represent a unique country, interpreting environmental issues in light of their political, economic, and social realities. Point out that each member needs to teach peers about the environmental issue so they can all debate environmental issues expertly.

Students may need help in drawing up resolutions. Have them locate existing resolutions, such as United Nations and congressional documents. It may also be a good idea to assign one student as parliamentarian and one as secretary/moderator for the debate.

Assessment

Resolutions form the basis for assessment. Theoretically, those resolutions that are passed demonstrate the most compelling arguments and logical stances.

As a closing assessment, the class can discuss what implications political decisions about the environment have on the world—and science.

Activity Variations

1. The entire class may concentrate on one continent.
2. The entire class may concentrate on one aspect of the environment (e.g., water or air, developing a set of resolutions based on each country's perspective).
3. The debate may be videotaped.
4. Decision charts may be generated to show how one environmental decision impacts other decisions.

MACHINATIONS

Activity Description

Each group creates a complex machine and identifies the physics concepts involved in making it work.

Content Outcomes

Students will:

- Identify physics principles.
- Relate physics principles to machines.
- Identify which physics principles affect machine operations and how they affect them.
- Create a complex machine and describe how it operates.

Information Literacy Outcomes

Students will:

- Locate and select information about machines and physics principles.

- Make predictions and draw inferences based on abstract concepts.
- Determine cause-and-effect relationships.
- Transform information into diagram form.

Prerequisite Skills
- Conceptualize a complex machine and diagram it.

Rationale for the Process
Physics describes the workings of the world around us. In particular, it identifies the forces and properties that make man-made objects operate.

This activity enables students to become aware of the variety of these physics principles and apply them to describe how complex machines work. This activity is useful as an introductory unit or as a synthesizing exercise.

Activity
Grade level: middle school and up
Time frame: three to four days
Resources: information about physics and machines, CAD or physics software (optional), clear transparencies and writing tools
Grouping: concrete and abstract thinkers, sequential and holistic processors, visual and kinesthetic learners, analytical and creative thinkers
Group tasks:
1. Design a complex machine.
2. Identify the physical principles that make the machine operate.
3. Diagram the machine, and label the physics principles of each part on an overlaid transparency.
4. Predict how the machine will work.
5. Change one part of the machine, and, again, predict how the machine will work.

Tips: To begin this activity, share diagrams of Rube Goldberg machines. Have the class describe how they think the machine works. Then talk about the physics principles behind the machine's operations. Some of the principles generated should include:

- Gravitational forces
- Simple machine principles (e.g., lever, pulley, wedge)
- Optics
- Electricity
- Magnetism

As groups design their machines, encourage them to incorporate a variety of physics principles. To structure the activity, a minimum of ten different principles may be required.

Assessment
Groups exchange their machines and overlays but keep the predictions. Have each group predict how the machine works. The original group then shows the altered machine, having their paired group predict the operational consequences. Groups then cross-evaluate the principles and predictions for accuracy and thoroughness.

As a check, groups may present their machines and have the paired group independently label the physics principles underlying the machine's operations.

In conclusion, the class discusses how changes to one part of the machine affect other principles, and how, in general, different physics principles interrelate.

Activity Variations
1. Groups may create actual machines.
2. Each group may focus on one set of physics principles.
3. Groups may extend the activity by having jigsaw groups change each machine.
4. Machines may be human.

MORE IDEA STARTERS
1. Create a card game using names of animal parts.
2. Develop ecowebs.
3. Develop a database of scientists, animals, plants, etc.

4. Produce word puzzles and riddles using scientific terms.
5. Play Pictionary using scientific terms.
6. Develop an anthology of literature or quotations about science.
7. Develop a board game or card game using the periodical table.
8. Give true and false uses for technical equipment.
9. Locate origins of plants, such as potatoes, using a world map.
10. Examine careers that apply scientific knowledge.
11. Describe a "day in the life" for an ant, algae, or virus.
12. Trace the water cycle or other ecosystem.
13. Hold a science awards night for historical discoveries.
14. Morph biomes electronically.
15. Create a science firsts calendar.
16. Locate science fiction stories, and determine which futuristic predictions have come true or are feasible.
17. Create a "bluff" game based on plant uses.
18. Contrast different types of maps that describe the same area (e.g., political, topological, various projections).
19. Trace what happens to trash.
20. List laws and regulations dealing with one issue in science (e.g., air pollution, nuclear waste).
21. Develop a slide–tape show or multimedia presentation on the history of conservation.
22. Create a hot-linked map showing endangered species.
23. Create popular articles about some scientific controversy, in terms of coverage and bias.
24. Create a card game using feasible and incorrect chemical solutions.
25. Draw physically sound and unsound bridges.
26. Develop a skit showing what would happen if there were no more trees.
27. Develop a skit about living under the sea.
28. Compare constellations of different cultures.
29. Locate science records (e.g., most abundant metal element, largest lake, first woman in space).
30. Diagram the physics principles involved in a sports movement (e.g., hitting a ball, skating on ice, windsurfing).

CHAPTER 16

Activity Plans for Social Studies

TIME CAPSULE

Activity Description
Each group produces a newspaper, multimedia program, or slide–tape show for a specific time in history.

Content Outcomes
Students will:
- Identify significant facts and details about a specific time in history.
- Identify key visual and verbal descriptions about a specific time in history.

Information Literacy Outcomes
Students will:
- Use a wide variety of media, particularly visual, as sources of information about a specific time in history.
- Use content analysis techniques to identify key facts.
- Identify main ideas and details about a specific time in history.
- Organize information using topic or thematic patterns and techniques.
- Integrate two or more forms of information in presenting ideas.
- Use a slide–tape format or newspaper medium to present their findings.

Prerequisite Skills
- Use library catalogs and indexes to locate relevant information.
- Use applicable presentation tools (e.g., desktop publishing for newspaper, authoring program for multimedia presentation, photographic and audiocassette equipment for slide–tape show).

Rationale for the Process
History is a fascinating compendium of facts and faces, a mixture of the whimsical and the tragic, the incidental and the momentous.

As students research the various aspects of a time period, they develop a richer sense of history and realize the interdependence of the various aspects of each era. In interpreting their findings using two or more forms of media, students experience the interdependence of presentation modes as well.

Activity
Grade level: high school
Time frame: one to two weeks
Resources: historical sources, especially visual; equipment to produce a slide–tape show; equipment and materials (including desktop publishing computer program) to produce a newspaper; equipment (including authoring program, scanner, other AV peripherals and connections) to produce a multimedia presentation

Grouping: students who receive information differently (aurally, visually), creative and analytical learners, sequential and holistic processors

Group tasks:
1. Choose a specific time in history.
2. Locate and select a wide variety of information about that time.
3. Photograph, reproduce, or scan appropriate pictures.
4. Arrange visual elements.
5. Develop written or audio material to complement the visuals.
6. Integrate the written/audio and visual elements to create a newspaper, slide–tape show, or multimedia presentation.

Tips: You may introduce the activity by using a "time capsule" image and asking questions such as:

- What items would you include in a time capsule to exemplify this year?
- What images come to mind when thinking about the 1960s? 1950s? 1920s?
- What aspects of life affect and reflect any era?

Another approach is to use an end-of-the-year summary, as seen in magazines and yearbooks. You and the students may bring examples of sources to analyze, using these questions as guides:

- What people are included?
- What events are included?
- What forms of art and entertainment are included?
- How are science and technology reflected?
- How are occupations reflected?
- How are politics and government reflected?
- What fads or ephemeral information are included?

Students may discover other significant categories of information as they look at these documents.

Students should also brainstorm the wide variety of possible information sources: timetables, illustrations and photographs, audio sources, documentary film, and the riches of primary sources (e.g., diaries, letters, speeches, announcements).

You may also lead a brainstorming session on feasible subject headings for locating information (e.g., entertainment/leisure, personalities, politics, fashions and fads, media, social and economic conditions).

Groups may develop themes or topics before they begin locating information so they can tailor their search strategy. Some groups may want to browse the available material, deriving their themes from what they find. As they examine sources, they should keep in mind how visual and written/narrative information complement each other.

To simplify the activity, the entire class may concentrate on one year with each group looking at one aspect of the period. As you plan this activity, also consider the time and money involved in creating slides and audiotape tracks. The class may consider other formats for presentation, such as collages, scrapbooks, or a simulated magazine. If the entire class focuses on one time period, each group could limit its work to one aspect, such as science illustrations. Using a newspaper format, each group could be responsible for one section.

If a newspaper format is chosen, groups should consider these issues:

- What kinds of articles and sections are included in newspapers?
- How is each kind written?
- How are headlines used and written?
- What role do visuals play? How are they identified?
- Are advertisements included?
- How are articles and visuals arranged?

If a slide–tape show is produced, groups should consider these issues:

- Who is responsible for each task: scripting, shooting, editing/sequencing, audiotaping?

- What equipment is needed to photograph pictures and create an audiotape track? Who will supply it?
- Is technical help available?
- Can existing filmstrips be cut into slides?
- Will sound be included: narrative, music, sound bites of famous speeches? Who is responsible for each task: locating sounds, sequencing, taping, synchronizing with slides?
- What funding is available? Who will keep track of it?
- How much time is available for each task? Will work be done outside of class time? Are delays taken into account (i.e., lost film, illness)?

If a multimedia presentation is produced, groups should consider these issues:

- Who is responsible for each task: storyboarding, designing, choosing and importing visuals, choosing and importing audio, choosing and importing video clips, writing, sequencing, and linking?
- What equipment is needed for each task? Are components compatible?
- How will the work be scheduled?
- Is technical help available?

Assessment

Each group presents its time capsule. Groups may exchange their projects for cross-assessment, or the entire class may assess results together. The following Time Capsule Assessment Rubric provides a guideline for both designing and evaluating the project.

As a closing activity, the entire class discusses time capsules and summaries. Ask leading questions such as:

- What makes an event or person significant?
- How have different time periods emphasized different aspects of life?
- What aspects of life have changed the most, the least?
- How might our views today about a time period differ from those of that period?

To expand the activity, as each group researches a time period, each member may specialize in one aspect of the times. The evaluation activity would include grouping the specific subject experts (e.g., all those focusing on music) from each time period to compare that one aspect through the ages. They may develop a timeline or sequence slides, which could then be cross-compared by the class.

Time Capsule Assessment Rubric

Time Period
Group Members
Presentation Format
Content

- Main points (people, events, ideas)
  - Chooses relevant facts
  - Relates facts to correct time period
  - Presents information accurately and objectively
  - Covers material thoroughly
- Research
  - Uses a variety of sources
  - Cites sources accurately
  - Avoids plagiarism
- Organization
  - Arranges information logically
  - Coordinates text, graphics, and sound
  - Clearly states purpose
  - Substantiates analysis

Technical Skill

- Range and versatility
  - Chooses appropriate technology tools throughout activity
  - Uses a variety of media appropriately
  - Communicates ideas proficiently
- Technical control
  - Uses technological conventions appropriately
  - Uses technical skills to transform information
  - Uses various types of technological structures for appropriate effect
  - Coordinates technologies to organize and present ideas coherently

- Presentation
  - Product is appropriate to the audience and assignment
  - Technology accurately represents the ideas and findings
  - Product is technically and mechanically competent
  - Information matches the presentation mode

Ratings for Each Descriptor

4: Fully accomplishes the purpose of the task/well-done/exceeds requirements

3: Substantially accomplishes the purpose of the task/adequate/meets requirements

2: Partially accomplishes the purpose of the task/needs revisions/meets limited requirements

1: Makes little or no progress in accomplishing the purpose of the task/restart/meets few or no requirements

Activity Variations

1. The entire class may concentrate on one time period. Each group may choose one aspect, such as sports or arts.
2. The entire class may concentrate on one aspect of history, such as science or personalities. Each group may choose one specific time period.
3. Each group may choose a different form of presentation.
4. The entire class may concentrate on primary sources.
5. Each group may focus their presentation using one medium: written, audio, visual.

IMMIGRANTS ALL

Activity Description

Each group produces a skit about a unique ethnic group's major migration to the United States.

Content Outcomes

Students will:
- Identify major migration movements.
- Accurately describe an immigration movement to the United States.
- Compare immigration movements.

Information Literacy Outcomes

Students will:
- Recognize and use a variety of sources, especially primary sources, of information about a specific ethnic group's major migration to the United States.
- Assess information from a variety of sources to verify facts, recognize forms of bias, and determine adequacy of information.
- Synthesize and organize findings into dramatic form.

Prerequisite Skills

- Use library catalogs and indexes to locate information.
- Interview people (optional).
- Create a skit.

Rationale for the Process

Immigration stories transcend number to encompass human responses to the challenges of a new land and different cultures. By developing a skit about immigration, students learn to crystallize and humanize facts. By acting out the experience, they learn to share the immigrants' feelings and actions.

Activity

Grade level: middle school and up

Time frame: one week

Resources: sources about history, culture, immigration, law; primary resources; human resources and agencies; materials for dramatization

Grouping: concrete and abstract processors; visual, aural, and kinesthetic learners; analytical and creative thinkers; introverts and extroverts; mixed ethnicities; American and non-American born

Group tasks:

1. Choose an ethnic group or immigration movement.
2. Locate and select information, especially primary sources, about the ethnic group's migration to the United States.
3. Determine one significant period of their migration.
4. Locate information about the United States at that time.
5. Based on the analysis of information, summarize the immigrants' experiences and challenges.
6. Dramatize the experience.

Tips: Introduce the activity by leading a class discussion about contemporary immigration movements, asking questions such as:

- Who are today's new Americans?
- Why are they immigrating to the United States?
- What problems do they encounter?
- How do you feel about these new immigrants?
- When did your family immigrate to the United States?
- What challenges might they have encountered?

Remind groups to search for information from various angles: by ethnic groups, by time period, by geographic region, and by social topic (e.g., women, labor, family). Explain how details can make the dramatization more effective by discussing a typical day and its factors: food, transportation, clothing, homelife, money. This will help students ferret out interesting aspects of the immigrant experience.

Groups should also use a variety of information formats, especially primary sources such as eyewitness accounts, film documentaries, recordings, oral histories, illustrations, and realia. The Library of Congress has an "American Memory" collection available on the Internet, which is very valuable for this activity. Groups may also visit museums and historical societies, as well as interview immigrants firsthand.

Assessment

Each group presents a skit, which is assessed for accuracy, thoroughness, credibility, and technical skill. The class discusses the immigration experience, comparing various time periods and immigration movements.

Activity Variations

1. The entire class may concentrate on one ethnic group or continent. Each group may choose one time period or geographic region of settlement.
2. The entire class may concentrate on one time period. Each group may choose one ethnic group or geographic region.
3. The entire class may concentrate on one immigration movement. Each group may choose one type of family.
4. Groups may present findings in different formats, such as videotape, multimedia, slide-tape, diary.

1776 NEWS BREAK

Activity Description

Each group produces a simulated news broadcast about an historical event.

Content Outcomes

Students will:

- Identify key facts about historical events.
- Interpret historical events from different points of view.
- Recognize the context and implications of an historical event.

Information Literacy Skills

Students will:

- Locate and use a variety of historical sources, especially primary sources.
- Assess information to verify facts, recognize points of view, and determine adequacy of data.
- Distinguish between fact and opinion.
- Synthesize and transform findings into broadcast format.

Prerequisite Skills

- Use library catalogs and indexes to locate relevant information.
- Storyboard, videotape, and develop a skit or simulated broadcast.

Rationale for the Process

History may sometimes seem abstract and disconnected from the present. Yet, its decisions continue to influence today's politics. Additionally, history books may cover historical events from a limited perspective, sometimes in an effort to present an objective point of view or synthesize all information.

Broadcast journalism has an immediacy that captures people's attention. Using that style of reenactment can engage the students viscerally and help them see history as a "live" presence. Covering an historical event from several points of view also fleshes out events and allows the student to come to his or her own conclusions.

Activity

Grade level: middle school and up

Time frame: one week

Resources: resources about historical events and contemporary life, particularly in primary sources; equipment for videotaping, editing, and viewing (optional)

Grouping: concrete and abstract thinkers; visual, aural, and kinesthetic learners; introverts and extroverts; sequential and holistic processors

Group tasks:

1. Choose an historical event.
2. Locate and select information, especially primary sources, about the historical event and its context.
3. Determine different points of view of groups with different perspectives.
4. Research the event in light of the different points of view.
5. Develop a news broadcast simulation, either "live" or videotaped.

Tips: To focus the activity, lead a group discussion on a recent historical event, such as a treaty, assassination, revolution. Ask open-ended questions such as:

- What happened?
- How did television cover the event?
- Which people were interviewed?
- What angles were explored?

Encourage students to analyze broadcasts in terms of content and approach. Lead a follow-up discussion about broadcast techniques.

Students should storyboard their broadcast, making sure to include different key figures and angles. Encourage students to research the clothing and figurative speech of the time to make the broadcast look more authentic. They may even want to include commercials to add some social context.

Assessment

Each group presents their historical broadcast. The viewers assess it for content and presentation technique.

As a follow-up assessment, the class discusses the documentation of history and various points of view. They may also discuss the responsibility of broadcasting and viewing.

Activity Variations

1. The entire class may concentrate on one period of time or one event. Each group broadcasts from a different country.
2. The entire class may concentrate on one country and develop a series of broadcasts on that country's major historical events.
3. The class may present their findings in multimedia format.

MAPPING THE ECONOMICS PICTURE

Activity Description

Each group produces a map transparency illustrating an economic factor.

Content Outcomes

Students will:

- Identify factors that contribute to the economic conditions of a country.
- Analyze and compare the relative status of an economic factor.
- Analyze comparative economic factors.

Information Literacy Outcomes

Students will:

- Locate and select information about economic factors for a specific political region.
- Interpret statistical and graphical information.
- Use symbolic patterns and techniques to synthesize and organize findings.

Prerequisite Skills

- Read maps.
- Use simple descriptive statistics.
- Use a computer paint program (optional).

Rationale for the Process

The economic health of a country depends on a variety of factors: labor, education, agricultural conditions, distribution of industries, energy, natural resources, government spending, and so on. Each factor provides a different perspective, and collectively, or in relationships, these factors create significant scenarios.

Additionally, within a country, or a continent, the distribution of economic wealth varies. Again, the interplay of factors emphasizes relative economic health.

By mapping economic conditions, students see the different factors at work. By visually comparing these factors, with transparencies, students grasp sophisticated economic relationships quickly.

Activity

Grade level: high school

Time frame: three to four days

Resources: economic sources, color pens and transparency materials for maps, computer paint program (optional)

Grouping: analytical and creative thinkers, detail-oriented and holistic learners, students with numerical and visual abilities

Group tasks:

1. Choose a set of economic factors for a specific political region.
2. Locate and select information about the factors.
3. Interpret statistical information to calculate the relative status of the factor within the region.
4. Chart the relative status on a map, producing a transparency.
5. Compare economic maps.

Tips: To help groups clarify their tasks, lead a class discussion by asking questions such as:

- What factors affect and reflect a nation's economic health (e.g., labor, patterns of saving and spending, industry distribution, energy and environment, agriculture)?
- Where can you find statistics about these economic factors (e.g., almanacs, encyclopedias, economic and political references)?
- How can you differentiate the relative status of an economic factor (e.g., by color, density of line or dots, different directional lines)?

To facilitate comparisons, have students find an outline map of their area. Students may also share models of comparative maps. It is easier for each group to assign one factor per student and then make congruent maps. The class may also consider developing a set of similar economic factors to facilitate cross-assessment between countries.

If students work with specific chart information, they will need to translate the figures into statistical form. If necessary, show them how to calculate the mean (sum/# of items) and the range (highest minus lowest figures). To create a color-coded map, students may divide the figures into five to seven groups. For example, one person may chart the number of head of cattle output per state in the United States. The figures may vary from 20,000 to 200,000 head in a state, a range of 180,000. Consequently, six different colored groups would be: 20,000–50,000; 50,000–80,000; 80,000–110,000; 110,000–140,000; 140,000–170,000; 170,000–200,000. Groups should also be reminded to include a scale or legend on their maps.

Assessment

Each group compares its maps and presents their conclusions and justifications for assessment by another group.

If the same set of economic factors is used across groups, new groups composed of one representative from each original group are formed. These jigsaw groups compare their maps and draw conclusions based on the data. The class assesses each conclusion in terms of the data and their inferences.

As a closing assessment activity, the class draws conclusions about economic factors in general.

Activity Variations

1. The entire class may use the same kind of legend.
2. The form of presentation may be a bar graph or other graphical form.
3. The entire class may analyze factors other than economic.
4. The entire class may concentrate on the same factors. Each group may graph a different decade.
5. The entire class may concentrate on one country and subdivide by region.

MORE IDEA STARTERS

1. Develop an historical recipe file.
2. Develop a compendium of historical songs, poems, or slang.
3. Examine ethnic stereotypes.
4. Create a database for a women's hall of fame.
5. Write history from the point of an outside or a disenfranchised person.
6. Create bingo games on topics such as women's studies, Native Americans.
7. Explore cemeteries as primary sources.
8. Trace the history of transportation, communication, religion, etc.
9. Interview senior citizens about life in the 1920s or other period.
10. Find international symbols; create some.
11. Compare rites of passage throughout time or in different cultures.
12. Create hyperlinked maps showing current or past peace efforts.
13. Research conditions for peace.
14. Examine situations where different cultures have come into contact for the first time.
15. Create hyperlinked maps of diasporas.
16. Collect current or past political cartoons from around the world.
17. Create timelines for social justice issues.
18. Debate an historical decision in light of the circumstances of the times (e.g., the decision to use the atomic bomb).
19. Explore history through novels.
20. Create historical or geographic databases for analysis.
21. Adapt commercial games to explore history or geography.
22. Create Utopias.
23. Hold a mock Senate or Supreme Court session.
24. Create a mobile about a country or time in history.
25. Trace legislation for a social justice issue.
26. Reenact a typical day for a refugee.
27. Develop a decades simulation.
28. Create an historical sociogram (e.g., French Revolution, establishment of communism).

CHAPTER 17

Activity Plans for Technology

READ MY CHIPS

Activity Description

Each group develops a chart that compares two sources (e.g., science fiction, nonfiction article, video) in terms of the perspectives on computers.

Content Outcomes

Students will:

- Identify the computer's role and operation within a work of science fiction or nonfiction.
- Identify the attitude toward the computer within a work of science fiction or nonfiction.
- Compare perspectives on computers between two sources.

Information Literacy Outcomes

Students will:

- Locate and select two sources (from science fiction or nonfiction) that feature a computer.
- Analyze sources in terms of the computer's role and operation and in terms of the author's attitude toward the computer.
- Use a chart format to synthesize interpretations of information.

Prerequisite Skills

- Identify science fiction and nonfiction sources.
- Use an index and catalog to locate fiction and nonfiction sources.
- Identify an author's bias.

Rationale for the Process

Computers have changed radically since they were invented. Likewise, human attitudes toward the computer have changed over the years. As these changes have occurred, they have been documented in periodicals and monographs. Science fiction authors, too, serve useful roles as reflective observers and forecasters. Science fiction predicts how a technological society may respond and change if present-day trends continue. It also reveals current attitudes about technological advances. Both science fiction and documentary treatments about computers have been recorded in movies and television programs as well. In these visual media, the viewer can see the computer in action—and its affect on the human environment.

By reading and viewing fictional and factual accounts, students relate technology to human values. They may predict their own future in the process.

Activity

Grade level: middle school and up

Time frame: two to four days

Resources: science fiction, scientific, and general news sources in print or nonprint format; bibliographies and indexes; paper and writing material to make charts

Grouping: students with different learning styles (auditory, visual), creative and analytical thinkers

Group tasks:

1. Locate two sources that feature a computer.
2. Read/view the works.
3. Identify the role that the computer plays and the human attitudes toward the computer.
4. Translate interpretation of sources into chart form.

Tips: To begin the activity, have students define "computer." Then ask their opinions about the roles that computers play now and student attitudes toward computers. You may ask questions such as:

- Where do you get your information?
- How do you develop attitudes about computers?
- Have your attitudes and knowledge changed? Why? On what basis?
- Do your parents or other adults hold different ideas? Why?
- How might nonfiction and science fiction works differ in their description of computers?

While nonfiction information about computers may be easy to locate, students may need guidance to specialized bibliographies and anthologies of science fiction works featuring computers. For time's sake, students may want to concentrate on short stories or poetry rather than novels and may need help using indexes to those sources. Some students may want to analyze comic books. Other students may want to examine nonprint sources such as films, television, or recorded speeches.

Since two sources are being compared, the connection between them may vary. Brainstorm with the class to generate logical pairings. Some examples follow:

- Two nonfiction articles written at the same time
- A science fiction short story and a science fiction novel written at the same time
- A nonfiction account and a science fiction work written at the same time
- Two similar sources written at the same time but in different countries
- A nonprint and a print source created at the same time
- Two similar sources written ten years apart
- Two sources by the same author written ten years apart

The entire class may use the same pattern of comparative works, or each group may choose a different approach.

To help students in each group structure their charts and summarize their ideas about their sources, you may ask leading questions such as:

- Why is a computer featured in the source?
- What does the computer look like?
- How does the computer operate?
- What can the computer do and not do?
- What is the computer's potential?
- How important is the computer?
- How influential is the computer?
- What happens to the computer in the account?
- Who uses or has access to the computer?
- How do the characters or the author relate to the computer?
- Is the computer considered "good" or "bad"?
- If the computer could be characterized as a person, what kind of person would it be?

To simplify the activity, produce and distribute a check sheet of questions for all groups to follow. For more sophisticated classes, you may lead a discussion on likely questions to ask so that the students structure their own research. The entire class may use the same points, thus standardizing the charts for easier comparison, or each group may develop its own categories of comparisons.

Assessment

Groups exchange their charts for cross-evaluation. Groups should consider the sources chosen and the accuracy of interpretation.

Group pairs may compare their charts in terms of computer role/operation and attitudes toward the computer.

The class discusses the roles of the computer and the attitudes toward the computer in general:

- What changes in computer roles and operations have occurred over time?
- What changes in attitudes have occurred over time?
- What relationships exist between computer operations and attitudes toward computers?
- What differences occur between nonfiction and science fiction treatments?
- How accurate are science fiction sources over time?
- What trends do you foresee in the ways computers will operate or be viewed?

Activity Variations

1. Each group may choose a story from a different decade (or five-year span).
2. The entire class may concentrate on science fiction during a specific decade. Each group may choose a different author or different media.
3. The entire class may concentrate on nonfiction accounts.
4. Groups may present their interpretations in different ways: oral report poster, poem, collage, drama, diagram, comic book, video, multimedia presentation.
5. Students may write original science fiction works.
6. Students may survey the community about their opinions and attitudes toward computers.

WEBQUESTS

Activity Description

Each group develops a Web-based lesson about technology.

Content Outcomes

Students will:

- Develop a Web page (layout and content).
- Identify appropriate Web sites.
- Incorporate relevant graphics (optional).
- Draw inferences about technology.

Information Literacy Outcomes

Students will:

- Locate and evaluate appropriate Web sites.
- Extract main concepts from resources.
- Summarize Web sites.
- Transform concepts into a Web page.

Prerequisite Skills

- Operate and manipulate computer hardware and applications.
- Develop Web pages (optional).
- Use Internet browsers and search engines.
- Develop a lesson plan (optional).

Rationale for the Process

Web pages offer an exciting new way to present research findings on a topic. Historically, bibliographies have provided this information. The reader could look up the source material used by the researcher if interested in pursuing that topic more deeply. The unique idea about a Web version of a bibliography, or Webliography, is that the user can access supporting research directly and simultaneously.

Similarly, bibliographic essays offer a running narrative about research sources. The bibliographer chooses relevant sources, sequencing them, to present an overview of the pertinent literature in the field. Such a research essay basically comprises the first part of most theses and dissertations. A WebQuest acts as the graphic equivalent. The WebQuest developer sequences and describes high-quality Web sites to develop an interactive review of Internet sources on a topic. Using this approach, students concentrate on source evaluation and discipline content rather than cut-and-paste research reports.

WebQuests provide valuable information for burgeoning researchers. The product can serve as a useful end product as well as the starting point for in-depth theses and ensuing research.

The technology emphasis furthers knowledge in the field.

Activity

Grade level: high school
Time frame: three to five days
Resources: Internet access, Web page development tools (optional), variety of resources on technology, bibliographic essay exemplars
Grouping: analytical and creative thinkers, verbal and visual processors, technology novices and experts
Group tasks:

1. Determine WebQuest technology topic.
2. Locate potential relevant Web sites and other resources.
3. Evaluate resources.
4. Develop a logical sequence for resources.
5. Describe relevancy of sources in essay form.
6. Transfer information into a Web page format.

Tips: Begin the activity by leading a class discussion about the research process. Focus on the value of the literature review stage. Then have students connect that stage to the generation of bibliographies. Introduce the concept of a Web-based bibliography and have students generate a list of critical features for each product.

Next, describe a bibliographic essay, showing an example of it, if possible. Show a bibliographic essay or literature review and a bibliography on the same topic and allow students to compare them. Then have students develop a Web-based framework.

Point out different types of Web sites: those which basically provide Web links, those which give overviews of topics, and those which cover a specific aspect of a topic. Note how a general Web site might offer valuable background information or contain sections that relate to the topic at hand. Have students locate examples of each type of Web site. Students then discuss quality Web sites and generate a list of criteria by which to evaluate them. Also discuss how to describe or extract the relevant information from a Web site.

Encourage students to bookmark good sites and take notes on them. Show them how to copy notes onto the computer's notepad or word processing program, if available. Some programs, such as Word 98, can save a document in HTML form, thereby saving a step. Otherwise, students need access to a Web development tool—or know how to use HTML.

The class may limit their WebQuest to Internet sources or decide to include non-Net items. With more types of resources, each person in the group can concentrate on one format. Another way to divide work is to assign one student to site evaluation, one to extraction, one to organizing sites, and one to oversee Web design.

Assessment

Groups assess each other's Web pages for content and format. Groups should be able to get an overview of the technology covered by examining the WebQuest. The assessment itself should also be analyzed for its thoroughness; this step may be considered a metacognition activity.

Students may extend the activity by continuing to research their chosen technology or use another group's Web page to pursue the topic. Indeed, this activity can be used as a jigsaw activity to facilitate technology knowledge.

Activity Variations

1. Students may choose other topics besides technology.
2. Students may incorporate other types of resources into the WebQuest.
3. Students may create hypermedia stacks about technology.

MIRROR, MIRROR ON THE WALL

Activity Description
Each group explores a special career to discover what impact computers have made in that field.

Content Outcomes
Students will:
- Identify job functions that incorporate computer technology.
- Determine the impact made by computer technology in specific career fields.

Information Literacy Outcomes
Students will:
- Recognize and use a variety of sources of information about computer technology in a specific career field.
- Identify main facts and details.
- Organize information to express patterns and relationships.

Prerequisite Skills
- Use library catalogs and indexes to locate relevant information.
- Interview experts (optional).

Rationale for the Process
Careers today involve connections with computers, whether for management, development, or communications. Yet, different careers demand different computer skills.

In completing this activity, students learn how pervasive computers have become. They may also begin to make decisions about their educational paths in the field of computer science.

If this activity includes an historical survey, students discover how quickly the computer science field has grown. They may extrapolate future trends as well.

Activity
Grade level: middle school and up
Time frame: two to three days
Resources: career and computer information
Grouping: analytical and creative thinkers, technology experts and novices
Group tasks:
1. Locate and select information about a specific career.
2. Determine what role the computer has played in this career.
3. Present the group's findings.

Tips: To help students clarify and summarize their findings, ask leading questions such as:
- How long have computers been used in this career field?
- How has the role of the computer in this field changed over time?
- In which specific aspects of the career are computers used: operations, management, training, communications, other?
- To what extent are computers used for specific projects: periodically, daily, constantly?
- Are computers used differently according to the specific rank or function of the employee in the field?
- What kinds of functions does the computer do: calculating, information processing, automating operations, word processing, telecommunications, networking?
- What trends are forecast in the use of computers in the field?

Each group may choose a career cluster, such as environmental careers, so each person can research computer impact for one specific career or function.

Groups should locate sources by looking at career materials and computer-oriented items. Encourage groups to examine career databases and nonprint resources and interview people in the field.

The class may brainstorm ways to present group findings: chart, skit, videotape, display, multimedia presentation.

Assessment

Each group presents its findings, which are assessed in terms of content accuracy and completeness. The class discusses general implications about computer technology impact on careers.

Activity Variations

1. The entire class may concentrate on one major field, such as business. Each group may choose a different specific career, such as accounting or advertising.
2. Groups may visit a company or institution and interview personnel. Students may interview family members.
3. Groups may develop timelines for computer use within a career field.
4. Groups may locate specific program titles used in different careers.
5. Groups may compare hardware/software use across career fields.
6. Students may focus on different types of technology.

COMPUTER ETHICS

Activity Description

Each group develops a computer technology code of ethics with related scenarios.

Content Outcomes

Students will:

- Determine the ethical use of computer technology.
- Apply technology ethics to controversial situations.

Information Literacy Outcomes

Students will:

- Locate and select information on ethics, particularly as related to computer technology.
- Make inferences about computer use by applying information about ethical principles.
- Substantiate their stance with adequate support.
- Organize and translate conclusions into a code of ethics.

Prerequisite Skills

- Use library catalogs and indexes to locate information.
- Develop scenarios.

Rationale for the Process

The computer presents issues of morality, rights, responsibilities, and controls that are made difficult by the technical intricacies of the computer itself.

Ultimately, we must ask whether the most is being made of the opportunity to adapt computers to our use rather than the opposite. Whether any such progress contributes to our general spiritual or emotional condition is determined by what we do with computers as individuals.

By locating information about the ethical use of computers and developing associated scenarios testing those ethics, students examine the value-laden issues of technology and develop a personal ethical stance. Additionally, they should also explore the issues of ethics enforcement.

Activity

Grade level: middle school and up
Time frame: three to four days
Resources: sources on computer technology, ethics, and designing scenarios
Group tasks:

1. Locate information on ethics and ethical codes.
2. Locate information on ethical issues in computer technology.
3. Decide what constitutes ethical use of computer technology.
4. Develop a scenario that tests ethical use of computer technology.
5. Present and assess the scenario.

Tips: To begin the activity, lead a class discussion on the ethical issues related to computer technology, such as privacy, copyright, access to information, system security. To help form the ideas, you may suggest situational questions, such as:

- Would you break a computer security code to examine confidential records about yourself or others?
- Would you copy a computer program for a friend?
- Would you use a password to gain access to a computer for class work, even if you were unauthorized to use it?

You may also need to discuss the concept of a code of ethics and its enforcement and provide examples of such codes. As one option, half of the class may develop codes of ethics, and half may develop enforcement regulations.

Assessment

Group pairs exchange scenarios, responding to them according to their own codes of ethics. Scenarios, responses, and codes are assessed for credibility and ethical stances. The class then develops one code of ethics for computer technology and discusses how the code would be enforced.

Activity Variations

1. Each group may concentrate on one ethical issue in technology.
2. The class may develop a Webliography or database of sources on ethical issues in technology.
3. The class may compare different computer acceptable use policies.
4. Groups may present their codes in different ways: poster, display, logo.
5. Groups may develop case studies on ethical issues in technology.
6. Groups may debate issues on ethical uses of computer technology.
7. Group pairs may develop codes of ethics and enforcement regulations.
8. Groups may produce flowcharts of decisions and consequences related to technology ethics.
9. Groups may produce multimedia Q&A issues on ethical issues in technology.

MORE IDEA STARTERS

1. Create a scavenger hunt with computer science terms.
2. Create a skit about historical events in technology.
3. Design the perfect computer. Determine which features are now available commercially, which are being developed, which are feasible in the near future, and which are improbable.
4. Create a database of significant people in technology.
5. Compare computer languages.
6. Compare search engines.
7. Compare how different periodicals cover computer technology.
8. Anthologize poetry or cartoons about technology.
9. Design an original computer language.
10. Produce an audiotape for the blind, explaining how they may use computers.
11. Locate articles and stories about the role of computers in the twenty-first century. Make your own predictions.
12. Develop a Turing test.
13. Present information about computerized music.
14. Explore computer effects in film.
15. Locate articles written over the last 50 years about computer technology and its influence. Assess their accuracy in light of present-day developments.
16. Research the year 2000 computer issue.
17. Draw the typical computer "hacker," based on research findings.
18. Research gender issues as they apply to technology.
19. Compare different technology-aided training methods and products.

20. Research expert systems. Determine for what kinds of jobs or decision-making functions expert systems are, or could be, efficient.
21. Debate the issues of reality and copyright when images are changed using technology.
22. Create a database or Web page of computer organizations or user groups.
23. Compare an operation or function done manually and by computer.
24. Create three lists: functions that computers now do more effectively than people, functions that computers might do in the future, functions that computers are not likely to do ever.
25. Debate whether computers should be developed to run government offices.
26. Compile historical statistics about computer technology: costs, users, availability.
27. Explore adaptive technology.
28. Trace the evolution of the chip.
29. Research computer animation.
30. Produce hyperlinked cross-sections of technology hardware.

CHAPTER 18

Activity Plans for Vocational Education

MINDING YOUR OWN BUSINESS

Activity Description
Each group develops a business plan.

Content Outcomes
Students will:

- Identify business and financial competencies needed to start and maintain a business enterprise.
- Identify legal implications of starting and maintaining a business enterprise.
- Develop a feasible business plan.
- Recognize and identify interpersonal skills needed to start and maintain a business enterprise.

Information Literacy Outcomes
Students will:

- Recognize and use a variety of resources about starting and maintaining a business enterprise.
- Gather data by interviewing business experts.
- Determine main facts and concepts.
- Determine cause-and-effect relationships.
- Transform findings into a plan.

Prerequisite Skills

- Use library catalogs and indexes to locate information.
- Interview for facts (optional).
- Write a plan.

Rationale for the Process
One of the fastest-growing sectors in the economy is entrepreneurship. In 1995 alone (the most recent year for which government statistics are available), 768,000 new businesses were incorporated. What skills are needed to start a business? What kind of start-up money is needed? What obstacles must be overcome?

This activity gives students an opportunity to examine the specific steps in establishing a business while becoming aware of the challenges and opportunities that young people face in the business world. The activity also examines how business affects people's personal lives.

Activity
Grade level: high school
Time frame: up to two weeks
Resources: business persons and organizations, business and legal sources
Grouping: sequential and holistic processors, analytical and creative learners, students with interpersonal and numerical intelligences, verbal and writing expressers

Group tasks:

1. Locate and select information about one factor in starting a business.
2. Create a chart that shows details needed to be considered when starting a business.
3. Form a new group to research a specific type of business.
4. Develop a business plan for the specific business.
5. Present the business plan as a simulated promo for investors.

Tips: To focus the activity, lead a class discussion about starting a business by asking questions such as:

- What are the advantages and disadvantages of starting your own business?
- What skills would help you start a business?
- What kind of help would be useful in starting a business?

The class then brainstorms various processes involved in starting a business enterprise. Points that should arise include:

- Legal issues: permits, incorporation documents, etc.
- Finances: buying vs. leasing property, start-up costs, labor, investment sources
- Site issues: use of space, seasonal use, square footage, utilities
- Produce/service: marketing, staffing, accountability
- Communication: networking with other businesses, advertising, etc.
- Impact on personal life

Students may need to consult business sources first in order to get ideas on how to establish a business. The Small Business Administration has a good Web site on this topic.

The second group arrangement consists of one representative from each original group. The second groups gather information about a potential specific business, using the expertise derived from the first research to develop the plan.

Students should also be encouraged to seek professional advice and examine existing business plans and promotions. It may be useful for students to watch business presentations on television to analyze the important points in promoting a new business.

Assessment

Groups give an oral business presentation about their new enterprise. Groups cross-assess business plans in terms of sources used, inclusion of steps, conclusions drawn, and thoroughness of plans. The class as a whole discusses business issues in general.

Activity Variations

1. Business experts may assess the groups' business plans.
2. The entire class may focus on one shopping area and research business practices of those merchants.
3. The class may work with the Junior Achievement club.
4. The class may develop a set of documents (e.g., advertising, press releases) about a business opening.

BEHIND THE JOB SCENE

Activity Description

Each group job-shadows a person, videotaping the day.

Content Outcomes

Students will:

- Identify and analyze typical functions and their time distribution of a specific job.
- Compare job functions.

Information Literacy Outcomes

Students will:

- Determine main facts about a specific job through interviewing techniques.
- Represent a typical day through videotaping techniques.

Prerequisite Skills

- Videotape job functions.
- Interview for facts.

Rationale for the Process

While visiting a job site is certainly a good way to learn about a career possibility, it's usually hard for students to visit very many sites. Even commercial videos often do not satisfy the viewer because they do not answer the questions that students have.

This activity allows students to shadow jobs, interviewing to get relevant facts. With the videotape, students can share their experiences with others and compare job functions.

Activity

Grade level: high school
Time frame: three to five days
Resources: sources on interviewing techniques and careers, videotaping and editing equipment
Grouping: visual and verbal learners, analytical and creative thinkers, videotapers and interviewers
Group tasks:

1. Select a company to visit.
2. Create a set of interview questions related to the company.
3. Videotape the visit to the company, interviewing the employees.
4. Present the videotape, editing if possible.

Tips: To focus the activity, lead a class discussion on job shadowing by asking questions such as:

- What would you want to know about a job?
- How would you find out the information?
- How would you share that information?

Students may need help in scheduling visits, in locating companies, determining whom to contact, and how to telephone for appointments.

Students may also need help with interviewing skills. The entire class may develop a set of interview questions, which may be customized based on the preliminary research done. Then students may try a dry run interviewing peers before the actual visit.

Because students may spend a whole day visiting the company, they should be selective about videotaping. The easiest way to edit the visit video is to edit in camera, which requires that the group storyboard the visit ahead of time and choose which scenes will likely be the most interesting or telling: shots about the facility, details about key procedures, images of typical work.

Assessment

Groups share their videotapes, cross-assessing them for accuracy and thoroughness. Groups may produce a classwide videotape of company visits, using visual images to compare career information.

Activity Variations

1. The entire class may concentrate on one occupational field or corporation.
2. Groups may interview companies through video conferencing.
3. Groups may take photographs and audiotape interviews of company visits and create slide–tape shows.

TRENDY CAREERS

Activity Description

Each group creates a chart or timeline that shows historical trends by tracing a specific career over time.

Content Outcomes

Students will:

- Trace historical trends for a specific career.
- Compare historical trends across careers.

Information Literacy Outcomes

Students will:

- Locate and select historical information about a career.
- Recognize trends and patterns when analyzing information.
- Extrapolate trends based on their analysis.
- Use symbolic patterns and techniques to organize and synthesize their findings.

Prerequisite Skills

- Use library catalogs and indexes to locate relevant information.
- Sequence information.

Rationale for the Process

Job descriptions and career status change over time. For example, people's perceptions of teachers and doctors have changed over the years.

By tracing historical trends in careers, students develop a better idea of "image" and preparation. They also realize the instability of some occupations relative to others.

Activity

Group level: high school
Time frame: three to four days
Resources: career sources, statistical references
Grouping: students with numerical and visual abilities, analytical and creative processors
Group tasks:

1. Choose a career.
2. Locate and select historical information about the career.
3. Analyze the career in terms of trends (e.g., number of practitioners, job descriptions, and status or prestige of the career within society).
4. Based on the analysis, predict the future of the career.
5. Summarize findings in chart form.

Tips: Groups may consider themselves cultural archaeologists, digging up facts about their particular career. They may imagine that they live in the twenty-first century and are reporting on these "found" careers.

The time parameters to place on the "dig" must be determined. For example, should it be limited to the twentieth century, or could it date back to the days of Plato or Socrates?

The class should also decide what geographic parameters to place on the "dig." Probably groups should concentrate on U.S. trends.

To help groups clarify their tasks, you may lead a discussion about trends in careers by asking questions such as:

- What careers are held in high esteem now?
- What careers have changed in status or function in the last century (e.g., nursing, teaching, dentistry)?
- What careers are almost obsolete? What careers have come into existence in the last fifty years (e.g., carriage repair versus computer repair)?

You may also lead a brainstorming session on possible sources of information, such as magazines, career materials, almanacs and statistical records, and interviews.

Groups may present their findings in various ways. The entire class may choose one method, such as line graphs, skits, career brochures, slide–tape programs, timelines, or multimedia presentations.

Assessment

Group pairs compare their presentations. The class compares trends across careers, noting factors such as:

- Representation by age, gender, education, nationality
- Fluctuations in functions, status, economics, quantity
- Length of changing cycles

Activity Variations

1. The entire class may concentrate on one career. Each group may examine one time period.
2. The entire class may concentrate on twentieth century trends.
3. The class may examine trends worldwide. Each group may choose one country, one career, or one time period.
4. The class may choose different presentation methods.

BIOGRAPHY RESUMES

Activity Description
Each group writes a resume of a famous person. (This activity could also be used for social studies.)

Content Outcomes
Students will:
- Identify significant experiences and backgrounds of a famous person.
- Write a resume.

Information Literacy Outcomes
Students will:
- Locate and select information about resumes.
- Locate and select information about a famous person.
- Identify main ideas and supporting details about a famous person.
- Categorize information following a resume format.
- Use classification patterns and techniques to synthesize and organize information.

Prerequisite Skills
- Use library catalogs and indexes to locate relevant information.
- Follow a resume format.

Rationale for the Process
Resume writing is an important skill when applying for a job. Yet, this task may seem daunting to students with little volunteer or work experience. Writing the resume of a famous person provides information for "filling in the blanks."

In addition, students may assume that career paths are straight and narrow. By looking at the careers of famous people, students develop a more realistic perspective on career changes within one's lifetime.

Activity
Grade level: high school
Time frame: two to three days
Resources: resumes, biographical sources
Grouping: analytical and creative thinkers, detail-oriented and holistic learners
Group tasks:
1. Choose a famous person, preferably one associated with achievements in a career.
2. Locate and select biographical information about the person.
3. Locate and analyze resume forms.
4. Analyze the person's biography, categorizing information according to resume form.
5. Organize the biographical information into resume form.

Tips: To help groups clarify their tasks, introduce the activity by asking questions such as:
- Who are some famous people who have accomplished much in their career fields?
- How would you chart their career paths?
- What is the purpose of a resume?

When choosing a person to research, groups should be encouraged to consider historical figures as well as contemporary ones. You may want to encourage students to find good role models.

To provide more depth, each group may choose an occupation and have each group member research one major figure in that field. In that way, comparisons may be made within the group about career paths.

A fun way to present the resume is to omit the name of the celebrity. The rest of the class can then guess the person's name and decide if that person would be good to hire for a particular job now.

Assessment
Each group presents its resume(s), omitting any names. The entire class discusses the resumes and persons along with the careers they represent. Students may compare different careers, paths, and types of people.

Activity Variations
1. The entire class may write an ideal person's resume for any one career.
2. The entire class may concentrate on one occupational field.

3. The entire class may concentrate on one period of history.
4. Half of the groups may write resumes for famous women, while the rest may write resumes for famous men in parallel.
5. Each group may choose a different cultural background to examine.
6. Each group may concentrate on one person, with each member writing a different job-related document: a letter of application, an application form, a cover letter, a follow-up letter, an interview framework.
7. The entire class may fill in application forms or write letters of application for famous persons.

MORE IDEA STARTERS

1. Create a card game similar to Authors that uses pictures of equipment associated with different jobs.
2. Select a controversial topic, such as nuclear energy, and hold a mock panel discussion according to the views of different career fields (e.g., science, politics, utilities [electric], conservation).
3. Create a game about career jargon.
4. Develop a job hotline for teenagers.
5. Compare interviewing techniques.
6. Produce a map showing the distribution of industries by state.
7. Compare vocational guidance tests, such as interest versus aptitude.
8. Make career collages.
9. Explore public images and connotations or stereotypes of different occupations.
10. Develop a timeline based on women's roles and achievements in professional occupations.
11. Locate and analyze laws and regulations related to equal opportunities in occupations.
12. Develop an anthology of poems or songs related to jobs.
13. Develop a bibliography of biographies, divided by occupational fields.
14. Develop Webliographies on career information.
15. Produce a skit that shows the typical day for a specific job.
16. Compare different ways to get a job.
17. Hold a career day, where each group explains a different career.
18. Compare the same occupational field across cultures.
19. Analyze fictional representations of occupations.
20. Collect and analyze cartoons and editorials about different occupations.
21. Write effective and ineffective resumes or letters of applications.
22. Role–play effective and ineffective interviews.
23. Trace child labor laws.
24. Create a career mobile.
25. Create a career board game.
26. Analyze job ads.
27. Analyze career choices of different ethnic groups.
28. Develop career pathways for different occupations.
29. Group careers by time shifts.
30. Analyze job choices by educational level.

Glossary

Affective. Pertaining to feelings and emotions.

Assessment. Evaluation of a behavior at one specific time under one specific condition.

Authentic assessment. Assessment based on performance, closely approximating a real-life situation.

Authoring program. A computer software program that enables the user to combine and sequence text and images (and sometimes sound and motion) in a series of "cards" or "screens."

Authority file. A reference list of names and terms used in a library media center to maintain consistent headings.

Benchmark project. A learning activity that involves a complex set of experiences, and applies that knowledge by presenting the results in an original manner.

Bias. A distortion from the objective view; a systemic error introduced when sampling a population.

Bibliographic citation. A formalized brief description of an information source, such as is found in book lists.

Boolean logic. A means to represent relationships logically, using the terms "and," "or," and "not" in combination between items. For example, "Students AND NOT teachers" defines a group of students that excludes all teachers.

CAD. Computer-aided design. Refers to software programs that enable the user to create 2-D and 3-D images on screen.

Case study. A portfolio of descriptions and information about an individual behavior or condition.

Classification. Grouping items according to characteristics such as color or grade.

Cognitive. Pertaining to factual knowledge.

Composition. In a work of art, the visual arrangement of the elements in a relationship that creates a unifying and harmonious whole.

Consensus. Decision supported by the entire group, rather than by a majority.

Content analysis. Analysis of a document by classifying, tabulating, and evaluating key themes and ideas.

Continuum. A continuous line or scale of values.

Cross-check. To check data from various sources to determine validity and accuracy.

Cross-reference. To refer to another source or subject; this process links concepts.

Cross section. One stratum, representing a whole, from the concept of cutting across something, such as a tree trunk.

Cycle of inquiry. The process of posing significant questions about a situation or behavior, then collecting and analyzing data about it, proposing a plan to change the condition, implementing and evaluating the plan, and finally closing the cycle by posing new questions resulting from the inquiry.

Database. A collection of related information, often used or produced by a computer program.

Deduction. A conclusion about a specific phenomenon drawn from general premises.

Demographics. Statistics about human populations.

Desktop publishing. Sophisticated word processing program that enables text and graphics to be combined in a publishing format.

Entry format. In a database program, it refers to the design of the record format.

Expert. One with special skills and knowledge representing mastery of a particular subject.

Extension name. A three-letter designation at the end of a computer file name, which clarifies its meaning.

Extrapolation. To infer or predict outcomes based on known data.

Fact-finding. The process of gathering facts, often to test a hypothesis.

Feedback. Information about a person or system given to the source of that action.

Field. In a database program, it refers to one piece of data within a record; for example, "author" is one field in a record for a bibliographic citation.

Holistic. Pertaining to the whole, rather than parts; assumes that the whole includes the inter-relationship of parts.

Hypermedia. An information environment for a computer; it stores and links different kinds of information in many ways.

Hypothesis. An educated guess about a phenomenon taken as a base for fact-finding and decision making.

Icebreaker. A game that helps people get acquainted.

Induction. Inference of a generalized conclusion as a result of examining particular facts.

Jigsaw. A cooperative learning structure in which one member from each original group becomes part of a succeeding group, thereby facilitating cross-fertilization of expertise.

Kinesthetic. Related to sensory experiences.

Layout. The arrangement and design of the elements of a product, such as a brochure.

Mainstream. To include students with special needs in a general educational program.

Module. An educational unit that covers one specific topic or concept.

Monograph. A single book or other written work; not part of a series.

Periodical. A work that appears regularly in a series, such as a magazine or newspaper.

Primary source. A document based on firsthand knowledge, such as a diary or eyewitness account.

Realia. Real objects, such as models and specimens.

Record. In a database program, one complete unit of information, such as a bibliographic citation.

Role–play. To act out a role, usually to experience feelings about a situation or relationship.

Sampling. Examining a small part of a population.

Search. In a database program, the process of finding all records that match specific criteria.

Simulation. A learning experience that resembles a real-life or historic event; students often role–play during simulations.

Sort. To arrange in order (e.g., alphabetically).

Sound bite. A short, effective quote that may be incorporated into an audio production.

Spreadsheet. A computer ledger program.

Stack. In a computer program, a group of related hypermedia cards.

Storyboard. A sequential set of visuals and narrative outlining a media story.

Symbolic patterns. A visual representational system, such as computer icons or the international system of signs.

Venn diagram. A graphic representational system that aids in reasoning; usually circles are used to represent groups.

Verify. To confirm as true, usually by consulting another source.

Visual literacy. The ability to perceive, understand, and interpret visual images.

Web. A graphical interface of the Internet.

Webliography. A Web-based bibliography.

Wide game. A game consisting of several stations; the game has a theme or story, and each station relates to the wide game theme.

Bibliography

Chapter 1: The Nature of Cooperative Learning

Adrini, B. *Cooperative Learning and Math: A Multi-Structural Approach.* San Juan Capistrano, Calif.: Resources for Teachers, 1989.

American Association of School Librarians. *Collaboration: Lessons Learned.* Chicago: American Library Association, 1996.

———. *Teaching Through Collaboration.* Chicago: American Library Association, 1996.

Breeden, Terri. *Middle Grades Teacher's Handbook for Cooperative Learning.* Nashville, Tenn.: Incentive Publications, 1991.

Costa, Arthur L. *Supporting the Spirit of Learning: When Process Is Content.* Thousand Oaks, Calif.: Corwin Press, 1997.

Cramer, S. *Collaboration: A Success Story for Special Educators.* Needham Heights, Mass.: Allyn and Bacon, 1997.

Davidson, N. *Cooperative Learning in Mathematics: A Handbook for Teachers.* Reading, Mass.: Addison-Wesley, 1989.

Dishon, Dee, and Pat Wilson O'Leary. *Guidebook of Cooperative Learning: A Technique for Creating More Effective Schools.* Holmes Beach, Fla.: Learning Publications, 1994.

Ellis, Susan S., and Susan F. Whalen. *Cooperative Learning: Getting Started.* New York: Scholastic, Inc., 1996.

Glasser, W. *Control Theory in the Classroom.* New York: Harper and Row, 1986.

Graves, Nan, and Ted Graves, ed. *Cooperative Learning: The Magazine for Cooperation in Education.* Santa Cruz, Calif.: International Association for the Study of Cooperation in Education.

Hamm, M., and D. Adams. *Cooperative Learning: Critical Thinking and Collaboration Across the Curriculum.* Springfield, Ill.: Charles C. Thomas Pub., 1996.

Hertz-Lazarowitz, Rachel, and Norma Miller. *Interaction in Cooperative Groups: The Theoretical Anatomy of Group Learning.* New York: Cambridge University Press, 1992.

High, Julie. *Second Language Learning Through Cooperative Learning.* San Juan Capistrano, Calif.: Kagan Cooperative Learning, 1993.

Holt, Daniel, and Jeanne Rennie. *Cooperative Learning: A Response to Linguistic and Cultural Diversity.* McHenry, Ill.: Delta Systems, 1993.

Jaques, David. *Learning in Groups.* 2nd ed. Houston, Tex.: Gulf Publishing, 1992.

Johnson, D. *Cooperative Learning in the Classroom.* Alexandria, Va.: Association for Supervision and Curriculum Development, 1994.

Johnson, D. W., and R. T. Johnson. *Learning Together and Alone.* 4th ed. Needham Heights, Mass.: Allyn and Bacon, 1997.

———. *Cooperation and Competition: Theory and Research.* Edina, Minn.: Interaction Book Co., 1989.

Johnson, D., et al. *Circles of Learning.* 4th ed. Edina, Minn.: Interaction Book Co., 1993.

Kagan, Spencer. *Cooperative Learning Structures.* Rev. ed. San Juan Capistrano, Calif.: Kagan Cooperative Learning, 1992.

———. *Cooperative Learning Resources for Teachers.* San Juan Capistrano, Calif.: Resources for Teachers, 1989.

Kolb, D. *Experiential Learning.* Englewood Cliffs, N.J.: Prentice-Hall, 1984.

McDonald, Penny. *Cooperation at the Computer.* Des Plaines, Ill.: Looking Glass Learning Products, 1989.

Moll, Luis C., Carlos Velez-Ibanez, and Charlene Rivera. *Community Knowledge and Classroom Resources.* Washington, D.C.: U.S. Department of Education, 1990.

O'Malley, C. *Computer-Supported Cooperative Learning.* Heidelberg, Germany: Springer-Verlag, 1991.

Pederson, J., and A. Digby, ed. *Secondary Schools and Cooperative Learning: Theories, Models and Strategies.* New York: Garland Publishing, 1995.

Putnam, J. *Cooperative Learning in Diverse Classrooms.* Columbus, Ohio: Merrill, 1997.

Sharan, S. *Handbook of Cooperative Learning Methods.* Westport, Conn.: Greenwood Press, 1994.

Sharan, S., ed. *Current Research on Cooperative Learning.* New York: Praeger, 1990.

Sharan, S., and Y. Sharan. *Expanding Cooperative Learning Through Group Investigation.* New York: Teachers College Press, 1992.

Slavin, Robert E. *Cooperative Learning: Theory, Research and Practice.* 2d ed. Baltimore, Md.: Johns Hopkins University, 1995.

———. "Synthesis of Research on Cooperative Learning." *Educational Leadership* (Feb. 1991) 71–82.

———. *Using Student Team Learning.* Baltimore, Md.: The Center for Social Organization of Schools, the Johns Hopkins University, 1980.

Stahl, R. *Cooperative Learning in Language Arts: A Handbook for Teachers.* Reading, Mass.: Addison-Wesley, 1994.

Stone, J. M. *Cooperative Learning and Language Arts: A Multi-Structural Approach.* San Juan Capistrano, Calif.: Resources for Teachers, 1989.

Totten, Samuel. *Cooperative Learning: A Guide to Research.* New York: Garland Publishing, 1991.

U.S. Department of Labor. *Secretary's Commission on Achieving Necessary Skills.* Washington, D.C.: Government Printing Office, 1991.

Chapter 2: Inclusive Ways of Learning

Anderson, R. C., et al. *Becoming a Nation of Readers: The Report of the Commission on Reading.* Urbana, Ill.: University of Illinois, Center for the Study of Reading, 1985.

Areglado, Ronald J. *Learning for Life: Creating Classrooms for Self-Directed Learning.* Thousand Oaks, Calif.: Corwin Press, 1996.

Armstrong, Thomas. *Multiple Intelligences in the Classroom.* Alexandria, Va.: Association for Supervision and Curriculum Development, 1994.

Barrs, Myra, and Anne Thomas, eds. *The Reading Book.* London: Centre for Language in Primary Education, 1993.

Belenky, Mary Field, et al. *Women's Ways of Knowing.* New York: Basic Books, 1986.

Bloom, Benjamin S., and D. R. Krathwol. *Taxonomy of Educational Objectives: The Classification of Educational Goals.* New York: McKay, 1956.

Bruer, John I. *Schools for Thought: A Science of Learning in the Classroom.* Cambridge, Mass.: MIT Press, 1993.

Byrnes, James P. *Cognitive Development and Learning in Instructional Contexts.* Needham Heights, Mass.: Allyn and Bacon, 1996.

Caine, Renate Nummela, and Geoffrey Caine. *Making Connections: Teaching and the Human Brain.* Reading, Mass.: Innovative Learning Publications, 1994.

Calvin, William. *How Brains Think.* New York: Basic Books, 1996.

Calvin, William, and George A. Ojemann. *Conversations with Neil's Brain: The Neural Nature of Thought and Language.* Reading, Mass.: Addison-Wesley, 1994.

Costa, A. *Developing Minds: A Resource Book of Teaching Thinking.* Alexandria, Va.: Association for Supervision and Curriculum Development, 1985.

Costa, A., and R. Garmston. *Cognitive Coaching: A Foundation for Renaisssance Curriculum.* Norwood, Mass.: Christopher Gordon Publishers, 1994.

Costa, A., and B. Kallick. *Assessment in the Learning Organization: Shifting the Paradigm.* Alexandria, Va.: Association for Supervision and Curriculum Development, 1994.

Dame, Melvina Azar. *Serving Linguistically and Culturally Diverse Students; Strategies for the School Library Media Specialist.* New York: Neal-Schuman, 1993.

de Bono, E. *de Bono's Thinking Course.* New York: Facts on File Publications, 1986.

———. *Six Thinking Hats.* Boston, Mass.: Little, Brown, 1985.

Driscoll, Marcy, and Mary P. Driscoll. *Psychology of Learning for Instruction.* Needham Heights, Mass.: Allyn and Bacon, 1994.

Dunn, Rita Stafford, and Shirley A. Griggs. *Multiculturalism and Learning Style: Teaching and Counseling Adolescents.* Westport, Conn.: Greenwood Press, 1995.

Erikson, Erik. *Childhood and Society.* New York: Norton, 1950.

Farmer, Lesley S. J. *Informing Young Women: Gender Equity Through Literacy Skills.* Jefferson, N.C.: McFarland, 1996.

Gallagher, James John, Mary Jane Aschner, and William Jenné. *Productive Thinking of Gifted Children in Classroom Interaction.* Washington, D.C.: Council for Exceptional Children, 1967.

Gardner, H. *Creating Minds.* New York: Basic Books, 1993.

———. *Multiple Intelligences: The Theory in Practice.* New York: Basic Books, 1993.

———. *Frames of Mind.* New York: Basic Books, 1983.

Gilligan, Carol. *In a Different Voice.* Cambridge, Mass.: Harvard University Press, 1982.

Harmin, Merrill. *Inspiring Active Learning: A Handbook for Teachers.* Alexandria, Va.: Association for Supervision and Curriculum Development, 1994.

Hergenhahn, B. R., and Matthew H. Olson. *An Introduction to Theories of Learning.* 5th ed. Englewood Cliffs, N.J.: Prentice-Hall, 1996.

Hoover, J. J. *Classroom Applications of Cognitive Learning Styles.* Boulder, Colo.: Hamilton Publications, 1991.

Hutchison, M. *Megabrain.* New York: William Morrow, 1986.

Jonassen, David H., and Barbara L. Grabowski. *Handbook of Individual Differences, Learning, and Instruction.* Mahweh, N.J.: Erlbaum, Lawrence Associates, 1993.

Krapp, J. V. "Teaching Research Skills: A Critical-Thinking Approach." *School Library Journal* (Jan. 1988), 32–35.

Latrobe, Kathy Howard, and Mildred Knight Laughlin. *Multicultural Aspects of Library Media Programs.* Englewood, Colo.: Libraries Unlimited, 1992.

Lazear, David. *Seven Ways of Knowing.* 2d ed. Palantine, Ill.: Skylight Publishing, 1991.

LeDoux, Joseph. *The Emotional Brain: The Mysterious Underpinnings of Emotional Life.* New York: Simon & Schuster, 1996.

Lewis, Rena B., and Donald H. Doorlang. *Teaching Special Students in the Mainsteam.* 2nd ed. Columbus, Ohio: Merrill, 1987.

Lutz, John. *Introduction to Learning and Memory.* Pacific Grove, Calif.: Brooks-Cole, 1994.

Marzano, R. J., et al. *Dimensions of Thinking.* Alexandria, Va.: Association for Supervision and Curriculum Development, 1990.

McGilly, Kate. *Classroom Lessons: Integrating Cognitive Theory and Classroom Practice.* Cambridge, Mass.: MIT Press, 1994.

McPeck, John. *Teaching Critical Thinking.* New York: Routledge, 1990.

Mikel-Brown, Lyn, and Carol Gilligan. *Meeting at the Crossroads: Women's Psychology and Girls' Development.* New York: Charles Scribner's Sons, 1994.

Miller-Lachman, Lyn. *Schools for All: Educating Children in a Diverse Society.* Albany, N.Y.: Delmar Press, 1995.

Minsky, Marvin. *Society of Mind.* New York: Simon & Schuster, 1986.

Oech, R. von. *A Kick in the Seat of the Pants.* New York: Warner Books, 1984.

Perkins, David. *Smart Schools: Better Thinking and Learning for Every Child.* New York: The Free Press, 1992.

Reiff, Judith C. *Learning Styles.* Washington, D.C.: National Education Association, 1992.

Restak, Richard M. *The Modular Brain.* New York: Charles Scribner's Sons, 1994.

Resnick, L. B., and L. E. Klopfer, ed. *Toward the Thinking Curriculum: Current Cognitive Research.* Alexandria, Va.: Association for Supervision and Curriculum Development, 1989.

Scarcella, R. *Teaching Language Minority Students in the Multicultural Classroom.* Englewood Cliffs, N.J.: Prentice-Hall, 1990.

Schunk, Dale H. *Learning Theories: An Educational Perspective.* Englewood Cliffs, N.J.: Prentice-Hall, 1996.

Shah, I. *Learning How to Learn.* New York: Harper and Row, 1981.

Smith, R. *Learning How to Learn.* Chicago: Follett, 1982.

Sternberg, R. J. *Beyond IQ: A Triarchic Theory of Human Intelligence.* Cambridge, Mass.: Cambridge University Press, 1985.

Stiggins, Richard J., et al. *Measuring Thinking Skills in the Classroom.* Rev. ed. Washington, D.C.: National Education Association, 1988.

Sund, R. B. *Piaget for Educators.* Columbus, Ohio: Merrill, 1976.

Tiedt, Pamela, and Iris Tiedt. *Multicultural Teaching.* Needham Heights, Mass.: Allyn and Bacon, 1989.

Walker, James Thomas. *The Psychology of Learning: Principles and Processes.* Englewood Cliffs, N.J.: Prentice-Hall, 1995.

What Works: Research about Teaching and Learning. Washington, D.C.: U.S. Dept. of Education, 1986.

Wonder, J., and P. Wonder. *Whole-Brain Thinking.* New York: William Morrow, 1984.

Wood, Eileen. *Cognitive Strategy Instruction for Middle and High Schools.* Cambridge, Mass.: Brookline, 1995.

Wycoff, Joyce. *Transformation Thinking.* New York: Berkley Books, 1995.

Chapter 3: Outcomes-Based Education

Airasian, P. W. *Classroom Assessment.* New York: McGraw-Hill, 1991.

Bernhardt, Victoria L. *The School Portfolio.* Larchmont, N.Y.: Eye on Education, 1994.

Brown, F. G. *Principles of Educational and Psychological Testing.* 3rd ed. New York: Holt, Rinehart and Winston, 1985.

California Assessment Collaborative. *Charting the Course Toward Instructionally Sound Assessment.* San Francisco, Calif.: Far West Laboratory for Research and Development, 1993.

California Department of Education. *Science Framework for California Public Schools.* Sacramento: Calif.: California Department of Education, 1990.

Cawelti, Gordon. *Challenges and Achievements in American Education.* Alexandria, Va.: Association for Supervision and Curriculum Development, 1993.

Costa, A., and R. Liebmann. *Envisioning Process as Content: Towards Renaissance Curriculum.* Thousand Oaks, Calif.: Corwin Press, 1996.

Crowell, R., and P. Tissot. *Curriculum Alignment.* Washington, D.C.: Office of Educational Research and Improvement, 1986.

Derich, Barbara, coordinator. *Technology Planning Guide for Curriculum Integration.* Larkspur, Calif.: Education Task Force, 1996.

Fosnot, C. T., ed. *Constructivism: Theory, Perspectices and Practice.* New York: Teachers College, Columbia University, 1996.

Kendall, J. S., and R. J. Marzano. *The Systematic Identification and Articulation of Content Standards and Benchmarks: Update.* Aurora, Colo.: Mid-Continent Regional Educational Laboratory, 1995.

Levine, D. V., and associates. *Improving Student Achievement Through Mastery Learning Programs.* San Francisco, Calif.: Jossey-Bass, 1985.

Mager, Robert F. *Measuring Instructional Intent.* Belmont, Calif.: Fearson Publishers, 1973.

Marzano, R., D. Pickering, and J. McTighe. *Assessing Student Outcomes: Performance Assessment Using Dimensions of Learning.* New York: Elsevier, 1993.

McTighe, Jay, and Steven Ferrara. *Assessing Learning in the Classroom.* Washington, D.C.: National Education Association, 1994.

National Council of Teachers of Mathematics. *Curriculum and Evaluation Standards for School Mathematics.* Reston, Va.: National Council of Teachers of Mathematics, 1989.

National Education Standards and Improvement Council. *Promises to Keep: Creating High Standards for American Students.* Washington, D.C.: National Goals Panel, 1993.

National Research Council. *National Science Education Standards.* Washington, D.C.: National Research Council, 1996.

Parrott, Charlene, et al. *Common Threads for the Future.* Farmington, Mich.: Farmington Public Schools, 1989.

Perrone, V., ed. *Expanding Student Assessment.* Alexandria, Va.: Association for Supervision and Curriculum Development, 1991.

Pressley, Michael, and Christine McCormick. *Cognition, Teaching, and Assessment.* Reading, Mass.: Addison-Wesley, 1995.

Rothman, R. *Measuring Up: Standards, Assessment and School Reform.* San Francisco, Calif.: Jossey-Bass Publishers, 1995.

Stiggins, Richard J. *Student Centered Classroom Assessment.* Columbus, Ohio: Merrill, 1994.

Tamalpais Union High School District. *Student Outcomes.* Larkspur, Calif.: TUHSD, 1995.

U.S. Department of Labor. *Secretary's Commission on Achieving Necessary Skills.* Washington, D.C.: Government Printing Office, 1991.

Wiggins, G., J. Brown, and H. Houston. *Standards, Not Standardization.* Stow, Mass.: Greater Insights Productions, 1991.

Wilson, Brent G., ed. *Constructivist Learning Environments: Case Studes in Instructional Design.* Phoenix, Ariz.: Oryx Press, 1996.

Chapter 4: Information Literacy

Anderson, M. A. *Teaching Information Literacy Using Electronic Resources, for Grades 6–12.* Worthington, Ohio: Linworth, 1996.

Breivik, P. S., and J. A. Senn. *Information Literacy: Educating Children for the 21st Century.* New York: Scholastic, 1994.

Bromley, Kearn, Linda Irvin-De Vitis, and Marcia Modlo. *Graphic Organizers.* New York: Scholastic, 1995.

California School Library Association. *From Library Skills to Information Literacy: A Handbook for the 21st Century.* Castle Rock, Colo.: Hi Willow Research & Publishing, 1994.

California School Library Association. *Information Literate in Any Language.* Castle Rock, Colo.: Hi Willow Research & Publishing, 1995.

Eisenberg, M., and R. Berkowitz. *Information Problem Solving: The Big Six Approach to Library and Information Skills Instruction.* Norwood, N.J.: Ablex, 1990.

Eisenberg, Michael B., and Doug Johnson. *Computer Skills for Information Problem-Solving: Learning and Teaching Technology in Context.* Syracuse, N.Y.: ERIC Clearinghouse on Information and Technology, 1996.

Farmer, Lesley S. J. *Informing Young Women: Gender Equity Through Literacy Skills.* Jefferson, N.C.: McFarland, 1996.

Fitzgerald, Mary Ann. "Misinformation on the Internet: Applying Evaluation Skills on Online Infomation." *Emergency Librarian* 24:3 (Jan. 1997), 9–14.

Garrett, Linda J., and JoAnne Moore. *Teaching Library Skills in Middle and High School.* Englewood Cliffs, N.J.: Prentice-Hall, 1993.

Gilster, Paul. *Digital Literacy.* New York: John Wiley & Sons, 1997.

Herring, James E. *Information Skills: The PLUS Approach—A View from the UK.* Copenhagen, Denmark: International Federation of Library Associations Conference, 1997.

Hyerle, David. *Visual Tools for Constructing Knowledge.* Alexandria, Va.: Association for Supervision and Curriculum Development, 1996.

"Information Literacy: A Position Paper on Information Problem Solving," *Emergency Librarian* 23:2 (Nov. 1995), 20–34.

Kolb, D. *Study and Information Skills Across the Curriculum.* London: Heinemann, 1995.

Kuhlthau, Carol Collier. *Teaching the Library Research Process: A Step-by-Step Program for Secondary School Students.* Englewood Cliffs, N.J.: Prentice-Hall, 1985.

Marland, Michael. *Information Skills in the Secondary Curriculum.* New York: Methuen, 1981.

Mendrinos, Roxanne. *Building Information Literacy Using High Technology: A Guide for Schools and Libraries.* Englewood, Colo.: Libraries Unlimited, 1994.

Pappas, Marjorie, and Ann E. Tepe. "Preparing the Information Educator for the Future." *School Library Media Annual* (1995), 37–44.

Pitts, Judy M. Personal Understanding and Mental Models of Information (Ph.D. dissertation). Tallahassee, Fla.: Florida State University, 1994.

Routman, Regie. *Literacy at the Crossroads.* London: Heinemann, 1996.

Soska, Matthew. "Educational Technology Enhances the LEP Classroom," *CABE Newsletter* (Nov. 1994), 6, 17.

Stripling, B. K., and J. M. Pitts. *Brainstorms and Blueprints: Teaching Library Research as a Thinking Process.* Englewood, Colo.: Libraries Unlimited, 1988.

U.S. Department of Labor. *Secretary's Commission on Achieving Necessary Skills.* Washington, D.C.: Government Printing Office, 1991.

Wright, Kieth. *The Challenge of Technology: Action Strategies for the School Library Media Specialist.* Chicago: American Library Association, 1993.

Chapter 5: Building a Learning Community

Allen, Janet. *It's Never Too Late: Leading Adolescents to Lifelong Literacy.* London: Heinemann, 1995.

American Association of School Librarians and the Association for Educational Communications and Technology. *Information Power: Guidelines for School Library Media Programs.* Chicago: American Library Association, 1988.

———. *Information Power: Building Partnerships for Learning.* Chicago: American Library Association, 1998.

Bazeli, Marilyn J. *Technology Across the Curriculum: Activities and Ideas.* Englewood, Colo.: Libraries Unlimited, 1997.

Bell, Irene Wood, and Jeanne E. Wieckert. *Basic Media Skills Through Games.* 2d ed. Englewood, Colo.: Libraries Unlimited, 1985.

Brooks, J. G., and M. G. Brooks. *In Search of Understanding: The Case for Constructivist Classrooms.* Alexandria, Va.: Association for Supervision and Curriculum Development, 1993.

Cochran-Smith, Marilyn. *Inside/Outside: Teacher Research and Knowledge.* New York: Teachers College Press, 1993.

Farmer, Lesley S. J. *Creative Partnerships: Librarians and Teachers Working Together.* Worthington, Ohio: Linworth Publishing, 1993.

Haycock, Ken. *School Library Program in the Curriculum.* Englewood, Colo.: Libraries Unlimited, 1990.

Higgins, Barbara J., et al. *Reaching Out: Cooperative Activities for the LMC and Art, P.E., Home Ec, Music, Health, and More.* Englewood, Colo.: Libraries Unlimited, 1990.

Johnson, Roger T., and David W. Johnson. *Structuring Cooperative Learning: Lesson Plans for Teachers.* Minneapolis, Minn.: Interaction Book Co., 1984.

Jweid, R. H., and M. Rizzo. *Library-Classroom Partnership.* Metuchen, N.J.: Scarecrow, 1988.

Larson, C. E., and F. M. J. LaFasto. *Team Work.* Newbury Park, Calif.: Sage Publications, 1989.

Loertscher, David V. *Taxonomies of the School Library Media Program.* Englewood, Colo.: Libraries Unlimited, 1988.

Meyers, Chet. *Teaching Students to Think Critically.* San Francisco, Calif.: Jossey-Bass, 1986.

Oakes, J., and K. H. Quartz. *Creating New Educational Communities: Schools and Classrooms Where All Children Can Be Smart.* Chicago: National Society for the Study of Education, 1995.

U.S. Department of Labor. *Secretary's Commission on Achieving Necessary Skills.* Washington, D.C.: Government Printing Office, 1991.

Urbanik, M. *Curriculum Planning and Teaching Using the Library Media Center.* Metuchen, N.J.: Scarecrow, 1989.

Vandergrift, Kay. *Power Teaching: A Primary Role of the School Library Media Specialist.* Chicago: American Library Association, 1993.

Winn, P. G. *Integration of the Secondary School Library Media Center into the Curriculum.* Englewood, Colo.: Libraries Unlimited, 1991.

Zingher, Gary. *At the Pirate Academy: Adventures with Language in the Library Media Center.* Chicago: American Library Association, 1996.

Index

AASL. *See* American Association of School Librarians
Academic objectives, 2
Accountability, 4
Acting. *See* Dramatizations
Activity plans, 53–54. *See also* Benchmark projects
   art, 55–62
   domestic sciences, 63–70
   English, 71–78
   foreign language, 79–87
   health, 87–93
   mathematics, 95–101
   music, 103–12
   physical education, 87–93
   psychology, 113–19
   science, 121–28
   social studies, 129–36
   sociology, 113–19
   technology, 137–44
   vocational education, 145–50
AECT. *See* Association for Educational Communications and Technology
Affective learning, 18–19, 151
Aging, 116–17
AIDS, 91–92
Aligning instruction, 31–32
American Association of School Librarians (AASL), 35–36, 45
American Memory, 133
Architecture, 63–64
Art activities, 55–62
Artistic brochures, 58–60
Aschner, Mary Jane, 155
Assessment, 151. *See also* Activity plans; Forms
   of activities, 8–9
   of groups, 7–8
   of learning, 47–48, 54
   of standards, 29–30, 33–34

Association for Educational Communications and Technology (AECT), 45
AT&T Learning Network, 12
Authentic assessment, 151. *See also* Assessment
Authoring programs, 151
Authority files, 151
Authors, 72–74
Autonomy, 3

Benchmark projects, 48–50, 151. *See also* Activity plans
Benefits of cooperative learning, 1–2
Berkowitz, Robert, 35
Bias, 137, 151
Bibliographic citations, 151
Bibliographies, 100–101
Big Six model, 35
Biographies, 149–50
Blocks to learning, 21
Bloom, Benjamin, 18
Body. *See* Human body
Book League on Books for Schools, 36
Boolean logic, 106, 151
Brain, 17
Brochure designing, 58–60, 121–24
Business plans, 145–46
Businesses, 145–46
Buzz sessions, 10

CAD. *See* Computer-aided design
California School Library Association, 37
Card games, 48–49, 109–10
Careers, 141–42, 146–48
Cartooning, 84–86
Case studies, 151
Categories game, 49(fig.)
Centre for Language in Primary Education, 18

Child rearing, 65–66
Classification, 79, 151
Climate, 121–24
Clothing design, 66–68
CNN, 12
Code of ethics, 142–43
Cognitive learning, 18, 151
Communications model, 13(fig.)
Complex machines, 126–27
Composition, 104–9, 110–11, 151
Computer aided design (CAD), 61, 63, 151
Computers. *See* Technology
Conceptual tempo, 18
Conflict resolution, 14–15
Consensus, 106, 151
Constructivist teaching, 33
Content analysis, 79, 103, 117, 129, 151
Content standards. *See* Standards
Continuums, 79–82, 151
Cooperative learning
   activities. *See* Activity plans
   benefits of, 1–2
   community, 43–51
   definition of, 1
   elements of, 2–4
   and information literacy, 39–40
   and libraries, 44, 50–51
   models, 9–12
   and outcomes-based education, 32
   planning for, 44–45, 51
   teaching factors, 4–9
Costa, Arthur, 10, 17
Costume. *See* Fashion
Countries, 49(fig.), 79–83, 125–26, 132–33. *See also* Travel
Creative thinking, 24–25
Creative writing. *See* Writing
Critical thinking, 20, 24
Cross-checking, 106, 151
Cross-fertilization grouping, 11(fig.)
Cross-references, 151
Cross section concepts, 79, 81(fig.), 151
Crossword puzzles, 97–99
Curriculum standards. *See* Standards
Cycle of inquiry, 108, 151

Database creation, 104–9
Database fields, 105, 151
Dating, 115–16
Debating, 125–26
Decision making, 19
Deduction, 106, 151
Designing
   brochures, 58–60
   clothing, 66–68
   computer aided, 61, 63
   housing, 63–64
   machines, 126–27
   masks, 61–62
   Web pages, 12, 139–40
Desktop publishing, 152
Dictionaries, 83–84
Dinosaurs, 124–25
Disabilities, 15
Distributed leadership, 3
Diversity in groups. *See* Heterogeneous groups
Domestic sciences activities, 63–70
Dramatizations, 76–78, 132–33
Dynamic/changing knowledge, 19

Economics, 134–36
Educable mentally retarded students, 15
Education
   outcomes-based, 27–34
   standards. *See* Standards
   technology, 22–23
Education Task Force (ETF), 28
Educators and learning, 23
Eisenberg, Michael, 35, 40
Emergency preparedness, 87–88
Emotionally disturbed students, 15
English activities, 71–78
Entrepreneurship, 145–46
Entry format, 105, 152
Environment and learning, 21–22, 45–46, 125–26
ETF. *See* Education Task Force
Ethics, 142–43
Ethnic groups. *See* Diversity in groups; Immigration
Etymology, 75–76
Evaluating. *See* Assessment
Exercising, 89–91

Extension names, 56, 152
Extrapolation, 147, 152

Facilitating learning, 46–47
Fact-finding, 74, 152
Family finances, 65–66
Farmington (MN) Public Schools, 27–28
Fashion, 66–68
Fast food. *See* Food
Feedback, 152. *See also* Assessment
Femininity, 117–18
Field guides, 124–25
Fields for databases, 105, 152
Financial planning, 65–66
First aid, 87–88
Fitness, 89–91
Fitzgerald, Mary Ann, 40–41
Food, 82–83, 88–89
Foreign languages, 79–87
Forms (assessment)
   brochure, 60
   database, 108
   database search strategy, 107
   housing, 64
   interview, 74
   travel agent promotion, 123
From Library Skills to Information Literacy, 37

Gallagher, James, 155
Games, 48–49, 109–10, 115–16. *See also* Interactive materials
Gardner, Howard, 19–20
Gender, 103–4, 117–18
Gender-equitable learning, 25, 51
Genres (musical), 103–4
Geography, 71–72, 79–82, 121–24
Global Schoolhouse, 12
Grade levels, 53
Group investigation, 11
Grouping, 11(fig.), 53
Groups
   accountability, 4
   autonomy, 3–4
   conflict, 14–15
   diversity in, 2, 13–14
   heterogeneous, 2, 13–14
   monitoring, 7–9
   processing, 5–7
   tasks, 54
Guest authors, 72–74

Health, 87–93
Hearing impaired student, 15
Herring, James, 37
Heterogeneous groups, 2, 13–14. *See also* Gender-equitable learning
History. *See also* Social studies
   drama, 76–78, 132–33
   word, 75–76
HIV, 91–92
Household repairs, 68–70
Housing, 63–64
Human body, 89–91, 116–17
   measurements, 95–96
Hypermedia stacks, 83–84, 152
Hypothesis, 152

Icebreakers, 12, 152
Immigrants, 132–33
Individual accountability, 4
Induction, 152
Information literacy, 35–41. *See also* Activity plans
Instruction
   alignment of, 31–32
   objectives, 28
   strategies, 37–38
   writing, 68–70
Instruments, 109–10
Intellectual access, 44
Interactive materials, 124–25. *See also* Games
Internet, 40, 82–83, 139–41
Interpersonal skills, 2–3
Interviewing, 72–74

Jason Project, 12
Jigsaw model, 10–11, 57, 92, 126, 136, 152
Jobs. *See* Business plans; Careers
Johnson, Doug, 40
Journaling, 42(fig.)
Junk food. *See* Food

Language problems, 15
Languages. *See* Foreign languages
Leadership, 3

Learners, 21
Learning
　assessment of, 47–48, 54
　communities, 43–51
　cooperative. *See* Cooperative learning
　disabled students, 15
　environment, 21–22, 45–46
　facilitating, 46–47
　process, 18–25
　resource-based, 43–44
Left brain, 17, 24
Librarian-teacher cooperation, 50–51
Libraries and cooperative learning, 44
Library of Congress, 133
Literacy, 35–41. *See also* Visual literacy
Literary tours, 71–72
Literature, 99–101. *See also* English activities
Locale memory, 18
Lyrics, 103–4

Machines, 126–27
Mainstreaming, 15, 152
Manual writing, 68–70
Map making, 134–36
Marin County (CA), 28
Marland, Michael, 36
Mask making, 61–62
Mathematics, 95–101
McREL. *See* Mid-continent Regional Educational Laboratory
McTighe, Jay, 29
Measurement, 95–96
Medical research, 91–92
Memorization, 18
Menus, 88–89
Metacognition, 20
Methodology. *See* Teaching: methodology
Mid-continent Regional Educational Laboratory, 28–29
Migration. *See* Immigration
Mind Extension University, 12
Mindstyles, 18
Models
　activity plan format, 54
　communications, 13(fig.)
　information literacy, 35–37

Money. *See* Financial planning
Monitoring groups, 7–9
Monographs, 105, 152
Multidimensional thought, 19
Multimedia presentations
　art, 55
　music, 110–11
　psychology, 115–16
　social studies, 129–32
Multiple intelligences, 19–20
Museums, 55–57
Music activities, 103–12
Musical genres, 103–4

National Forum on Information Literacy, 35–36
News broadcasts, 133–34
Newspapers, 129–32. *See also* Periodicals
Novellas, 84–86
Numbered heads together, 10
Numbers. *See* Mathematics
Nutrition, 88–89

Objectives, 2–3
Observing groups, 7–9
Occupations. *See* Careers
Old age, 116–17
Online resources. *See* Internet; Technology
Outcomes-based education, 27–34
Outfits. *See* Fashion

Pappas, Marjorie, 36
Periodicals, 152
Personal problems, 113–15
Persuasive art, 57–58
Photo novellas, 84–86
Physical education, 87–93
Physics, 126–27
Physiology, 89–91
Pitts, Judy, 36
Planets, 96–97
Planning process, 44–45, 51
　financial, 65–66
Plans. *See* Activity plans; Business plans
Playing instruments, 109–10
Primary sources, 132–133, 145, 152

Problems
   language, 15
   solving, 113–15
Processing data, 19–20
Project-based learning, 32–33. *See also* Activity plans
Promotion assessment, 123(fig.)
Psychological differentiation, 18
Psychology, 113–19
Puzzles, 97–99. *See also* Games

Realia, 152
Recipes. *See* Food
Repair procedures, 68–70
Research journal, 42(fig.)
Research process. *See* Information literacy
Resolving conflicts, 14–15
Resource-based learning, 43–44
Resources, 45–46, 53. *See also* Primary sources
Resumes, 149–50
Right brain, 17, 24
Role-play, 11–12, 152
Rubrics, 30, 33, 131–32

Safety, 87–88
Sampling, 79, 81, 152
SCANS. *See* Secretary's Commission on Achieving Necessary Skills
Scenarios, 87–88
Science, 121–28. *See also* Domestic sciences
Science fiction, 137–39
Search, 107(fig.), 152
Secretary's Commission on Achieving Necessary Skills (SCANS), 2, 29, 35, 43
Senior citizens, 116–17
Shelter. *See* Housing
Simulations, 133–34, 152
Skill line spectrum, 9(fig.)
Skills (interpersonal) 2–3
Skits. *See* Dramatizations
Slide-tape shows. *See* Multimedia presentations
Small businesses, 145–46
Snowballing, 10
Social objectives, 2–3
Social studies, 129–36

Sociology, 113–19
Soska, Matthew, 39
Sound bites, 131, 152
Space travel, 96–97
Spreadsheets, 91(fig.), 152
Stacks. *See* Hypermedia stacks
Stages of research, 37(fig.)
Standards, 28–29
Sternberg, R. J., 156
STL. *See* Student team learning
Stock market truth table, 32(fig.)
Storyboards, 134, 147, 152
Student team learning, 10
Surveys, 88–89
Symbolic patterns, 152

Tamalpais Union High School, 28
Taxon memory, 18
Teacher-librarian cooperation, 50–51
Teaching
   constructivist, 33
   cooperative learning, 4–9
   methodology, 46
Technology, 137–44
   and learning, 12, 22–23
   and research process, 40
   rubrics, 30(fig.)
Teen problems. *See* Personal problems
Tepe, A., 36
Thinking processes, 20. *See also* Creative thinking
ThinkQuest, 12
Time capsules, 131–32
Time frames, 53
Tours, 55–57, 71–72
Tracking. *See* Assessment
Transparencies, 134–36
Travel, 96–97, 121–24. *See also* Countries
Trends in information literacy, 38

U. S. Department of Education, 23
U. S. Department of Labor, 2, 35

Venn diagram, 106, 152
Video conferencing, 12
Videotaping, 72–74, 146–47

Virtual tours, 55–57, 71–72
Visual dictionaries, 83–84
Visual literacy, 152
Visually impaired students, 15
Vocational education, 145–50
Voyages, 96–97

Wardrobe design, 66–68
Web page design, 12, 139–40, 152
What Works?, 23

Wide game, 50, 152. *See also* Games
Women, 117–18
Word studies, 75–76
Writers. *See* Authors
Writing
    brochures, 58–60, 121–24
    field guides, 124–25
    instructions, 68–70
    mathematical, 99–101
    resumes, 149–50

www.ingramcontent.com/pod-product-compliance
Lightning Source LLC
Chambersburg PA
CBHW080938300426
44115CB00017B/2865